Last Dance

Last Dance

"And a Loving Mother"

STEPHEN MANNING

ISBN-13: 978-1-7346240-0-7

This book is dedicated to my lovely
wife and "Loving Mother" to my children.........
Mary Ann Manning

Table of Contents

Preface

I authored this story with a heavy heart. It's the story of a beautiful person, wife, and *Loving Mother*, Mary Ann Manning.

I want this story to be about her. I want it to be about the beautiful person she was. How she grew into motherhood and how she developed the critical, basic instinct of a *Loving Mother*. I believe those basic instincts develop within a mother's womb during pregnancy. It forms the basis of what is called a mother's love for her child. A mother's love is potent. It has helped define and guide civilization from its very beginnings. I watched how this delightful reality formed and how it shaped my wife's approach to caring for our four lovely children. Fatherhood is also a vital element of the family unit and needs to be acknowledged as well. In my experience, the family unit's center is driven by the love and guidance from *the mother's love for her children*.

As with every new couple, when they get married and start to think about a family, they always question if they have what it takes to raise a child. They can, and often do, read books. They talk to their parents and to their friends that have children. At the end of the day, how do they know if they have the instincts required to raise a family? Whether it be one child, or as in our case, a family of four?

The following chapters will tell the story of how Mary Ann and I took that family journey together. It will describe how I was fortunate enough to meet and then marry the woman of my dreams. It will discuss the many joys and challenges of that journey for 37 years. It will also tell of some tremendous sadness and losses along the way. Along that journey, Mary Ann once asked me, "What is your ultimate goal in life?" I told her I wanted to raise a family with her, retire, buy a cabin in the mountains, and author a book. I never thought my first book would be about her and, earlier, our son Kyle Raymond Manning's tragic death.

I outlined this story only a few weeks after Mary Ann passed, but I could not get past my grieving to write it for several years. The thoughts of her loss and the pain I saw in our children were just too strong. As time passed, I started to gather my thoughts of our life together, and with the help of my children, the extended family, and many of our friends, I started the journey of writing *Last Dance*. As I started writing, I would pass the chapters on to our children -- Kristie, Karie, and Ryan to make sure they thought I was authoring the story as their mother would have wanted it written. As they helped me through the writing, correcting the words and sentence structures, the book began to form. As I completed the first edition, I then shared it with other family members including, my brother Mike, sisters Stephanie and Kim, and cousins Tish Smiley and Tom Manning. I also had the help of a young man named Thomas Pak early on. I then shared it with others who knew Mary Ann, including her close friends and the Reidy family, whom you will get to know through this reading. They all gave me invaluable input that helped form this remarkable story of love, friendships, family, and the tragedy of losing a son and a life partner.

LEAVING FOR CHICAGO

I grew up in a beautiful town in the Midwest: Lincoln, Nebraska, a city at the time of around seventy thousand people. Lincoln wasn't a large city but a great city and a great state university with a powerhouse football team. These factors made it an easy decision to stay at home for college.

I graduated from the University of Nebraska in 1974 with a B.S. in Economics and Finance and a minor in Accounting. At the time, I knew that degree was going to offer me some great career opportunities. I started on-campus interviews at the beginning of my senior year. I also sent resumes to companies located in larger cities in the West and Midwest. I thought that a larger company's corporate office would offer me the best long-term opportunity given my degrees. I knew I did not want to go into public accounting, or government work, even though that would have been a typical career path. I was hoping to lock down an offer early in my senior year and use the last semester to study for the CPA exam, which I was to take in June.

As I got closer to graduation, I sat down with my mom and dad to discuss my plans post-graduation. I told them that I would be leaving Lincoln shortly after graduation after sitting for the CPA exam. I told them that I had accepted an offer from the Inland Steel Company in the Chicago area. My father, who was a traveling salesman, perked up and said, "I love Chicago and have traveled there often on business. But son, are you sure you want to leave Lincoln and be so far away from your family and friends?"

My mother took a deep breath and then began to cry. Of course, that brought tears to the eyes of both my dad and me. She got up and left the room.

When she reappeared, she said, "Stephen, I have known for a long time your career would take you elsewhere. Please know we will miss you every day. Please remember that you will always have a bed in this house."

She then gathered herself and said, "Son, I know you will be successful in Chicago. You will likely meet someone special and start a family there. Chicago is a big city, and you will meet many women there. The one thing I ask of you is when you meet that special someone, please make sure *she is the one you want to raise your children.*" My mother was a special person who had a powerful influence on all of us. She was, in many ways, the quintessential *"Loving Mother."*

As I packed my car and said my final goodbyes to the family and close friends, my mother pulled me aside. With a big hug, she whispered in my ear, "Remember what I said to you, and good luck finding that special lady someday soon."

As I started my long drive to Chicago, I felt anxious, both for what lay ahead and sorrow for what I was leaving behind. I left a great family with loving and caring parents, a brother who was away at law school, and three sisters. Not to mention friends that I had been with, some since grade school, and many from high school and college. Many of these friends I am still in contact with all these years later. I knew my ultimate goal was to move somewhere warm, where snow shovels were seldom ever sold, but Chicago was a good starting point for now.

I moved in with some college classmates and another individual from Iowa, Dan Donahue. Dan soon became my best friend and later the godfather to my second daughter. All in the accounting profession, the four of us lived in a singles complex called Four Lakes Village in Lyle, Illinois. We either spent our free time at Four Lakes Village or took frequent weekend trips into the city.

Inland Steel was a great starting point for my career. They treated me well, and I recognized that the company would give me a chance to advance my career. The Controller was a graduate from Nebraska and was the one that recommended my hire. My first assignment at Inland was at their Harbor Works in East Chicago. It was quite a long hike from Four Lakes Village.

However, I knew that if I worked hard and kept my nose clean, I would be getting a shot at a position at the corporate offices in Chicago. That opportunity appeared the next year. I soon moved into a one-bedroom apartment in the city and started working at the corporate offices; it proved to be my young life's best decision.

The move to the city and the corporate offices was exciting. I spent a lot of time in the city with Dan on weekends and was comfortable with city life. Public transportation was good in Chicago, so I sold my car and started taking the bus to work. The corporate offices at Inland were centrally located in downtown Chicago. It was full of new hires, as the company was strong in the late sixties and was hiring recent college graduates and MBAs. The employee group in the offices in Chicago was mostly sales, finance, accounting, and HR. The company had a social planning group called the Inland Steel Club. It was staffed with volunteer employees and funded by the company. The club did an excellent job of planning social events for the employees like ski trips, bowling leagues, and golf tournaments. This worked out well because many of the recent hires were from outside of Chicago and were looking to meet new people.

Meeting Mary Ann

$\mathcal{M}$y new assignment happened to be on the accounting floor, and it gave me a clear line of sight to the cashier's desk at Inland. That would not usually be a big deal, except that I could see a frequent visitor to the cashier. This regular visitor was the secretary to the VP of Sales. As it happens, the sales teams would take out cash advances to support their customer entertainment events. The salesmen would request a cash advance to the VP of Sales, and, after approval, his secretary would come down to the accounting floor to get the money. So, I would frequently see a beautiful young lady standing in front of the cashier, waiting to complete the transaction. My only thought at the time was that the sales department is not entertaining enough!! For weeks, this went on, and I asked all my fellow "bean counters" if they knew who that lady was. The usual answer would be, "Someone from the sales department," which meant that I would have to take it upon myself to figure out who exactly she was. With little interaction with that group or reason to go up to that floor, I had my work cut out for me.

My new apartment on the Near North Side of Chicago, next to Lincoln Park, was a decent-size one-bedroom apartment. It was on the seventeenth floor of a high rise that provided me a striking view of the city and Lake Michigan. The bus had to stop about ten or twelve times between my apartment and the office and was on a busy route. It was challenging to get a seat during rush hour, but that didn't bother me one bit. I was living in the big city and, at the time, one of the best singles areas of the city, so standing was something I could handle.

The bus stop was right outside of my building, and I was well into my daily routine of taking the 8 a.m. Route 40 city bus. It was a typical late fall morning in Chicago, winds howling and snow in the air. I was at the back of the line, but I saw the lady from the sales department standing in the front of the line. I remember thinking, *OMG, what should I do? Could this be a divine intervention or dumb Irish luck?* I entered the bus, and as always, it was standing room only, but it appeared a gentleman gave up his seat for her. That was OK because I could still see her and bad because everyone standing would get off first when we got to the Inland stop. That meant that there was no way I could wait by the door to introduce myself to her. She would think that I was stalking her. I can hear her now: "Wow, I got off the bus at work, and some bean counter from the accounting department was stalking me!" I knew I needed to go to plan B, which, at the time, did not exist!

As time went on, I started to see her more and more at the same bus stop. She was always ahead of me in line for some reason, but as I learned later, that was Mary Ann. If you tell her to be somewhere at 8:00 a.m., she will show up at 7:45. I later learned to adjust my schedule to hers. Well, the clouds broke open one morning when she turned around in line, looked back at me, and waved. I did the right thing and looked behind me to make sure she wasn't waving at someone else. Then I waved back, and I did so with a big smile. As usual on that bus ride, someone offered her their seat as soon as she got on. The good news was that the seat was not too far from where I was standing. When the person next to her got up, she motioned to me to sit down next to her. I didn't just run to that seat but put my shoulder down like Tom Rathman to make sure I made it to that seat. I later apologized to the lady I knocked over and made sure she got help as they took her off the bus.

Mary Ann was so sweet, she said, "I see you at work every time I go to the cashier. What do you do at Inland? You must be in either finance or accounting."

I resisted with all my strength telling her that I was sitting there waiting for her to come for cash advances every day. So, I gave her a broad description of what I was doing in accounting, hoping not to bore her. As it turned out, she took night classes in accounting and had some interest in what I was doing. Since she opened the door, I thought it appropriate to mention that I recently passed the CPA exam.

Mary Ann had recently moved to the Lincoln Park area, which was why I started to see her in the bus line. Unfortunately, she was dating someone on the sales team who lived in Milwaukee, Wisconsin. Living on the Near North Side of Chicago made it easier for them to see each other on weekends since it would only be an hour-and-a-half drive. I was excited to hear that she was a neighbor but not excited to hear she was dating someone. As she went on to describe that relationship, I had a feeling that it was not a strong one. As noted earlier, the social group at Inland was highly active. I pretty much got a pass into this group because of Mary Ann. Over the next few weeks, and many bus rides together, we started to socialize with that larger group.

The Near North Side in Chicago at that time was a unique social area. There was an area of bars and restaurants along the way home for us. If you got off the bus in this area, there were many choices to meet, drink, and have dinner. We would do that in the same group that we would make ski trips with and other events. While at the time we were not dating, we would generally check-in and say, "Are you going to this event or not?" We became close friends in that larger group. I was still dating others, and she was still dating that salesperson, but I knew it was not going well for her. As time went on, increasingly, the bus rides home was now just the two of us. On weekends, we would have lunch at one of the many unique neighborhood bars on the Near North Side of Chicago. We would spend the afternoons together and then go our separate ways in the evening. Nothing at the time was considered a date by Chicago standards. If we met on Sunday, we would discuss what we did on Saturday.

I always felt that Mary Ann was way over my pay grade. She was a beautiful, caring woman who I deeply admired. While I cherished our friendship, I never thought that I would qualify for her true love and affection.

Things started to change on one of the Inland ski trips. These trips usually involved two or three buses and an average of three to four hours of travel. We would usually go to Wisconsin or the Upper Peninsula of Michigan.

Inland would let us out early on Friday, and the buses would pick us up in front of the building. There were adult refreshments and snacks on the bus and plenty of music. Since I was on the accounting floor and a bean counter, I would not usually have been allowed on the sales bus. However, with Mary Ann's sponsorship, I was allowed to be on the sales-dominated bus. That was good because they had better adult refreshments, snacks, music, and of course, Mary Ann on that bus.

Once all buses boarded and we took off, the music and adult beverages got going, and we went off to the ski slopes. Once the buses were out of the city, dancing in the aisle was not only allowed, it was encouraged. As the energy of the trip started to wear down, people began to take their seats. As I looked for a seat, I got the nod from Mary Ann, much like I did on our first bus ride to work, to share the seat with her. Given the friendship we had built, that was not surprising to me.

What happened next set my life in the most fantastic direction that I could ever imagine. I told her that I was surprised that a particular salesperson was not on the ski bus. (Not that I wanted to meet him, but I just thought he would be there.) She said, "No worries, we broke up a few weeks ago; it was just not working for me. I found that I was having more fun with another person. Please put your arms around me, and I will tell you who that person is. I think you might know him!"

I put my arms around her, and she whispered in my ear, "Mr. Manning, I want to be with you." With my body melting, I thought, *OMG is this happening, and if so, am I ready for this?*

For the first time since I had been in Chicago, and after many dates and relationships, I heard my mother's words: "The one thing I ask of you is when you meet that someone special, please make sure *she is the one you want to raise your children.*" The feeling at the time was fantastic. Mary Ann was so impressive. All I could think about was what a great person and what a good friend she was. I never thought I would qualify for anything other than a trusted friend, but now I was holding her in my arms.

On the first day, the snow was surprisingly good, but I was the only person on the trip who thought they were on top of the world.

As we made our way back to Chicago, I knew my life was about to change, and it did. Mary Ann and I started dating and eventually moved in together. We started riding the bus together to work, and of course, as we boarded the bus, someone would always stand to offer her their seat. I would remain to stand, smiling at her all the way to work.

Life was good and about to get a whole lot better.

Meeting the Parents

As we continued our new life together, I started to think again about my mother's words not that long ago. Knowing that this relationship was growing in ways that I had not expected, I knew I would soon have to answer the question: Is this the woman I want to raise my family with and be *the mother of my children*?

I finally decided to call my mother to tell her I had someone I would like to bring home. Edna, being the great mother that she was, could only say, "Son, I am so excited for you and Mary Ann, please bring her with you as soon as you two can get away." As it happened, Nebraska was well into its football season, so we planned a trip around their next home game.

I had already been training Mary Ann on the art of being a Nebraska football fan. She often joined me in front of the TV on most football Saturdays. Nebraska had an excellent record while I attended school there, with two NCAA championships in 1970 and 1971 and two top ten finishes. So, to say my expectations for every game was a little over the top was an understatement. I don't think I was always that pleasant to be around during a game that Nebraska was not winning by a large margin. Mary Ann always seemed to find something else to do in another room when Nebraska was losing a game.

Nonetheless, when I asked her to join me on a trip back to Lincoln to meet my parents and catch a Nebraska game, her eyes lit up. She knew how close I was to my family, and taking her to meet them was a big step for us both. I think she was of mixed mind about going to the game on Saturday, but curious to meet my family and friends. I am sure she was hoping for a match-up against a non-conference pushover to make it even more enjoyable.

The trip to Lincoln takes about eight hours and is boring, to be honest. The weather was good for us, so that made the trip more comfortable but still dull. Yet, we were both excited about the trip and anxious about it. We knew where this next step in our relationship was taking us. While a very self-confident person, Mary Ann knew she would be tested in front of my family. Not in a threatening way, but a test. She also knew how important my mother and family were to me. I knew she would pass the test with flying colors, but she remained nervous. I also wanted her to meet my dear friends from Lincoln, many of whom I had known since grade school. So, I also arranged a get-together the Friday night before the game, and I picked one of the local bars we used to frequent while at college. I thought this would take some of the pressure off her of just meeting the family. As good friends always do, I also knew that they would accept her with open arms, and they certainly did.

We had started the journey early on that Thursday morning. We wanted to arrive in Lincoln before dinnertime. Since I had sold my car earlier that year, we took Mary Ann's car. Mary Ann referred to her car as the "Green Pea," mostly because it looked in color as a green pea! It was one of those colors that looked better when it was a little dirty. It was generally not a problem in Chicago, especially when you must park the car on the street, which was the Green Pea case. It was a two-door Dodge sedan that her dad helped her buy after she graduated from high school. Her dad always helped her keep it in good working order, and it was free of rust or any visible body damage. I often became grateful for the Green Pea since I would occasionally need access to her. I would usually borrow her car when I needed to drive out of the city. I thought returning to Lincoln in the Green Pea was going to cause me some interesting issues.

One of my jobs in college was selling cars, sports cars. I did that for my final two years in college. The one thing that happens when you are selling sports cars: buyers would always ask you what kind of car do you drive. Before I started working for that company, I had bought a used Triumph Spitfire from them. At the time, it was the lowest-cost Triumph you could buy, but a sports car, nonetheless. So, when people asked me what I was driving, I would take them out to the back lot and to show them my car. More times than not they would say, "will you sell me that one?"

At first, I would say no. I can only sell you what is on the floor. I finally figured out that the customers assumed I had the opportunity to buy the best-used sports car on the lot. So, they thought my car was their safest buy. With that in mind, I took the next offer and sold my current car at a decent profit. I then bought the next-best used sports car on the lot that I could afford. It started happening increasingly. Eventually, by the time I graduated and left for Chicago, I drove the car I always wanted, a Porsche 911.

But now, returning to Lincoln to celebrate my success in Chicago, I would be arriving in the Green Pea. All my friends were going to get a kick out of this. No problem for me, because the Green Pea's passenger seat would be the woman of my dreams. My mom and dad were both quite excited about the visit and excited to meet Mary Ann. Unfortunately, my older brother Mike and my sisters Michele and Stephanie, would not be there. They were all living elsewhere at that time. Mary Ann would soon become as close to them as she was to her brother and sister. As we pulled into the driveway that day, I could see the nervousness on Mary Ann's face. I parked the Green Pea, reached over to give her a hug and kiss, and said, "No worries, sweetheart, my family is going to love you!"

Everyone came out to the car to greet us and help with the luggage. When we got inside, I said, "Mom, Dad, Kim Ann, I want you to meet Mary Ann Lesin; she is from Chicago."

My parents and little sister could not have been nicer to Mary Ann, and whatever tension there was in the room quickly dissipated. As my mother greeted Mary Ann and took her to her room to freshen up, my dad pulled me aside. He asked me how the drive was and how work was going. He then turned to me and said, "Mary Ann appears to be a delightful person. Congratulations on finding her. You know how worried your mother was about you dating in Chicago."

As soon as Mary Ann reappeared into the living room, she asked my mom how she could help with the dinner. My mother gratefully accepted her offer for help, and they both went off to the kitchen. I continued talking with my dad and little sister, Kim Ann, who was eighteen years younger. We all started discussing the upcoming game on Saturday. We then discussed the season in general and our disappointment that Nebraska had no path to the National Championship game. Nebraska fans had been spoiled by the years of success in the early seventies. Of course, we knew it was only a matter of time before we got back to being ranked number one in the NCAA.

It was now five p.m., and in the Manning household, that indicated that the bar was open. No liquor would be served in the Manning household before five p.m. After that magical time, all restrictions were removed, and the Manning Bar, my favorite door in the kitchen cabinet, was opened. I offered to make my dad a cocktail. With that and my curiosity, I went to see how the ladies were doing in the kitchen. As I turned the corner into the kitchen, I saw my mom and Mary Ann chatting away. They were talking away like old lost friends, and I couldn't have been happier or more relieved. I knew they would eventually get along. Their personalities had so much in common. I offered them both a drink and delivered them along with hugs; not wanting to get in the way of what I was sure was a great ice-breaking conversation, I left them to themselves. I took the drink to my dad, and he asked how Edna and Mary Ann were getting along. I told him great and bet him $5 that dinner was going to be late!

Dinner was late, as forecasted. My mother did her typical excellent job of delivering a fantastic home-cooked meal. I was so impressed with how well Mary Ann had interacted with the family that first night. I remember going to bed that night thinking that this special lady from Chicago would play a significant role in my life. I was confident I would get the seal of approval from my family when we packed up and headed back to Chicago on Sunday.

The next day was filled with more Mary Ann time with the family. That night, we gathered at one of the favorite nightspots in Lincoln with many friends from school. It was nothing special, just a place we went to in college. Cheap beer, decent food, and full of young adults getting ready for the game on Saturday, of course, all dressed in red and cheering for victory. The next day, Mary Ann had her red on! I had gotten her a red shirt with "Nebraska Fan in Training" that she wore under some protest. As always, it was good to

be with all the friends I loved and missed. I was more than happy to introduce them all to Mary Ann. More than once, I got the comment from them
that they had never seen me happier. Also, many congratulations on finding
such a lovely person. Now all that was needed to make the weekend visit a
complete success would be a Nebraska victory, then a safe journey home on
Sunday.

Football Saturdays in Lincoln are as good as they get. Nebraska has a
fantastic group of fans who come out every football Saturday, all dressed
in red and anxious for the game to start. It was a brisk fall day in Lincoln,
perfect football weather. We were both dressed appropriately in our red
garb as we started our journey to the game. Gameday usually gets into
full steam around 10 a.m. on a football Saturday, with plenty of tailgating and campus visits. I took Mary Ann for a walk around the campus
and visited some of the buildings where I had classes. We also stopped
by my fraternity house, Pi Kappa Phi, to pick up tickets for the game.
Many of the underclassmen I knew from the fraternity were now in their
final years of school. They were getting ready to graduate and start their
careers. Of course, they all wanted to know how life was outside of the
daily grind of college.

As we walked to the stadium, Mary Ann seemed a little down, so I
stopped, and I asked her what was bothering her. She looked up to me with a
bit of tear in her eye and said, "Steve, I am so happy that you got a chance to
attend college. I know you cherish your memories; unfortunately, I never got
that chance. I wanted to attend the University of Illinois in Champagne, but
my family couldn't afford it. No one in my family ever attended college; for
them, it was not considered a priority. Instead, I went to a one-year business
school, and that is how I ended up at Inland Steel."

I felt terrible for Mary Ann for the first time in our relationship. Mary
Ann was a smart person and did very well in school. She had above-average
grades, was a cheerleader, and a good athlete. She would have enjoyed university life to its fullest, no doubt. I hugged her and said, "Listen, all things in
life happen for a reason. Had I not graduated from Nebraska, Inland Steel
would have never hired me. Had you gone off to the University of Illinois,

you would never have started working at Inland Steel. Given that, we never would have met."

With that, she gave me that delightful bright-eyed smile, and we hugged then headed to the stadium to watch the game.

The one thing you see when you enter Memorial Stadium in Lincoln is the Sea of Red. All patrons are dressed head to toe in their red and white, and the stadium is always full. In fact, to this day, they have the longest record of sellouts in NCAA football history. I don't think that record will ever be broken, even though they have not performed consistently with their past in recent years. On every football Saturday, Memorial Stadium itself becomes the third-largest city in Nebraska! We were right in the middle of it all, sitting in the student section. I had gotten the tickets from a couple of my fraternity brothers; tickets for a home game were tough to come by. Many students sold them to help offset the cost of campus housing and books. The student section was always crowded and always fun. The enthusiasm there was electric. Pre-game, the band fills the field, 98 strong, and plays all the fight songs. Mary Ann never really got excited about one song over the years was "There Is No Place Like Nebraska." I won't bore you with the words, but every college has one of these songs. They do many other music renditions to fire up the crowd and then, of course, the National Anthem.

The crowd and the student section were fired up and not all that sober. Most had been tailgating, which happens at most college football games. I failed to mention to Mary Ann that the student section does not take their seat until Nebraska scores their first points, whether a safety, field goal, or touchdown. After the kickoff, Mary Ann went to sit down. I looked at her, still standing, and said, "Sorry, sweetheart, we can't take our seats until Nebraska scores a point."

She gave me her famous "What!" and got back on her feet. She would complain about this habit every time we watched a Nebraska football game on TV for years to come.

The game started slowly, and I saw Mary Ann kept looking back at the seat, and she wanted to take advantage of it. Finally, Nebraska scored, and at that moment, everyone let go of their red balloons; with the sky now full of red balloons, Mary Ann looked and asked, "Wow, that is cool, why didn't we get a red balloon?"

After finally getting into her seat, Mary Ann enjoyed the whole game experience. I behaved because Nebraska won the game, much to the relief of Mary Ann. With smiles on all faces, we walked back through campus and headed back to my parents' house. We enjoyed a final meal and celebration before we packed up and headed back to Chicago that next morning.

The ride back to Chicago was, as always, a long drive. We talked more about what Mary Ann had missed by not going to college. We also talked about how well she was doing with her studies at night school. I told her if she decided to go full time, I would find a way to support her on that journey. She then turned to me and said, "Stephen" (I knew she was serious, because when she was serious or mad at me, or both, she frequently called me Stephen), "I can't tell you how much I enjoyed your family. I know you know how nervous I was about this visit, but your family made me feel right at home the entire time. Now, if you are OK with it, I would like to take you down to Tinley Park next weekend to meet my family."

I squeezed hard on the steering wheel, thinking, *my god, things are starting to move fast in the right direction.* I said, "Sweetheart, I would love nothing better than to meet your family next weekend." We both knew what was unfolding between us; she reached over and gently squeezed my hand.

Mary Ann's family was a splendid example of the middle-class families in Chicago. She had two great parents, a younger sister, Peggy, five years younger, and a brother, Mike, two years younger. Ray, (her father) was a tool and die maker at Allis-Chalmers in Chicago. Allis-Chalmers had a great history during the industrial revolution. It was a great company, but its markets were affected by foreign competition, mostly from Japan and Germany. Times became tough for Allis-Chalmers, which was threatened by what the new owners were doing to the workforce. The company soon became a victim of the early private equity deals that started to unfold in the seventies. Someone would buy a company, strip the cash, load it up with debt, and lay off all the employees they could. Checking the papers, Allis-Chambers was an excellent example of how that does not always work, especially for the shareholders or the employees. As a tool and die maker, Ray was considered a valuable employee there. As with every manufacturing company, tool and die makers are the ones that keep production going; because of this, Ray was never at risk. They needed Ray's skills to keep the machines up and running, but as he sat on the shop floor, he had a clear line of sight about what was going on with his fellow workers... and he was worried.

Midge, Mary Ann's mother, was a stay-at-home *Loving Mother* like mine. That is an essential job, which does not exist in many communities today. Back in the 1950s and through the early part of the 1980s, this was a typical family structure element. Either due to economic pressures or personal desires, we don't see that many stay-at-home mothers today. Remember that the *Loving Mother's* instinct will always be to do whatever it takes to advance the family's health. Many women want to be both a mother and a teacher, doctor, employee, manager, or executive. In my opinion, a working mother is the most challenging job possible for any profession. Their education and their life desires drive them to do this. It is an essential option in this world, but it is a hard job. They have such valuable input on how to manage companies. And how governments and schools should be run. Some very accomplished women have run many countries around the world. I always respected and encouraged the women who were working mothers in my departments and companies that I managed. I did my best to allow them whatever time they also needed to be a mother. It was never a problem but a sign of their character and commitment to both.

As we started planning our visit to meet her family, she gave me the background on her family and asked, "Are you ready for this?"

I knew she wanted it to be a successful visit. I told her, "Mary Ann, I know you love your family, and it sounds like you have always been your dad's princess. You, in his eyes, could do no wrong, but with what your dad is going through at work, things may be difficult. If he views me as part of management at Inland Steel, he will have a problem. I am, in his eyes, management, and in his eyes, he is blue-collar. I know he will be nice to me because he loves you. How can we make sure this goes well this weekend?

These are exceedingly challenging times for your dad and Allis-Chambers; I know, it's been in all the papers."

Mary Ann knew this, and I could tell she was worried about the planned visit. She said, "Let's go see my mom first." Midge was due for a medical procedure that next week and Mary Ann wanted to take some time to see her after the operation anyway. She suggested, and I agreed that we would see her first and check on how she was doing. She was to have a three-day recovery from the procedure, so we planned to see her on Friday afternoon.

Like any Loving Mother, Midge would never pass up a chance to meet her eldest daughter's new boyfriend. Midge was in full recovery mode, and as I got to know her later, she was very much Midge. As soon as we walked in, Midge was on fire! After giving Mary Ann a big hug, she looked at me and said, "Great to meet you, Steve; Mary Ann hasn't brought anyone home to meet me since high school! Damn, I always knew that sales guy she was dating was not stepping up!"

Mary Ann already knew she could not control anything that came out of Midge's mouth, but that was Midge. If she felt something or thought something, she said something. Midge was more than enjoyable. Mary Ann had already debriefed her on our trip to Lincoln, and I think she was a little jealous of how well Mary Ann said she had gotten along with my mother. Midge also knew from talking to Mary Ann how well our relationship was going.

Midge's dad was a highly successful salesman at Sherwin Williams and a Democratic alderman who worked and lived on the Southside of Chicago. There was no blue collar/white collar distinction in Midge's view. We all enjoyed the time together. I told her about my family, and she told me about her sister, brother, aunts, and uncles and, of course, her proud Dutch heritage. I met many of the family members in the next six to eight weeks on frequent follow-on visits to the Lesin household.

As we finished our visit with Midge, we got into the car and started to drive home. Mary Ann asked, "How did that go for you?"

I answered, "Honestly, it was great. Your mom has a great personality and is not afraid to say what she thinks, no filter!" I then thought for a moment and said, "While not having met your dad yet, I bet I may see more of you in your dad than your mom."

She said that she and her dad were close and that he always had a lot of influence over her; even though they didn't always agree on everything, he still had her back. "Except for not supporting my desire to go to the University of Illinois, although it was a key life decision for me, I understand why he made it. I still loved him and forgave him for that decision. After all, as you said, we would have never met at Inland had I had gone to college. Besides, I wasn't sure what degree I was going to pursue. I did want that college experience and a chance to choose a career based on that learning."

It was getting late and well upon dinnertime. Chicago is one of the greatest cities in the world for dining. There were many ethnic restaurants, given all the immigrant communities that developed over the years. All great and very authentic. Italian, Greek, Irish, French, Spanish, Mexican, Moroccan, and of course Dutch. About anything you could imagine. They were all based on original recipes but, over time, modified to Chicago taste buds. I asked Mary Ann where she wanted to stop for dinner. Mary Ann enjoyed all the Chicago cuisine. Not too far from our apartment was a great pizza restaurant called the Chicago Pizza and Oven Grinder. It was a fabulous restaurant that served an incredibly unique upside-down pizza with a delicious jumbo mushroom in the middle. We knew we could park her car somewhere on the street between the restaurant and the apartment, have a wonderful meal, and start to walk off some of our dinners on our way home. It was one of the first places we had eaten on one of our first real dates. So, I made the executive decision to suggest this location for dinner. I knew if I got the "Stephen" comment, we would make a quick mid-course correction!

Mary Ann was more than happy with the venue selection. We parked the car and started walking to the restaurant. Mary Ann, who was anxious for the meal, said, "Stephen, let's talk a little about my dad at dinner. I am sure our visit will go well, and I have some ideas on how this might play out for everyone."

Mary Ann had been talking to her dad about things at Allis-Chalmers for a while. He was upset and concerned about it. Labor and management issues were getting out of control in the early seventies at his company and most rust belt manufacturing companies. Historically, high inflation and increased dumping by Japan was turning manufacturing companies upside down. It drove labor unions to demand better satisfaction for their workers, and the companies were fighting back. It became a no-win situation for both adversaries.

Ray Lesin had worked at Allis-Chalmers for most of his adult life. He had an excellent pension that he had already qualified for. If the company were to go bankrupt, he would risk losing most, if not all of it, including his life insurance and family medical insurance. For his family and his co-workers, this was a huge issue. One of the qualities of Ray Lesin that I learned over time is that he didn't just worry about himself and his family, but also his fellow workers. He was also a union steward, so this all kept him busy, and he did it with his heart.

I saw this all happening at Inland Steel. We were preparing for our round of negotiations with the Iron and Steelworkers of America. We would run "what if" analyses with various terms that the union was demanding. As I looked at the results, I saw no clear path for success for the company or the Union, especially given Japan's dumping of steel products, which would worsen. Japanese companies were offering steel at less than our cost to produce. It was crazy; these steel products were heavy rolls of steel, and they were selling them, freight included, at prices below our costs to produce!

It set up the discussion we wanted to have on how my meeting her father would be a success. She said, "Steve, Allis-Chalmers is not the only thing my father thinks about right now. His other passions are his religion, his family, and sports. He is remarkably close to the Catholic Church, his brothers, sisters, cousins, and certain sports. Sports in his mind is NOT Nebraska football! More likely the Chicago Bears (who were awful during the mid to late seventies), golf and bowling."

I said, "No to baseball, hockey or basketball?"

"Not much," she replied, "but golf and bowling."

With that revelation, a plan was starting to take shape. I was an avid golfer growing up and started as a caddie. I then started playing junior golf, high-school golf, and even played for the Nebraska golf team for my first two years. Also, one of my short-list companies in Chicago that I had gotten an offer from was Brunswick. Brunswick was synonymous with bowling and pool, especially in Chicago. I thought if we could get the discussion off on the right foot, the meeting could go very well.

Mary Ann also had mentioned to her dad that my family could not afford to send me to college either. She told him that I worked three jobs while going to school: working at K-Mart automotive on Sundays, selling cars after class and on Saturday and Sunday, and bartending on Friday and Saturday nights. Ray was a hard worker and would respect challenging work. Most importantly, I knew I needed to leverage his love for Mary Ann and maybe have a little discussion about golf and my desire to learn how to bowl.

As we were setting the stage for my meeting with her father, dinner was served. It was great pizza, uniquely served as an upside-down pizza. Mary Ann's eyes lit up as she cut into one of her favorite dishes in Chicago. Her enthusiasm for the meal only increased mine. We enjoyed the meal along with a couple of cold beers. Before her first pregnancy, Mary Ann would enjoy a beer or two as she had not yet developed a taste for fine wine. While a good Manhattan was the drink of choice for the Lesin household, what kind of person would stand up a Manhattan with a good pizza? We finished our meal, packed up, and started our walk back to the apartment, with smiles on our faces and joy in our hearts. We decided Ray Lesin time would happen the following weekend in Tinley Park, Illinois.

That following Saturday, we took off for our visit to Mary Ann's parents. A little anxious about the trip, we started joking with each other. I asked what would happen if this did not go well? I suggested that she may want to ask her mom for some boxes if she needed to pack all her things that we moved from her apartment. One punch in my stomach by Mary Ann made it clear; I was not funny. It looked like we had gone to punches in the stomach rather than just an "Oh, Stephen." As with any new relationship, you must learn to adapt. It was not too bad, though, since I usually got a kiss, a very fair trade-off with the punch in the stomach. I didn't always get that kiss when she did the "Oh Stephen" thing.

Thankfully, Ray was not called into work that night. He had a strict schedule, 6:30 a.m. to 4:30 p.m., Monday through Friday, but he was always on call by the nature of his job. Ray got double time on weekends and seldom passed up a call-in. Even given the overtime, there was no way he would disappoint his little princess and not be there to meet her new boyfriend.

As with my parents' home, this was not the home that Mary Ann grew up in. They moved houses when Mary Ann was finishing high school. Much to Ray's disappointment, they decided to move out of the Chicago Pullman area on Chicago's south side. The neighborhood started to change, and crime began to increase. It had broken Ray's heart; they had bought the house when it was new during the post-World War II building boom. Like many in the Midwest, including my family, they had made many upgrades to it over the years. They had finished off the basement with a bedroom, a bathroom, and a workshop for Ray. That's what had to have made a move so discouraging: Ray felt that the house was finally what he and Midge had wanted after living there for eighteen years. Both Ray and Midge's brother, sisters, and cousins all lived close by in the same area. They all moved out of the neighborhood around the same time. With them, and others selling then, they found that housing prices had plunged. Most, including Ray and Midge, lost most of their equity in their home. They all pretty much had to start from nothing in Tinley Park. Fortunately, because of the GI Bill and Ray's willingness to work a lot of overtime, they could get a loan and buy a new home. While not as large as the one they had to sell, it would accommodate their family of five. They knew the kids would, like Mary Ann, soon be moving out on their own, so they were willing to accept the downsizing.

We pulled into the driveway around 3 p.m. We wanted to have enough time to meet Ray, and Mary Ann's sister Peggy and brother Michael. Ray was sitting in his favorite chair in the living room as he waited for our arrival. On future visits, I would learn that the regular entry into the house was the kitchen's side door off the driveway. For this occasion, Mary Ann said we would be entering through the front door. There to meet us was Midge, and as she greeted us, she turned to introduce me to Ray.

Ray was gracious and reached out his hand and said, "Steve, so glad to meet you. Mary Ann has told me quite a bit about you."

I said, "Ray, good to meet you as well, sir. I hope Mary Ann has only told you the good stories about me. She also has told me quite a bit about you and the rest of the family."

With that, we all sat on the couch, Ray turned off the TV, and Midge went to the kitchen to grab some snacks and iced tea for all. Ray asked how long I had been in the Chicago area and how I found my job at Inland Steel. I gave him the short story on this, wanting to move away from discussions about work. The conversation then went on to cover local events, the weather, and more small talk. It was all too comfortable. As things started to get a bit quiet, I asked Ray, "Was that the golf tournament you had on?" Back then, the networks only showed the back nine and followed the leaders, so the airtime was relatively short.

Ray seemed to light up a bit and said, "Yes, it was. Do you play golf?"

I answered, "Yes, in fact, I do, but haven't played much since I moved into the city and sold my car."

Ray jumped out of his chair and said, "You have to bring your clubs out next time. Get here a little earlier next time, and I will take you to one of the local courses. What's your handicap?" I replied, "It's hard to say right now since I haven't been playing much. But when I was playing golf for Nebraska, I was around a three or four handicap, not always good enough to play on the first team."

With that, Ray ran downstairs and reappeared with a seven iron in his hand, and Mary Ann's mother burst out in laughter. "Oh my God, Steve, he does this all year long. He is always changing his swing and practices it in the living room all the time. I don't even play golf, but he is always asking me to check out his new swing."

With that, we all laughed, other than Ray, of course.

Ray said, "No, seriously, Steve, please look at my swing and tell me what you see and what I am doing wrong." The living room was not noticeably big, but at least it had a high ceiling. I moved some furniture around. I wanted to stand behind him and offer whatever guidance I could. What I saw was an inferior grip on the club, but not too bad of a swing. I suggested that it would be better for us to get to the course early and spend some time on the driving range before we teed off; he was more than grateful. With that, Midge, who thought golf was the biggest waste of four hours in the world, chimed in, "Ray, enough about golf. Go make some Manhattan's for our guest!"

We then settled down over a nice Manhattan, the Lesin drink of choice. As we talked about some of our favorite golf stories, Ray said, "Steve, how is your bowling game?"

I told him I had never bowled until I got to Chicago and joined the Inland Steel bowling league.

He replied, "Perfect. I will teach you how to bowl, and you in turn, can teach me how to golf."

The evening could not have gone better as we all sat for a delicious meal at the dinner table. As it turned out, Midge, like my mother, was an excellent cook. I knew I would not go hungry during what turned out to be frequent trips to the Lesin household. The evening was getting late; after handshakes and a little hug from Midge and a big hug for Mary Ann from her dad, we headed home to the city. As we pulled out of the driveway, Mary Ann put her hand on mine. She said, "thank you for coming with me today. I think my dad likes you."

I told her, "I enjoyed meeting your dad; as I suspected, I see a lot of your dad in you. He seems to be a special and caring person, works hard, and cares about his family, friends, and coworkers. The only negative thing about your dad is that he has a bad golf grip!"

The family box was now checked for us both.

Our Engagement

*M*ary Ann and I continued to work at Inland Steel together, her in the sales department and me in finance and accounting. Everyone in the office knew we were dating seriously, and I found out later that if you want to keep something a secret, do not tell Mary Ann! I continued to work on the financial analysis, looking at what potential impact the pending new labor agreement would have on the company. The key variables were energy prices, labor costs, and inflation rates. If you included the rate of increase in Japanese steel imports, the numbers looked even worse. My analysis started to point to a severe risk in the steel industry's health in the United States. I knew energy had many important impacts on the steel industry. It takes a tremendous amount of energy to mold and form steel and more to transport it. As energy prices go up like they were in the mid-seventies, it would drive spiral inflation. My senior year paper in economics was on the compounding effect of an increase in oil price on inflation. I modeled four critical areas in the economy—first, the increased transportation cost and how it would affect all commodities' costs. Secondly, the increased cost of plastics since oil is a critical factor in the manufacture of plastics. Thirdly, the increased cost of steel production as inflation rolled through those parts of the economy. And finally, how this would impact all other parts of the economy. If not corrected, inflation would spiral out of control, and of course, it did just that later in the seventies and early eighties. It takes time for this compounding to take its full effect. Companies continued to raise prices to help make up for the added cost in their labor and supply chains.

Knowing this information, I had a tough decision to make. Inland could not have been better to me. I knew if the company stayed healthy, I would have a job for life there. With what I was doing with the financial analysis team, I got the opportunity to interact with the entire leadership team at Inland. They were all smart and decent people. I knew I would have their support if I stayed at Inland. Yet, I could not get out of my mind my analysis on energy inflation and what might lay ahead for Inland. Not today, not even next year, but in the future. In fact, at the time, Inland was the best-performing steel company in the industry. However, over the next ten to twelve years, life in the steel industry would worsen, even for a professionally managed company like Inland. I did not mention my concerns to Mary Ann, as I did not want to upset her. I also didn't know what I was going to do about it. I had not been out of college that long, and changing jobs back then was not always looked on with pleasure. I did know that I would be more marketable with my CPA now in hand, but I didn't know any headhunters.

One day I got a call. It was from a headhunter; how he got my name, I do not know. He had an exciting opportunity that I thought I should investigate further. It was a position at a conglomerate called Rockwell International, based in Pittsburgh. The job was in its Operational Audit Group, which had four regional offices. One of those was in Schaumburg, Illinois. To qualify for this position, you had to either have a CPA or an MBA, with an engineering undergraduate degree. In that role, you would be teamed with either a CPA or an MBA, or preferably one of each. The team would perform operational and financial audits at its manufacturing sites. These sites were in North America and Western Europe. You would be on-staff for eighteen to twenty-four months. After that, you would be placed in a senior-level role at one of the operations or division headquarters. One thing guaranteed was heavy travel and eventual relocation. It was somewhat of a development position. It was modeled after the GE and IBM training program for young, high-potential executives.

From a career point of view, the position looked ideal. I was beginning to like manufacturing, and I felt pure accounting and finance were not long-term. I always believed that those disciplines were a solid foundation for any career. Accounting for me was still a beginning position, not the ending position in my career.

After taking a few days to think about the opportunity, I called the head-hunter back to let him know that I was interested. Unfortunately, the interview was going to be at their offices in Schaumburg. I would need to have a car to get there. It was not my intent to hide the opportunity from Mary Ann. I wanted to feel better about it before I started to worry her about it. But, since I needed to borrow her car so I had to tell her about the interview. I told her not to worry; I wanted to find out more about the job to see if it was the right fit for me. Of course, she said yes, but I could tell she was concerned about what was happening. I then told her about my concerns about Inland and how its future was waning on my mind. I said, "This is not about tomorrow or next year. But over the next ten or so years, the U.S. steel industry is headed for trouble."

She said, "Stephen, you are still young in your career. Everybody loves you at Inland; even my boss in Sales told me you are considered high potential in the company. Why are you in such a hurry to leave?"

I said, "Mary Ann, you know I love my dad, but the man you met back in Lincoln is half the man he was. He was a high-flying salesman for his company. He was highly successful early in his career, making good money. Always the best dressed, playing golf at the country club, all the trappings of success. The industry started to change around him while he was in his late forties. The apparel industry went from a model of field salespeople calling directly on stores to holding regional shows. They called these "apparel markets." The primary store owners would travel to major cities like New York, Chicago, Minneapolis, Denver, and Kansas City. There they would be entertained by company executives and would buy their goods there. Over time they reduced my dad's commissions on those sales. The floor fell out from under him, and it was too late in his career to make a career change. He was one of the best salesmen in a dying industry. As I watched this happen, I told myself I would never let that happen to me. This change did not happen overnight, which was unfortunate. Had he seen it coming earlier in his career, he could have changed course while younger. Like your father, he is a proud man, and you would never know this story by talking to him. He knew he did not cause this to happen but became a victim of it and had no options other than to suck it up. That is why my mom went back to work at the university to help make ends meet. I walked into the kitchen one Saturday morning and saw them cutting coupons and food stamps. When my dad saw me, he looked down and cried. He was embarrassed, and he should never have been. It wasn't his fault. Let me run out to Schaumburg and look at what they have to offer. I won't make any decision until we have time to talk about it."

She took the keys out of her purse, handed them to me, and said, "you know where it's parked; good luck on the interview."

I was learning in our relationship. Sometimes you need to give Mary Ann a little time alone to process unexpected news. I left her alone that night.

I went out to Schaumburg for the interview with Rockwell. There I met an interesting gentleman named Ron Sanderson. Ron was unique in so many ways. Highly intelligent and well-traveled, he had moved up from Dallas to start the office with his lovely wife, Cheryl. Cheryl was a flight attendant with American Airlines at the time. You could tell from the start that Ron had no patience for the status quo. For him, change was more than what you carried in your pocket. He once said, "If you are not changing, you're not moving forward."

Ron and I were getting along well. He started to tell me stories of many of the audit engagements that he worked on. He was trying to give me a feel for what life was like as an Operational Auditor at Rockwell. Before moving up to Chicago to start that office, he was an auditor on the Dallas audit team. He thought putting together an audit team with financial and engineering expertise was a great combination. The finance person would learn more about manufacturing, and the engineer would get exposed to finance. Both would become better business managers. Ron was also intrigued by manufacturing. He said, "Rockwell was the best place to be for that right now. On one assignment, you may go out to audit Saberliner (brand) and watch them build business jets. For the next assignment, you may go to Admiral and watch them build either refrigerators or TV. Next assignment, you may watch them build avionics for the F-111 bomber or parts for the Apollo space program. The company was amazing and very diversified. This position I am talking to you about is like getting a free 18-month education. You will get exposed to all aspects of American manufacturing, and we will pay you a lot of money when you are taking the class, but be aware, there are some risks. We only hire high-potential candidates. If you are not up to the task, we will take you out very quickly. It's a high-risk/high-reward opportunity, and the washout rate is pretty high."

Overall, the one-hour interview lasted a little over two hours. I left there pumped.

As I started my drive back to the city, I thought. *Who takes a job after the first interview? What about the high-risk/high-reward statement? Who is Rockwell International anyway, and what do I know about them? The one thing I did know is that I would love to work for that Ron Sanderson guy, but is that enough? Leaving Inland was in the cards, but that was a long-term issue for me, not one I had to deal with today.*

Another critical issue was how this would affect my relationship with Mary Ann. I did not feel that we would get married anytime soon, but I was hoping that it would be the case sometime in the future. I was hoping that she felt the same way, but we had never broached the subject. I hoped that if I took the job, we could continue our relationship. The interview was long but started early enough in the day that I got home before Mary Ann got back from work. Although as it happened, she got back early. I asked her if something was wrong. She said she just could not work any longer today, told her boss she had a headache and needed to leave work early. She immediately asked how the interview went and if I would take the job; clearly, she was concerned.

I told her. First, I cannot accept the job until they give me an offer. So no, not yet. Second, I would not do anything until we had a chance to talk. The conversation was not going well. When Mary Ann had something serious on her mind, she wanted answers, and then she needed her quiet time to process everything. I suggested that we take advantage of Lincoln Park and take a walk. I told her we could talk about the job and the interview and discuss the next steps. I was glad she got home early from work that day because this would be a long walk.

Spring had come early in Chicago, which is seldom the case. The Park was beautiful. Trees and spring flowers were starting to bloom. There wasn't too much wind in the air, and with a light jacket, the temperature was perfect. I was not too sure how Mary Ann's temperature was at that moment. But I knew if we got a chance to talk, she would calm down, and we could work things out. As we walked through the park, I started to tell her more about this position's details, told her some of the stories that Ron said to me about the job, and what excited me most about the position. I told her that it would be quite a significant increase in salary for me, far larger than I would be getting from Inland. Mary Ann said that she was overly concerned about the amount of travel I would be doing and that I would not be with her every night. She said, "I am not going to be able to sleep at night if you are not there to hold me."

That statement struck home with me. Not only that she felt that way, but also by the sense of loneliness that would affect us both.

We then started to talk about the larger issue: moving onto a new role somewhere other than Chicago and what that might mean to our longer-term relationship. This was going to be a more challenging issue for us to address. I told her, "I was always OK with leaving Chicago at some point in my career. And long term, I wanted to end up somewhere where people do not need a snow shovel."

I could see this discussion was not going well for Mary Ann, and she asked, "What about after eighteen months? What do we do then?"

I told her, "I'm not sure. I know how close you are to your family and how much you love Chicago." She had never expressed a desire to leave the area. "I feel it's too much for me to ask you to leave Chicago and your family. So, I am not sure exactly, and by the way, I don't even have an offer from Rockwell yet."

She said, "This is now not just about Rockwell; it's about us." In her best Chicago accent, she said, "If you think I am just going to pack up and move with you wherever you decide to go to work, without a ring on this finger, you have another thing coming."

That statement caught me way off guard. Did she say what I think she said? The words of my mother jumped right back into my head, "marry the person you want to be *the mother of your children.*"

I said, "Mary Ann, are you sure you would be willing to leave Chicago and your family?"

She looked up to me and said, "Stephen, we are talking about us starting our own family, and yes, I would."

I said, "Sweetheart, I always hoped that our relationship would take us here. I just didn't know when." With that, I pulled her close to me and said, "Mary Ann, will you marry me?"

When I held Mary Ann, I would always have different sensations. The first time on the ski bus was a good one, but this time it was the best! I sometimes, even today when I am in Chicago, drive-by that exact spot in Lincoln Park. It is down the street from the Chicago Pizza and Oven Grinder and right outside our apartment.

The wheels were now in full motion. From that extraordinary walk in Lincoln Park, we jumped into the role of Wedding Planning. Things were happening fast. I did receive and accept the offer from Rockwell. And after asking Ray and Midge for their daughter's hand in marriage, Mary Ann and her mother started planning for the wedding. A couple of weeks later, Mary Ann went to see her parents. Mary Ann called that afternoon from Tinley and asked, "Stephen, June 10th or July 23rd?"

I responded, "Other than both those days being our birthdays, what are you asking?"

She said, "I know you would want to have our wedding party at a country club if possible, and we are here at Cherry Hills Country Club in Flossmoor, Illinois, and those are the only two Saturdays they still have open for a wedding party next summer.

I said, "Wait a minute, that sounds expensive. Are you sure your parents want to spend that kind of money?"

She said, do not worry. My dad was a great saver, and he had been saving since his little princess's birth for this special day. She then declared, "I am not going to get married on my birthday. I don't want to share that special day every year with our anniversary, so let's do July 23rd!"

I said, "Sweetheart, that is fine with me. Birthdays are no big deal to me. And anyway, it will help me always remember our anniversary!!"

I hung up the phone and thought, *Man, this thing is really happening. Stephen put on your seat belt.* Then it dawned on me, *Oh My God, I haven't even bought Mary Ann an engagement ring, and we have already set a date for our wedding!!* I grabbed the dictionary off the bookcase to look up the word "jerk." I wanted to make sure my picture or name wasn't included in the definition.

Mary Ann decided to stay the night at her parent's house. She wanted to go through more details of the wedding plan with her parents. When she came home that next day, I greeted her and told her she looked a little naked.

She said, "What are you talking about?"

I picked up her left hand and stared at it, and said it appears something is missing.

She looked at me and said, "You're right, Mr. Manning, and you had better put a ring on that finger before I change my mind!"

With that, we made plans to go ring shopping Monday after work. As was typical with Mary Ann, she had already been checking out where in Chicago was the best place to buy an engagement ring, not wasting time while she waited for me to figure it out. We left work, grabbed a cab, and set off to the jewelry store she had researched. The people in the store were great and well-practiced on how to handle the entire process. I would never have thought the process of buying a ring could be so complicated: gold or silver, what size diamond, what shape diamond, what color diamond? Well, Mary Ann had already thought about all these things. The way the engagement happened, ringless and all, she had a unique opportunity. She would be able to pick out precisely the kind of ring she wanted, and she did just that.

With the decision completed, the gentleman took us to the cashier. He looked at me and said, "How would you like to pay for the ring?"

"Mary Ann," I said, "I am sorry, but I did not know we were going to buy the ring tonight." I was more than a little embarrassed, as I did not bring my checkbook with me. It would not have mattered I did not have enough money in my checking account anyway. With that, I got one of those "Oh, Stephen" comments.

The jeweler did not want to cause a scene or add to my embarrassment. He said, "Mr. Manning, why don't you leave a $100 deposit, and we will set the ring aside for you."

I gave him the $100, and we grabbed a cab home.

Mary Ann was so excited to get the ring after waiting patiently for a few weeks. She said as we left, "We have to go back there tomorrow so they can get started making my engagement ring. I can't tell everyone that we are getting married and not have an engagement ring on my finger!"

I said, "I understand, and I love the ring you picked out, but that is a lot of money, and I am going to have to get a loan from the credit union to pay for it." Inland Credit Union was right in the building and offered great rates to the employees. The only problem with that plan was that you had to repay all your outstanding balances as soon as you left Inland. All payments had to be paid through payroll deductions. Knowing that I was about to resign at Inland, this was not a viable plan for me.

Mary Ann then said, "I can't believe I am now buying my engagement ring! I will go to the credit union and get the money first thing tomorrow morning, but you are paying me back for this!"

She went immediately to the credit union as soon as it opened that next morning to withdraw the money. A brief time later, she hopped on the elevator, pushed the button for the accounting floor. Instead of heading to the cashier, she turned and walked up to my desk. She handed me a piece of paper that showed the exact amount that I would pay her for that ring, basically equaling her payroll deduction to the credit union. In her mind, she wanted to leave no doubt that she was not buying her engagement ring.

I looked at the math, smiled, and said, "We have a deal!"

Later that day, it was back in the cab, and we headed to the jewelry store and gave them the money. Before we left, she turned to the jeweler and asked, "Can I see my ring one more time before we leave?" With all smiles, we left the jewelers. We decided to enjoy the evening with a walk to one of our favorite watering holes. We had dinner and a drink to celebrate this critical next step in our relationship. The jeweler put a rush on the order for Mary Ann, and we were able to pick the ring up early that next week. She could not wait to walk into work that next day, flashing her ring around and letting everyone know that we were getting married on July 23, 1977.

While we were still hanging out with our many friends from work, we did enjoy our time alone. We would take that time to start planning our future together, always wondering where the road would take us. Before I met Mary Ann, I had begun to take advantage of Sunday mornings by attending mass. There was a beautiful church, St. Michael's, not too far away from my apartment. I found this time memorable, and, like when I was in college, I wondered where life would take me post-graduation. I would often ask the Lord for his help and guidance. Now, as I was getting settled in Chicago, I would knock on that door once again. I would ask the Lord for his guidance in making the right life choices. While I would mostly ask God for professional and social advice, I would, on occasion, ask for his help in finding that person that *I would want to be the mother of my children*. At that time, I did not think that this was a high priority, well, not until I met Mary Ann. I knew from meeting Mary Ann and her family that Sunday mass was essential to them as well. While Mary Ann was still living at home, it was part of the weekly routine. They lived close enough to the parish that they would always walk together to church.

I enjoyed Sunday mass as well. When we first started dating, Mary Ann would occasionally stay the night with me. If it was a Saturday night, she would often see me up early on Sunday morning. I would be off to church for my special time with the Lord. One weekend I said to her, "Mary Ann, why don't you join me Sunday for church. St Michael's is such a neat church, and I would love for you to join me." As an added incentive, I told her that I would take her to brunch at Butch McGuire's, a great bar/restaurant on the near north side that we often frequented with friends after church. She loved their eggs Benedict, and their Bloody Marys to go along with it. It soon became a standard weekend date, not every Sunday, but many. Sometimes, if our Sundays were full, we would catch the Saturday evening mass. On

Saturdays after mass, oftentimes, we would walk to another famous restaurant in the area, the Twin Anchors. They had the best BBQ ribs in town, and like many great rib places, no reservations, and cash only. They also had a great bar to hang out. There was always a wait, often up to an hour and a half. Scattered around the bar were many pictures of Frank Sinatra and other celebrities. The Twin Anchors was known for where Frank Sinatra always went for ribs during his many stays in Chicago.

Before I started work at Rockwell, I had to resign from Inland Steel. That was going to be difficult for me because they had all been so good to me. Many would later either be in our wedding party or guests at our wedding. My direct boss sat right behind me, and we often talked, not always about the job, but also about family and life in general.

I turned my chair to him and said, "Dennis, let's go grab a coffee. I have something I need to tell you."

As we walked down to the cafeteria, he said, "Steve, I am a little nervous. You sound so serious; I hope nothing is wrong between you and Mary Ann."

I said, "No, things are fine with Mary Ann and me, but it is serious."

We grabbed our coffees and found a table. I said, "Dennis, I have taken another job and will be leaving Inland in two weeks."

Dennis was shocked. He said, "Steve, are you out of your mind? While you have only been here a brief time, the leadership team loves you, and while you are not supposed to know this, you are on the company's high-potential list. I know that because I must review your performance and our plans for you every quarter. You should know the company has some really exciting plans for you over the next three to five years." He paused and then asked, "Steve, why are you leaving, and where are you going?"

I told him about Rockwell and the operational audit position there. He asked if I had been out interviewing and how I came across this opportunity. I told him I had not been interviewing at all. I took a call one day from a headhunter and took the interview about a month ago. For the question of why I was leaving, I said, "Dennis, I will tell you as a friend, but please don't tell the leadership. It is about where the U.S. steel industry is going, and I think there is a great long-term risk here. I don't see inflation getting under control or the U.S. Government doing much about the Japanese steel indus-try's dumping. We both know they are getting more efficient in their produc-tion techniques, and their quality is improving. Simultaneously, the industry here in the U.S. is not making the kind of investments needed to modernize the mills. The country has gone through the biggest oil shock of its history. Gas shortages and rationing were rampant in the early seventies. With what I think are signs of runaway inflation caused by the oil shortage, labor costs are going to get out of hand, and the union will try to protect their members."

Dennis said, "Are you telling me you are going to throw away this terrific opportunity here at Inland because of your economic theory and what might happen?"

I told him the story I told Mary Ann about my dad and how he got caught short when his industry dramatically changed. Dennis said, "Steve, I understand and won't fight you on this.

It all called for some Mary Ann time. I also felt a call to my parents was required to bring them up to date. Back in those days, especially in Nebraska, having a job for life at a good company was the rite of passage. While this was slowly changing, it was much more the norm than the exception. Of course, one of my mother's first questions was, "What does Mary Ann think about all this?"

I told her that we were about to discuss this tonight. Mary Ann had gone out to get a pizza to give me some time alone to call my parents. She came back to the apartment with a take-out Chicago Pizza and Oven Grinder upside-down special. As I told her about my meetings, she said, "Stephen, we don't have to be rich. I will never be that demanding. As you know, I did not grow up in a family with a lot of money, and we did fine. Please do not think that I will ever judge you or love you less for how much you make, and if necessary, I can continue to work after we get married."

I told her that the salary increase and the signing bonus were not what was motivating me. It was still very much about the long-term health of the steel industry. I went on to say that I hoped after we got married, she would only continue to work until we had kids. Once we started having kids, I wanted her to stay-at-home and take on the critical task of caring for our children full time. It was also her desire. We agreed we would set that as our primary goal. I said, let's let the income level fall where it may. Neither one of our families had much, and we were both happy growing up. We both agreed that what was important was how we raised and cared for our children, just as our parents had raised us.

We desired to have a family-first marriage. We never discussed how many children we thought we were going to have. More than one for sure, but we never put an upper limit on it. We knew those details would play themselves out for us over time. She came from a family of three, and I came from a family of five, so we were pretty much comfortable with a number between three and five. As we continued to talk about my decision to leave Inland, she finally said. "OK, Stephen, if you believe that Rockwell is the best choice for your professional career, I will support you in that decision, but if things don't work out, please don't burn your bridges at Inland. I am sure they will take you back if it turns out you made the wrong decision."

I then called my parents back. I let them know that I would move forward with Rockwell and that Mary Ann was OK with that decision.

Our Wedding

*E*verything seemed to be moving as planned, although sometimes in reverse order. A marriage proposal was made. Both parents were informed of our plans. Wedding date set, the venue chosen. The engagement ring purchased. With that, we started sketching together the invitee list and wedding party. We were both getting overly excited about our future and our life together. Our relationship was only getting better.

One day Mary Ann came to me and said that she had a doctor's appointment. The doctor suggested I go with her on her follow-up visit. I could see she was upset, so I asked her, "What did the doctor say? Why would he want me to be with you at the next appointment?"

She started to cry and said that the doctor found a cyst on an ovary and that he might have to remove one or both of her ovaries.

I had little knowledge of women's health at the time and knew little about a woman's anatomy, so I had to ask if this was serious. She said that he wanted to do more testing, but an operation was likely. He also wanted to explain the possible outcome of the surgery.

I said, "I understand why that would make sense for you. Are you telling me this is life-threatening, and that is why he wants me there?"

"No," through her tears, she said, "but it may mean that I will not be able to have children. Since I told him I was getting married, he thought he should sit down with us both. He wants to explain the risk of surgery and possible outcomes."

I found out later from her mother that Mary Ann was worried sick that I would cancel the engagement when I heard this news. Mary Ann had told her to find out what the cancellation policy was at Cherry Hills. She was worried that her dad would lose his deposit if we canceled the wedding party. The story her mom told me broke my heart. She cared about everyone, especially her dad. She knew he could not afford this wedding and was worried that he would lose his deposit.

My immediate thought was, *oh my god, I always had plans to get married and have a large, healthy family.* Now the idea of a childless marriage had me stunned. Mary Ann could see she caught me way off guard and started to cry even more.

I held her and said, "Sweetheart, calm down, catch your breath, and let's talk about this." A thousand thoughts were going through my head; one of them was that I loved this lady. I had to be there for her. I knew if the roles were reversed, she would be there for me. As she started to calm down, I told her, "Mary Ann, this does not change a thing with us. I have loved you from the beginning, and I still love you now. Yes, I want you to be *the mother of my children,* and if God allows that, I know you will do an excellent job. If not, and you cannot have children, then we will adopt. I know you will still *be a great mother to our children.* Please set the meeting up with your doctor as soon as possible."

She said, "He can see us tomorrow."

I still did not know how I felt about this news, and she knew it. While we did not talk much about marriage while dating, she did know how I felt. Unless you were ready to start a family, I did not think getting married was of any urgency. This all had to be weighing on her mind. I am sure that is what prompted her to call her mother about wedding planning.

I thought *the doctor could not have been more thoughtful and caring to offer to consult with both of us.* He introduced himself to me and hugged Mary Ann as he took us into the exam room. He said, "Mary Ann, I now have all of the test results back. I would like to go through these with you and Steve. Are you OK with that since it's your personal medical history?"

She said yes, of course, and he proceeded. "Mary Ann, Steve, the diagnosis is not good, but you do have some options which we should discuss. That is why I wanted you both here. Mary Ann, you have a cyst on both of your ovaries. One cyst is large, but the other one is not too big. You should have the surgery very soon. The safest option for you, Mary Ann, is to remove both ovaries. That would remove the risk of cancer in the future. Option two would likely be to remove the one ovary that has the largest cyst. I would then try to save the second one by cutting away the cyst on it. If I am successful with that procedure, I may be able to save enough of the ovary, and you might have at least one child. Again, by leaving the ovary in place, you risk the chance of having cancer in the future. The good news is the cysts are not cancerous."

Mary Ann held my hand tightly, trying her best not to start crying in front of the doctor. My head was spinning out of control. I thought about my sweetheart and how devastating this news must be for her—even knowing how strong she was as a person, how terrified she must have been.

Mary Ann gathered herself. She looked up to me and told me, "Stephen, I have always wanted to have children, and I still want to try." Now with tears in my eyes, I looked at her and said, "Sweetheart, I will go along with whatever you decide. Please remember, I am OK with adoption. I love you, and I want to be with you for the rest of my life. I am worried about the future risk of cancer for you."

She hugged me and said, "Stephen, if you will stay with me, let us give this a try. If we can't have kids in the next few years, I will go back in for the complete surgery."

While I tried to be strong for Mary Ann, I was taken back by this news. We had only been engaged for a couple of months. It all came on fast, and I knew I loved her, but I wanted to build a family with her. I was not sure now if the marriage would be the right thing for us. I did not want to tell her that because she had enough stress at the time, and I did love her in so many ways. I was searching for the *mother of my children and* adopting children at the time was not what I was considering. I said nothing further about this subject; she had enough on her mind. It was later that I went back and forth in my mind about how to deal with this pending reality. Back then, I thought, you date to fall in love. You marry to have children and start a family. No question I was in love with Mary Ann and wanted to spend the rest of my life with her, but I also wanted a family with her.

The doctor scheduled the surgery two days later. We took a quick trip to St. Michael's after the appointment. We hit the Lord hard with a handful of prayers, asking for his help to get through the operation. We also asked for his help in letting us start a family.

The surgery was a success, and the doctor said he could save portions of each ovary. When Mary Ann had recovered from the surgery, the doctor came in to see her. We thanked him for everything, both medically and personally. We told him we were adding him and his wife to the wedding guest list. He thanked us and suggested that we should get on with it if we wanted to have kids as soon as possible. He was a very caring doctor. I so wanted his words to be right. I knew that Mary Ann would be a loving mother if she had a chance to do just that.

As I started to make the commute to Schaumburg, in the Green Pea no less, I thought at some point that a relocation to the Schaumburg area was likely. Leaving the city was going to be difficult. It was such an excellent place to be young and single. Mary Ann and I had met so many great friends there. I started to think about what life in the city would be like for a young married couple getting ready to start a family. As it turned out, Mary Ann was having some of the same thoughts. She said it had been a wonderful experience, and she had enjoyed her single life in the city. She thought she would want to start her family in a house in the suburbs once she got married. Given the advice of her doctor, we knew we would be trying to start a family soon.

That weekend we took another walk-through Lincoln Park. Mary Ann asked if I had taken any time to look around the neighborhoods by my new office. I told her no but thought that someday a move to the suburbs might make sense for us. She would have to commute into the city, but if you lived close to one of the commuter rails lines, the commute was not too bad. We decided to take a ride together the following weekend. We wanted to check out some of the neighborhoods around Schaumburg.

We found some nice areas and houses that we could afford to buy. The timing was right because my apartment complex was converting over to condos. That meant I would either have to buy my apartment or try to rent it from the new owner. We also looked at some property further north of the area where we were living. From what we could see, the only thing we could afford were fixer-uppers and little did she know that I was not that handy.

Once we decided a house in the suburbs was in our future, we had to figure out how this would work. Even though we were pretty much living together at this point, we had not shared this information with our parents. She kept her room in the house she shared with her two friends but seldom stayed there, only keeping her off-season wardrobe, skis, a bike, and some keepsakes. I contacted a local realtor to help find some listings in the area as well. We ended up finding a lovely townhouse a short drive from the commuter train station that had ample free parking for its commuter customers. It also meant that I would have to buy a car now since we would both need one to go to work. We had enough for a down payment with the signing bonus, and we qualified for a mortgage with our two incomes. The townhouse was three stories, with a small basement, three baths, the master on the top floor, and two bedrooms on the second story. I knew Mary Ann was already thinking about how she would decorate the baby room someday soon.

We were still about six months from getting married, and that was going to be a problem. To make this all work, we needed both salaries to pay the mortgage. So, Mary Ann had to move out of her apartment and into our new home. Both of our parents were deeply religious and devout Catholics. They were also both still recovering emotionally from Mary Ann's surgery along with the prognosis of having difficulties with childbearing. They were happy that plans were still in place for us to get married in July. Yet, they were not going to be pleased with this news. We both decided that this news had to be delivered in person. She would go to Tinley Park, and I would take that long ride to Lincoln. My mother knew something was up when I told her I would be coming home that weekend to see the family alone. I knew Mary Ann would have a more challenging job because her dad would be dead set against this move. I also knew my mother was going to have extreme heartburn about this as well. My mother loved Mary Ann, but she also loved the sanctity of marriage. I figured my dad would shake his head in disapproval, but my mother was going to be far more vocal.

When I sat down to discuss this move, she said, "Steve, I can't condone this. I love seeing you and Mary Ann together, and I so want to see you marry, but this is not right."

Not to add controversy to the discussion, I told my mother that I was still concerned about Mary Ann's ability to have children. I could see my mother was upset. She liked Mary Ann and was convinced that I had met the *woman I wanted to have my children.* In her best Catholic voice, she said, "My son" in an even stronger voice than Mary Ann's "Stephen." When my mother said, "My son," she was not only speaking for the family but also for the church. She said, "Son when you love someone, you love them for all of their goodness and all of their faults. No one is ever perfect, and if you think you are, I will share a few stories with you. Mary Ann has more character than anyone you have ever brought home before. She is loving, and I can see she loves you very much. When you come into the room, her eyes light up. A mother sees these things that you may not. Sure, it will be tough if you can't have kids together but think about all the kids that would love to grow up in your household. Do not lose this opportunity. She is the one for you. Take some time, say your prayers to the Lord. He will listen to you. He, like your father and I, think this is the right person for you and your future family, however that comes about."

My mother was so special, which is why I loved her so much. I saw so much of her in Mary Ann. I was still nervous, but these words helped so much. It also took the focus off us moving into the same house just a little bit. Five PM back in the Manning household could not come quick enough that first night back home.

In Mary Ann's case, it was her father who was the vocal one. Her mom was more accepting, knowing that July 23rd was fast approaching. It could not get here fast enough. One thing that seemed to make it a little more acceptable with Ray was that his daughter's name was on the mortgage, so he could be proud that she could buy a house at such an early age. Although the golf season was fast approaching, I figured my next golf game with Ray would be sometime after July 23rd.

So, neither of our parents approved our decision to move in together. But they knew our decision had been made. We both loved our parents, but we knew this was the right decision at the time.

Although tense, things started to settle down, and we moved into our new home. My parents had not planned to visit Chicago until the wedding, so no issue there. Ray Lesin told Mary Ann he refused to visit us in our new home in Roselle, Illinois, until we were married. But Midge could not resist; she wanted to see our new home. Since Midge did not drive, she talked one of her girlfriends into driving her. She was too nosey and came up many times after we moved in and started to decorate.

As we were getting settled in our new home, we decided to have a house-warming party. Beyond the many friends from the city, we had many friends outside the city we wanted to get together. There were still friends of Mary Ann, who I had not yet met, and friends of mine she had not met. As we started to build the list, I thought, w*ow, this is quite a unique set of people. I wonder how they would all get along since many did not know each other.* I came up with the idea of having a "hat party." In the invite, we told everyone that they needed to wear a hat to the party. My thinking was that we needed to loosen everybody up. My theory was when you wear a hat, you lose some of your apprehensions, especially about meeting new people, and by the way, the crazier the hat was, the better!

The idea worked out great. No one came without a hat, and they were all incredibly unique hats. Everyone mingled and had a wonderful time. That was good because everyone was going to be together soon at our wedding party.

As we started building our wedding list, we started worrying about how big that list would be. With Mary Ann's family being local, there would be many of them attending the wedding. I assumed that a large part of the Manning clan would also be traveling to Chicago for the wedding. I knew country club weddings were not cheap, and they all charged on a per-person basis. The invitee list was soon growing beyond the one hundred and fifty that Ray and Midge had budgeted for, and it was fast approaching over two hundred. In her mind, Mary Ann had been planning her big wedding day for some time. She wanted it to be the most special day of her young life. Mary Ann wanted everything to be perfect, and so did I. I suggested that we hire a wedding planner to help make the day as unique as she had dreamed of. It would take some pressure of her and help her not miss an essential detail of that special day. Mary Ann researched and found a wedding planner who had planned a wedding before at Cherry Hills.

As we started going through the wedding details, I could see the dollars beginning to mount up. I learned that the wedding industry was a money pit. Everything costs more when you put "wedding" in front of it. For example, Flowers were double the price if you said "wedding flowers" instead of a bouquet of flowers. Rather than disappoint Mary Ann and driving Ray and Midge into early bankruptcy, I suggested that I help defray some of the wedding costs. I asked the wedding planner to itemize the bill into two parts. What would the cost be for one hundred and fifty guests only, and two, the estimated total for two hundred or so guests.

Mary Ann turned to me and said, "Stephen, you know my dad is not going to accept any money from you for our wedding."

I said, "I know your dad is an immensely proud man, and I love him for it, but you are still his little princess. I know he would want you to have the wedding of your dreams. Please go sit down with him, and in your best little princess voice, convince him this is the right thing for all of us."

She had that discussion with him on her next visit home. Thankfully, he agreed to the new math and finalized the guestlist for that special day.

The next thing to complete was planning for the honeymoon. If it were not July, a ski honeymoon would have been truly relevant for us, but a snowy ski slope would be hard to find. We discussed many east coast and west coast venues and even thought about Europe. Having only about eight days left in either of our vacation times that year, we did not want to spend too much of that time on an airplane flying. The discussions continued about where we would go for our honeymoon. I suggested to Mary Ann that I would go to the travel agency we were using at work and hand them the problem. After all, Mary Ann had done most of the work on everything else related to the wedding. It was time for me to step up.

The next day I stopped by the travel agency and asked them for some ideas for our honeymoon. They were happy to help. A few of them in the office gathered around. They started asking questions about what I thought my bride-to-be would like. A beach somewhere? A big-city tour? A lake house? and on and on. They were really getting into it when I saw a poster on the wall advertising an ocean cruise line. I said, "That's it! Let's plan for an ocean cruise"!

They responded excitedly, "OK, where to?" and pulled out the brochures from one of the cruise lines they often used, and we looked at assorted options.

All sounded great, but we settled on a Caribbean Cruise. I figured I could not go wrong with the Caribbean? With islands like St. Croix, St. Thomas, and St. Lucia, it all sounded too perfect. It would be a wonderful place to honeymoon with my St. Mary Ann. Cross-Atlantic cruises had been enjoyed by the extraordinarily rich for many years. Holiday cruises to islands and back to the U.S. didn't start getting popular until the late sixties. In the winter months in Chicago, they were advertising heavily. I grabbed the brochure for the Caribbean cruise and later that day sat down with Mary Ann.

I said, "How about this for our honeymoon?"

She said this could not be more perfect other than that the ship sets sail on Saturdays. And we are getting married on a Saturday. I said, OK, let's take some time to enjoy all the out-of-town guests coming in for the wedding. Then we can leave for the cruise that following Friday. We would have to get some extra time off from work, but this is too good a plan to pass up.

Deal done and the honeymoon cruise was booked.

Time was moving fast, and our wedding day was around the corner. Most of the guests had already confirmed their attendance. We confirmed the final headcount to Cherry Hills along with our last deposit. I was starting to get cold feet about the wedding. The words "married for life" meant a lot to me, and I was getting nervous. I was still having thoughts about our ability to have children. I am sure a few weeks before getting married, and all couples have concerns about their big day. I must have been over-thinking it. I knew if I did not go forward with this wedding, I would suffer a lot of displeasure from all those who had made plans to attend. I also knew how lucky I was that Mary Ann had decided to participate in this event with me. I eventually got my head on straight, realizing how lucky I was. No matter what happened with Mary Ann's ability to have children, I was still the luckiest guy in Chicago. Being at the wedding altar with Mary Ann was a true gift from above.

The bachelorette and bachelor parties were all done. Close family and friends were starting to arrive for the big day. Ray and Midge had offered their home for a pre-wedding party. The families could get to know each other, which was great. I arranged for the catering and liquid refreshments, and we set up a bar in the basement of their house. The weather cooperated, so we were able to entertain in the home and outside. My dad and Mary Ann's uncle Bill operated the bar, and my mother and Midge served the food. It was going to be the first time my parents would meet Mary Ann's family. Thus, we all got there early so they could spend some time together before the larger crowd gathered.

My dad was a great storyteller. You could give him a subject or a location, and he would manufacture the best story possible, frequently injecting facts when available or what he called "likely facts" when necessary. Well, poor Ray Lesin got cornered by Ray Manning as he lit into one of his stories about the war. Both Rays had served in World War II, Ray Lesin in the Army, and Ray Manning in the Naval Air Command. Little did Ray Lesin know that war stories were fertile ground for my dad's use of "likely facts" in his story-telling. I finally had to pull Ray Lesin aside and said, "Ask my dad about golf. He will generally stick to the facts when talking about golf." Ray Lesin did, and they got along well, as they both loved the game.

Midge and my mother also got along well. They started to prepare the catered food and set the table for the soon-to-arrive guests. Uncle Bill was not the right person to pair up with my dad at the serving bar. Bill had a very cheerful personality and had never met a stranger, which was great for a mixed crowd. Bill, as it happens, was also a "storyteller." As the two got together at the bar, I noticed two things: One, they both tried to "out-story tell" each other in what I was sure a string of fact-light stories. Two, as I found out later when Uncle Bill makes a drink for you, he always likes to taste it first, to make sure he mixed it right, even on straight shots! It was not the bartender partner my dad needed. Dad got into his own taste verification mode along with Uncle Bill. It wasn't too long before we had to turn the bar into a self-service bar that night! The party ended earlier for some, like dad and Uncle Bill, and it went well into the evening for others. Everybody was anxious to meet all members of the Lesin and Manning clan.

My parents and sisters stayed at our house that week, and Mary Ann stayed with her parents. My brother could not make the wedding as he studied for his upcoming bar exam back in Topeka, Kansas. I had planned for him to be my best man, so I decided to keep that role in the family and asked my dad to do the honors. He was taken back by the request. He thought he was too old for the role but soon became excited about it. It was also crucial to me because we had a falling out when I started college. For a time back then, we were not even talking to each other. It was a sad time for both of us. If I were home and he walked into the room, I would get up and leave the room. It wasn't until my mom's mom grabbed me by the collar and said, "Steve, I want you and your dad to make up right now! If you don't, you will regret this for the rest of your life."

Gam, as we referred to her, would never get in the middle of a family argument, at least not in front of the grandkids. She was a strong woman of German descent and could pack a punch when mad. Gam only stood about five feet tall but had my full attention when she grabbed my collar. I loved her dearly, and I knew she was right. A brief time later, my dad and I sat down and made amends. I would not be surprised if Gam did not at some point grab his collar as well.

It is now the morning of July 23rd, and we need to make our way to Tinley Park for the wedding. My dad and I were in our tuxedos and my lovely mother in a stunning dress, as were my three sisters. Tinley Park was about an hour's drive from Roselle in light weekend traffic. We left early to ensure we got to the church in plenty of time. Everyone was excited about what was about to unfold. My parents kept talking about how much they enjoyed meeting Mary Ann's family and how beautiful she looked at the party. As we entered the church, my dad and I were ushered off to the back of the church. They wanted to make sure we did not sneak a glance at my beautiful bride.

I am now getting nervous about how big this moment was going to be. "Married for life" was ringing in my head, but I knew this was the lady I wanted to make that commitment to. As we walked out onto the altar, I could see the church was packed. Mary Ann had chosen some great music for the ceremony. When the music switched to the procession song, I had to take a deep breath. As the wedding party started their way down the aisle, I waited with great anticipation. I could not wait to see my lovely bride, and she did not disappoint. Mary Ann looked stunning in her white wedding gown, healthy, tan, and veiled. The closer she got to the altar, the more incredible she looked. She looked even better when she kissed her dad and looked up to me and gave me that great smile of hers. As I stood next to her, I could not have been prouder or happier. The ceremony was beautiful. When my dad handed me the ring, which by the way was now fully paid for, I looked into Mary Ann's eyes and smiled. I was again thinking, "married for life."

After many, many pictures in and around the church, we were off to Cherry Hills for the wedding reception. Everything was going as planned, and Mary Ann was more than pleased. We jumped in my dad's car as he drove us to the Country Club. The wedding mass was set later in the afternoon. Mary Ann wanted everyone to be able to go from the church directly to the reception. As we pulled up to the Country Club and past the golf course, I saw the clubhouse for the first time. The setting was terrific. It was a stately building, framed by some large oak trees and red roses, my mother's favorite, glowing in the afternoon sun. As the guests saw my dad's car pulling in, they all came out to greet us. Many of the guests took in the church's wedding ceremony, which I knew made Mary Ann very happy. She had planned everything to the tee, including the church's music and all the flower arrangements. With her cousins' help, we took the flowers from the church and spread them around the reception area. The reception dining area was quite impressive. All the windows and balcony overlooked the golf course, which was sparkling in a striking shade of green in the late afternoon sun. As we thought it would be, the reception was packed.

When you commit a final headcount to the wedding venue, you give a number, and you get a plus or minus 10% range at the price agreed. We were at the plus 10% end. Many friends and all significant relatives were there, anxious to celebrate our marriage with us. I was so happy to see and greet Mary Ann's surgeon and his wife, who had also attended the wedding ceremony. He had played a key role for us, as we would find out later in our marriage.

Dinner was served, speeches were made, and toasts were given by many people important to both Mary Ann and I. Mary Ann's dad did an excellent job introducing and toasting his lovely daughter. Ray did not like public speaking. He soon found out, when you are speaking from your heart about someone you love so dearly, public speaking is more comfortable. My dad was the opposite. He never found a podium he did not like standing behind. He gave a brilliant toast, and as I made him promise, "no storytelling."

I had warned the wedding planner to tell the club to make sure they put on extra bartenders. I knew from being around my family and some of Mary Ann's that the bartenders would be remarkably busy that night. Sure enough, the bar was the place to be before dinner and after the dancing started. Soon it was time for our first dance. As the music began, I looked at Mary Ann in her beautiful white gown. Her hair was perfect and still covered with her veil. And she had the most precious smile I could imagine, with that I held her close, and we started our first dance as Mr. and Mrs. Manning. Of course, Mary Ann had chosen a song from one of her favorite artists, Barbara Streisand, "Evergreen." Such a dream come true. I then handed her off to her father, who fancied himself as quite the dancer. She had them play his favorite song, which he often had sung to her, "Ave Maria," Ray had a great singing voice. He was happy with her song selection. We cleared the floor for what was a great father and daughter wedding dance.

After they glided around the floor, I took my mother's arm and led her to the dance floor as well. My mother was also a good dancer and loved to dance. She was light on her feet and wore a floral dress that helped light up her face and had a wonderful smile. Mary Ann and my mother had a similar music taste, and I know she collaborated with my mother on some of the early song selections. Mary Ann was so gracious; she danced that night with every male relative that I had at the reception. My dad, Uncle Tom, and Uncle Vince danced with her many times before I finally got her back into my arms.

As extraordinary events in your life go, the evening seemed to speed by. At the end of the night, I felt like it was over before it started. No one left the reception early. Unfortunately, it was so crowded I did not get a chance to spend the time I wanted to with many of the guests. With that, Mary Ann and I left for our hotel with full exhaustion. Mary Ann was so excited about how well the entire day went. She said before she went to bed, my face is sore from smiling so much today; I think I need to put ice on it!

The next day Mary Ann had planned a picnic. It would be at one of the local forest preserves for all friends and family still in town. The Chicago area had some tremendous well-maintained forest preserves that you could reserve for a small fee. She had found a spot at one of her favorite locations, that was big enough for everyone. It was a relaxing afternoon. There were hot dogs and hamburgers, a few kites, and Frisbees for the kids, and plenty of adults sitting comfortably in chairs still resting their feet from a night of dancing. As we wrapped up our little post-wedding picnic and prepared to head back to our house, Ray Lesin pulled me aside. He asked, "Steve, I am anxious to come to see the house you and Mary Ann bought; when can I visit?"

I shook his hand, put my other hand on his shoulder, and said, "Ray, our door is always open for you, dad." I knew this was a tough stretch for Mary Ann's dad, but he put up with it. He was as happy as I was that July 23rd came and that we were now a legally married couple.

My parents had stayed at our house during all the events. They had planned to stay a few days longer. They wanted to steal some time with Mary Ann before we took off for our honeymoon. It was remarkable how well Mary Ann was getting along with my parents. This significant relationship would only continue and grow. That Friday, my mom and dad took us to the airport to go to Miami and the cruise.

Our Honeymoon

We arrived in Miami midafternoon. We checked into a hotel close to where we were going to board the ship that next morning. I surprised Mary Ann and had gotten the bridal suite at the hotel. Since the hotel we stayed at after the wedding did not have a bridal suite, I thought that would be a nice treat. We ordered up a bottle of champagne and dinner and enjoyed just being alone. After having my family staying at our house, we were going to take full advantage of being alone and so very much in love.

The next day we made our way to the boarding area of the ship and started checking in. As we were checking in, the purser asked if there was anything special we were celebrating. With some immediacy, Mary Ann said, "Our honeymoon!" With that, the purser rechecked the passenger list and said, "I am sorry I missed that. I see you will be having dinner at the Captain's table on Monday night. He wants to toast you both. Please make sure you dress in a proper dinner jacket for that event." Luckily, I had packed a tuxedo and Mary Ann, a fancy dress for that event.

We made our way to our stateroom and started to unpack. Our room was not too big but well-appointed and had enough closet space for all Mary Ann's clothes. I would soon learn that Mary Ann never traveled light. She would always pack a little extra for those "just in case" moments. Those "just in case" moments where I never found out over the years, but I got used to it. We then got into our best cruise ship walking gear and headed out to see what a cruise liner looked like. We checked out the upper deck and then the pool area, bars, and restaurant, and then, to Mary Ann's displeasure, we found the casino area.

Mary Ann was not a gambler. One night I had some guys over to my apartment for a card game. Mary Ann was there to help me host the group. We were playing blackjack, and I was winning. As I went into the kitchen to get some beers, she asked, "How much are you winning?" I said about $100. Later after everyone had left, she asked how much I was ahead. I said it looks like $50. With that, she cried out in disgust, "I can't believe you lost $50!!"

I responded, "What?"

"Well, you said earlier that you were up $100," she responded. Now I was never a math genius, but I had taken a lot of math courses. And I was now learning Mary Ann's gambling mathematics. The family learned to call these Mary Ann-isms. You will read much more about those later. I would tell the kids 'don't argue with her'. No one got hurt; let it go.

It was getting time for dinner. The ship offered two seatings in the main dining room, and we had chosen the later seating. The travel agency told us that this cruise line was famous for its food and service, so we were excited to see the menu. It also had assigned seating, so we were also interested in meeting our new dinner partners for the week. As we entered the dining area, they asked for our names and then escorted us to the table. We were a little early, and only two ladies were at the table, so we pretty much got our choice of seats. The two young ladies had recently finished their second year of college. Their parents had sponsored the cruise for them. We introduced ourselves to them, and as we were making small talk, another couple came to the table. This was a couple a little older than us from New York, Barbara and Jan. Jan was a quiet guy, as it turns out not by nature. It was because Barbara never gave him a chance to talk. She would answer every question posed to either herself or Jan and had pretty much an answer for everything. Barbara could project a voice better than a studied opera singer. This would become evident not just at our table but at most tables around us.

By the time the cruise ended, everyone knew Barbara. As sweet as Mary Ann was, Mary Ann would just start shaking by the end of the cruise. Barbara would inevitably insert herself into somebody else's conversation. After cocktails at the table, the waiter brought over the menu. Mary Ann was beside herself with the menu's multiple choices: steak, lamb, fish, pasta, chicken, and pleasing appetizers and salads. She loved lobster, so that was going to be her first dinner choice. As advertised, the food was excellent, cooked to order, and in reasonable portions. The dessert menu was as delightful, with so many options. We decided we would each order a different dessert and share. I ordered coffee and an after-dinner drink as we sat, getting to know our dinner guests. About midway through the dinner, another lady showed up who was single and on the cruise by herself. She was from Texas, while the other two young ladies were from New Jersey.

As the dinner conversation wound down, we decided to retake a walk around the ship. We found some deck chairs where we could enjoy the night sky. As we stared into the sky, I said, "Mary Ann, I am sorry I forgot to ask you how you enjoyed your lobster?"

She said, "It was excellent, but I am mad."

I asked, "Honey, what are you mad about??"

She then let loose, "Can you believe it? We are on our honeymoon, and they sat us with three single women. Tables with couples surround us, and here I sit, having to share you with three young women and Barbara and Jan."

I said, "I am sorry sweetheart, tomorrow morning after breakfast, I will talk to the purser and see if we can get our table changed. It will be alright; let's enjoy the evening right now."

The next day we slept in and caught a late breakfast. Breakfast was relaxed, eat when you are ready with no assigned seating, which made Mary Ann happy. We found a table with two other young couples that were also on their honeymoon. One pair was from the Boston area and the other from Kansas City. We had a lovely chat with them both—sharing experiences from our recent wedding day and how all the events of that special day unfolded. To Mary Ann's delight, they had eggs benedict, which, as always, she topped off with a Bloody Mary. The food again was excellent, and the service top-notch. After breakfast, I went to see the purser about moving our table assignments at dinner. Unfortunately, there were no open tables at the last seating, and we didn't want to take the early seating. Mary Ann, gracious as always, said, "OK, I can deal with it and make the best out of it. It looks like Barbara, and I are going to become close friends, at least at dinner."

We sat by the pool that afternoon and grabbed a light lunch poolside. Mary Ann already had a tan that looked great on her, especially in her white wedding gown, and now in her striking yellow two-piece swimsuit. Not wanting to ruin such a great tan with a sunburn, she asked if we could move into the shade at the back of the ship. I was more than happy to oblige since, with my Irish skin, I usually went from white to bright red after being in the sun. The seas were calm as we sat there together, watching the wake of the ship as we headed to our first island stopover.

We started talking, really for the first time after her surgery, about when we should try to start a family. We knew that we would need her income for a while to help fund the mortgage. Both of us were worried about waiting too long, but we wanted to enjoy being a couple for at least a brief time, take some ski trips together, get some furniture in the house, and just be a couple for a few more years. We decided that afternoon that she would work for three more years before starting our family. Mary Ann had always been so easy to talk about our life together since our first date. She was never afraid to say what was on her mind and speak up when she did not agree with something.

Dinner was still a way off, and Mary Ann decided that she wanted to take a short nap before we got ready for dinner. I told her I would hang out for a little longer and then check out what the entertainment was at the nightclub after dinner. The ship had different entertainment every night at a lounge onboard. It was advertised to be surprisingly good, generally a comedian or a small song group. The entertainment would go from ship to ship at every port of call, so it was always different every night. She grabbed all her things and headed off to the room. I went to the bar, got a cold beer, and started looking for the theater. After checking out the night's entertainment schedule and making a reservation for the show, I went back to the room.

When I got back to the room, she was up and starting to get ready for dinner. I had already learned that Mary Ann takes a long time to get ready to go anywhere, she was such a perfectionist, but the wait was always worth it because she always looked stunning. As she was getting ready, she asked where I hung out and what was on the entertainment schedule tonight. I said, "I stopped by the night club, and they had a comic act on for the evening, so I made a reservation for us for after dinner. I also ran into the two guys we had breakfast with and had a beer with them."

She said, "OK, good, we can hang out with both couples after dinner and go to the night club together."

We got ready and went down to dinner. We decided to stop at the bar first and have our dinner cocktails there. That would give Mary Ann a little break before we joined our dinner guests at our assigned table. As Mary Ann said she would, she made the best of the dinner situation. She immediately engaged the three young ladies, asking about their college experiences, what they were studying, and if they were dating anyone special. I was enormously proud of how she handled the evening.

Looking at the menu, I knew we had some tough decisions to make. Everything on the menu looked outstanding. The waiter came by and could see we were having difficulties making a dinner choice. He said, "tonight I can recommend everything on the menu. If you can't make a choice, order three dishes, and you both can share."

I thought, *are you kidding me? Is the waiter telling us we can order three dishes for two people? And everything is inclusive, what a great deal.* With that, Mary Ann ordered a pasta dish that sounded delicious. I ordered a steak and a shrimp dish for us to share. The food was excellent and, of course, we both had dessert. I thought *we would be putting on a few pounds on this trip, but why not enjoy it now? We would both be going back to the gym when we returned to Chicago.* Barbara, of course, led most of the dinner conversation. As she started to ramble, the three young ladies finished dinner quickly and excused themselves. Jan sat there quietly as Barbara went on and on. Finally, Mary Ann turned to Jan and said, "Jan, tell me more about yourself and your family."

Jan perked up, looked at Barbara as if to say, is it OK for me to talk? Barbara attempted to tell Jan's life story; Jan interrupted her. "Barbara, I've got this," Jan turned out to be a good guy, quiet, at least around Barbara, but a good guy. Mary Ann took a liking to him. Throughout the rest of the cruise, she would always start the conversation with him first. Jan loved it, and I am sure Mary Ann did as well. We later met up with the couples from breakfast and enjoyed a good night of comedy.

The next day we would have our first island stopover. It was St. Croix. We took a tour of the main part of the island. Then walked around the area by the port where the ship was docked. We took a swim in the ocean, and the water was clear. In the shallow area, you could see all the way to the bottom. It was the first time I had ever seen water that clear. It was a fun spot, but we had to get back to the ship early. It was the night that we were going to be seated at the Captain's table. Mary Ann was going to need a little more time to get ready. As we walked back to the ship, I could see Mary Ann was getting a bit nervous about having dinner at the Captain's table that night. I asked, "are you ready for our special dinner tonight?"

She said, "I don't know, what do I even call him when we are introduced?"

I said, "I don't know, maybe, Captain?"

With that, I got one of those punches in the stomach but followed by a kiss!

When we got back to the room, Mary Ann jumped in the bathroom and started getting ready. I kicked back on the bed and put on some music, knowing that this would be a longer process than usual. When she finished, I jumped in the shower and started getting ready. As I came out of the bathroom, she had already gotten dressed. She looked fantastic; with her stunning white gown and beautiful dark tan, it took my breath away. It was not merely because she looked so good; the gown she brought with her was the same one that I had seen her in before we started dating. It was at one of the Inland Christmas parties. I remember seeing her there and thinking how attractive she was and how so far over my grade scale she was. Now I was taking my little angel to have dinner with the ship's captain to celebrate our wedding. It doesn't get any better than this.

As we entered the dining room, me in my black tux and her in her white gown, more than one eye turned to look at her. There was a small area off the Captain's table set up for pictures - First the two of us together, and then one with the Captain. I can see right away, the Captain couldn't take his eyes off Mary Ann, and for a good reason. Mary Ann kept that picture on our nightstand for years. She said it was her favorite picture of the two of us, and I am sure it was. She also knew she killed it that night, and she certainly did. Mary Ann was never stuck on herself, but sometimes you must give credit where credit is due.

The evening was a big hit for us. The dinner was as good as we had come to expect. Being at the Captain's table, we agreed to order one entrée each, which was a wise choice. One of the best things about being at the Captain's table was they served the best of the best wines there. I had started to get into fine wines with my travel with Rockwell. One of the auditors I would sometimes travel with was a wine connoisseur. Mary Ann was not yet fond of wine, but that night she decided that maybe the wine would be her drink of choice. Well, at least until the Captain decided to make his toast to all the newlyweds at the table. With that, they brought out their best champagne. It was Dom Perignon, and I am sure a good year. It was excellent, and Mary Ann had a glass of both the wine and the champagne in front of her all night. They always served flaming desserts at the Captain's table, which was exceptional. Mary Ann had ordered cherries jubilee; me the bananas foster. It was the first time either of us had ever had a flaming dessert. The dinner was excellent. The night was still young since the seating with the Captain was part of the early seating group.

With the wine and champagne, Mary Ann and I were feeling no pain. As we were leaving the dining room, Mary Ann looked at me and said, "I know you want to hit the casino on this trip; let's go there now."

It made me think, *oh boy, Mary Ann is a little bit lit up right now.* Mary Ann would seldom get anything close to tipsy. She always controlled her alcohol intake. I thought, *OK, let's try it and see how well she does with her gambling math tonight.*

We got to the casino, and I saw more older couples than I had seen before. The earlier dinner seating was far more popular for the older passengers on the cruise, as it turns out. Nonetheless, I found a seat at the blackjack table behind two gentlemen from New York. As we approached the table, they both stood up and offered Mary Ann their seat. She said, "No, I am not playing, just here to watch my husband play." They were very accommodating and moved their seats together so Mary Ann could take a seat next to me. With that, they stood to introduce themselves to Mary Ann. We all sat down, and the dealer started to deal.

The game did not start well for me. Soon I was well into my winnings for the trip. Mary Ann tried her best to keep her calm, but I could see she was getting a little upset. Not sure how her gambling math works when you are never up, but I am sure it's not right. The deal started to change, and I won like six hands in a row to go back up. I was waiting for the question, "How much are you up?" But she had gotten busy talking to one of the other player's wives, and she was losing track of the game, which was good. I did not want to have one of those situations that she asked me how much I was up and then leave the table still up but below that benchmark. The dealer continued to be cold, and we were all winning more than our fair share of hands. Often when a dealer is that cold, the house pulls in another dealer, which is exactly what they did. I decided to pick up my chips. Really for two reasons: they changed the dealer, but more because I was at my peak winnings for the night. I knew when I went through the game with Mary Ann and her gambling math, and I would be able to tell her that I won money.

With that, we decided the evening was getting late, and we needed to get up early the next day. This time we were going to explore St. Thomas. We both looked forward to seeing St. Thomas; it is a beautiful island, and they had some tremendous duty-free shopping on the island. We were looking forward to it. I was not a big shopper, but now with some real money in my pocket from a couple of nights of blackjack, I thought I might be able to buy something nice for Mary Ann.

The morning came early for both of us. Likely it had something to do with the wine and champagne. And likely excitement from winning at blackjack the night before. Mary Ann got up first and jumped in the shower. She wanted to start getting ready early for the island tour and shopping. I went down and got us some coffee and some excellent pastries. When I got back to the cabin, Mary Ann was finishing up getting ready. I showered, put on some walking shorts, and we headed off for the disembarkment. The ship was ported right off the center of St. Thomas and was a leisurely walk to the town center. There the stores were crowded. Another cruise liner had pulled into the dock earlier. Now there were passengers from both ships in all the stores. As we walked around to test some of the duty-free pricing, I turned to Mary Ann and asked, "What are you looking to buy?"

With that, she pulls out a list. Mary Ann always had a list. What surprised me that time was how long her list was. I would soon find out Mary Ann was a shopper. If something was on sale, she became a super-shopper. I should have known this. A few months after we got engaged, she came to me, with a little guilt on her face, and said, "Steve, I need to show you something." With that, she pulled out two account statements, one from Macy's and one from Carson Pirie Scotts. Both were stores near our offices in Chicago. She went on to say, "Steve, I want you to know I owe quite a bit of money on my credit cards." I looked at the outstanding balances and thought, *how did these stores allow her to build up such a bill based on her salary?* She was embarrassed by the amount that she owed, and frankly, she should have been. I thought then that I would pay off the engagement ring on time; it would take quite a while to pay these off. The good news was on this shopping trip, we would buy with cash, no credit cards. I figured I had won enough at blackjack to cover most of her list. We found more than enough from her list to buy; some nice outfits for her, mementos for our new home, and a lovely necklace for Mary Ann that was on my list.

As we were winding down our shopping, I turned to Mary Ann and said, "Mary Ann, one thing I would love to get into is photography, given all the great scenery that we have seen on the cruise, with the ocean, the night sky, and the islands. I want to get a single-lens camera, like the one our photographer used at our wedding."

She said, "I don't know much about photography, but I always liked to take pictures with my Kodak camera. Let's go shopping and see what they have."

That was a big step up from a typical Kodak camera, and the prices reflected it. Because we were both novices at this photography level, the camera store's salesman had his hands full. He showed us all cameras and lens levels until we settled on a genuinely nice camera and two lenses, one for close-in shots and one for longer-range ones. Our last purchase pretty much depleted all the cash we had but gave us some lasting souvenirs from our honeymoon.

We didn't realize that it gave us a camera that we would use for many years to capture our times together, like special pictures of our family and the kids growing up. Mary Ann would later put those pictures into albums that I still look at today.

With bags full of our shopping successes, we made our way back to the ship. What followed were more fun nights in the nightclub, other island stops, and more time together with my new bride. We then headed back to Miami and on to Chicago.

Our honeymoon could not have been more perfect. We got back to Chicago late that Saturday night. We unpacked the essentials, hung up Mary Ann's dress and my tux, and left the rest for the morning. As with every great vacation, we were thoroughly exhausted and in need of another break before returning to work, which, of course, never happens.

Finding Out We Were Pregnant

We were woken up the next morning with a call from my boss. Ron enjoyed his weekends as much as I did, so I was surprised by the early call. Ron said, "Steve, we have a problem."

I said to Ron, "I hope it is not anything serious. Are you and Cheryl alright?"

"No," he said, "not that kind of problem. It's a problem with Admiral's Mexico City operations."

I said, "I didn't know Admiral had a Mexico City operation."

"Yes, they do, and they had a fire there on Saturday morning."

I said, "Ron, what does a fire have to do with the audit team?"

He paused for a moment and said, "The problem is the fire started in the safe. That's where all the accounting records are stored."

"Wow, that is suspicious for sure. Since Mexico is in our region, what are you going to do about it?"

Ron said, "I am going to put you on a plane this afternoon. I want you there when the doors open on Monday. You will need to find out what the hell is going on down there. The controller will be expecting you in his office first thing Monday morning. I don't know him, but you need to find the underlying cause of this. You need to let us know if we have a financial problem down there. Fires in the safe are never a good thing."

I then reminded Ron that we had just gotten back from our honeymoon and asked him how long I would be gone. He said, "Get down there and assess the situation. Take a few days, then give me a call, so we can put together a game plan. Since you were out on your honeymoon, I had to assign all the other auditors to other audits. If I can pull someone off another audit, I will send him down to help. Pack up and get to the airport. Your flight leaves at 2 p.m."

I said, "OK, but Ron, you know I can't speak or read Spanish."

He said, "No problem, I am sure you will figure it out." With that, he hung up, and he likely went back to bed!

Mary Ann was hanging on my back in her cutest way, trying to listen to the phone call. She was worried that something was wrong with Ron and Cheryl. Mary Ann liked them both. Cheryl had become a big sister to Mary Ann, helping her cope with the life of being attached to an auditor. She was only getting every other word of what Ron was saying. She was hearing what I was saying and heard Mexico City. It would be the first time my audit job would take me outside the United States. Many of my audit assignments were either in the Chicago area or close by in Illinois, Indiana, or Iowa. Many that I could drive day to day or within a hundred and fifty-mile radius of Chicago, out on Monday and back on Friday. While we would be alone on some of the assignments, it was all very manageable, mostly because Mary Ann was a champ and supported my new job.

Traveling was hard back then. There were no cell phones, no email, and no public internet. The first commercially available cell phone did not appear until 1983, and both the cell phone and the cell service were costly. I remember my first cell phone was costing a dollar a minute. The government may have been developing something that would become the internet back then, but nobody would have known what it was. Nobody had personal computers. When I traveled, our one-on-one communications would usually happen when I got home on Friday. It's hard to imagine today how anyone had a relationship without those communication aids. The good news is that is how we were all conditioned back then. The fire in the heart was kept alive and relit when we were back together again.

After the call with Ron, I filled Mary Ann in on the details she missed with her ear to my ear on the phone. I told her that I would have to pack and go to Mexico City for what I thought would be a few days. She was not happy but jumped into her fire drill mode to make sure I had enough clean clothes for the trip. It was cute watching her running around the house, collecting the clothes while still in her honeymoon nightie. The good news for both of us is that we now had a washer and dryer in the house. Before that, we needed to head to the local laundromat with a handful of quarters to do our laundry. After she got the wash started, she came back upstairs. I was still packing for the trip. She came over to me and gave me a big hug, and pulled me back over to the bed. We laid down together, and she turned to me and said, "Stephen, after we start a family, we can't live like this. We had the best two-and-a-half weeks of our life with the wedding, time with our families, and the honeymoon. I was looking forward to our life together as a married couple, and now you are off to Mexico."

I told her not to worry, and I needed to go down for a few days and see what had caused the fire and why it started in the safe.

After lunch together, I caught the afternoon flight to Mexico City. The good news about traveling out of Chicago is that you can fly directly to most locations worldwide. Mexico City was no exception. With Ron's wife being with American Airlines, she was able to get me an upgrade to first class. I arrived late that Sunday night. Being late, I grabbed my bags and caught a cab to the hotel. I decided to get my U.S. dollars converted into Mexican currency the next day, figuring the Admiral site's finance staff could arrange for that. The following day, I got up and, from habit, turned on the TV. It was tuned to the local news. I did not understand that many words in Spanish, so I paid little attention to it. After taking a shower, I ordered some coffee and a plate of fruit; as I was putting on my tie, I noticed that whatever the news was, the announcer seemed quite excited about it. They started showing pictures of U.S. dollars and the Mexican peso. Charts were showing a steep decline in the Mexican Peso. I thought this was a story of some intensity on the local currency. I finished my coffee and fruit and made my way to the Admiral factory.

Mexico City is a massive city with over eight million residents. Traffic was very congested, and the air quality in the city was terrible. Pollution in the city was awful, especially on a calm day. Most cars in the city were older cars sent down from the United States. I do not think that any new vehicles were being produced in Mexico at the time; every car was imported. Most cars I saw on the road were six to eight years old. They were spewing smoke out of the exhaust pipe like they were spraying for mosquitoes. The standard of living was low in Mexico back then, and they had a small middle class. Most citizens would have been considered as lower working-class by U.S. standards. Unfortunately, like most Latin American countries at the time, corruption was rampant. If you were a high official in the government, a protected class member, your wealth was significant. The income difference from bottom to top was way out of line. It was disgusting. I saw many examples of poverty and was able to meet many of the Mexico City working class. These were beautiful people; friendly, hardworking, and deeply religious people. I often thought, *how does a country get away with treating its population like this?*

When I got to the Admiral offices I met with the controller, I could see he was nervous. To break the ice, he asked if I had seen the news this morning. I told him I saw something on the news at the hotel but was unsure what was going on. I thought from what I had heard, and it must have been something to do with the Mexican peso. With that, he jumped out of his chair and said, "Something??!! Are you kidding me? The Mexicana just devalued the Mexican peso by over 50% to the dollar. We are not sure where the exchange rate will end up by the end of the day. This is a serious situation.

He then asked if there was anything I needed other than an office to start my work. I told him that I got in late last night, and I had not yet converted any of my U.S. dollars to pesos, and asked if someone in his office could do so for me. He laughed and said, "Steve, you are a fortunate man. Had you exchanged your dollars when you arrived last night before they announced the devaluation, you would have lost at least half your money overnight." We keep a petty cash fund here, so I will arrange for whatever you need. Please see my secretary when you are ready."

He then asked, "Why did they send the corporate auditors in because of a fire in the factory?" I told him that I had gotten the call Sunday morning and was instructed to be here first thing today. Not yet benefiting from any calls with the General Auditor, I would imagine they want to know how the fire got started in the safe. They will want to know if any original accounting documents were destroyed or lost. I then asked him if he had done an inventory of documents yet or had any idea how the fire got started. He said he had not. With that, he got up and suggested we both see the safe and look at the damage. Then we got up and walked down the hall from his office to check out the safe. It was clear that the fire did not start by itself.

It took me a couple of days to complete the interviews, with the help of a local interpreter who I had hired from our public auditors. By now, I could see that this would be a very laborious effort, sure to go on for weeks, not days.

Thursday morning, I called Ron to bring him up to date on what I had discovered. He was interested in what I had seen to date and then went on to say that things have gotten a lot worse. Because of the Mexican currency's maxi-devaluation, the corporation would be recording a loss of at least $15 million. It had reached the attention of the entire senior staff. So much so that the CFO, General Auditor, and head of corporate security were going to be flying down to Mexico City first thing Monday morning. He said, "Instead of coming back to Chicago tomorrow, why don't you just stay there and work the weekend? It would be a great chance for you to meet the CFO and help Paul, my boss, brief him on the audit. It would be great exposure for you and your career."

I said, "Ron, I can't do that to Mary Ann. I need to get back to Chicago and let her know that my time in Mexico City will be long and extended. It was no longer going to be a couple-day audit. I told him that it was clear that fire in the vault did not start by itself. There is something serious going on here, and it's going to take some time to sort it out." I told him that I would need the help of a couple more auditors, at least one that speaks and can read Spanish.

The flight back to Chicago was uneventful, which is how I like to travel. Other than going through customs, getting on the plane was easy back then: no TSA, no long lines, and pretty much walk onto the plane and grab your seat. No first-class this time, but back then, even the coach seats had plenty of legroom. The aircraft was not too crowded, so I could get some work done on the plane. I decided to take my lovely bride to dinner that night to give her the unwelcome news about my need to return to Mexico City. Usually, after being on the road all week and eating out at restaurants, I would long for a home-cooked meal in my own home. In this case, I thought it would be nice to take Mary Ann out. One of our favorite dining spots in the area was T.G.I. Friday's. The first T.G.I. Friday's opened in Manhattan in 1965 and was an instant success. It was later in the sixties that they started to franchise the restaurant outside of New York. It was trendy, known for tasty food, and for being a younger generation hang out. There was always a line to get a table or seat at the bar. They had opened one in Schaumburg next to my office and a short distance from our house.

Mary Ann was happy with the choice, so when she got home, we took off for dinner, wanting to get there early since we knew there would be a line to get in. We ordered some drinks and dinner, and I started telling her the story of my trip. As I got into my story, she was figuring it out. It was not going to be a four-day visit to Mexico City. The field audit work was planned for about three weeks. I told her in my estimation, and if I got some help with a couple more auditors, it might take up to four to six weeks of fieldwork. She was not happy. I felt terrible; looking at the sadness on her beautiful face killed me.

I returned to Mexico City to complete the audit and got a couple of extra auditors to help, but none of us spoke or read Spanish. I took a couple of years of Spanish in school; over time, I started reading common phrases in the accounting records. The more we got into it, the more we knew that there was some fraud going on. Corporate security also came back with their early report that the fire in the safe was not an accident. All three of us on the audit team were from the Chicago office. We commuted down together on Monday and back to Chicago that Friday. Mary Ann stayed with her parents, and we met up at home on Friday.

Things were not great, but we knew we could get through this for only a handful of weeks. Then I got the call from Ron. "Steve, you are not going to like this, but my boss Paul saw your expense report and noticed that you were traveling home on weekends from Mexico. He said that only domestic audits allow for weekend trips home. For audits outside the United States, you are not allowed to travel back home. You will have to stay there until the audit is complete."

I said, "Ron, that is ridiculous. The flight to Mexico City from Chicago is only a little over four hours. How am I going to deliver that news to Mary Ann?"

He said, "I know it's ridiculous, but we are corporate auditors. We, of all people must follow all corporate guidelines. Let me see what I can do." He called Paul back to appeal my case, and the two of them came up with a plan. Ron said, "while you cannot travel home on a foreign audit, you can have your significant other make one trip to your location. You get, under normal circumstances, a week off to enjoy the R&R with your loved one." I thought that is stupid, and I did not want to extend this audit any longer than necessary. The more we were getting into it, the more it looked like this whole thing could take up to eight weeks to complete.

I said, "OK, let me talk to Mary Ann and see what she wants to do."

Mary Ann and I talked. We decided that she would fly down for a long weekend, arriving on Thursday that second week and flying back on Monday night. I called Ron back with the plan. I told him I also wanted a Spanish-speaking auditor for the rest of the audit. I wanted to make sure we got this thing done on time. He agreed, and we hired an auditor out of our public accountant's staff in Mexico City.

The good news about being in Mexico City at the time, after the maxi-devaluation of the Mexican currency, is that everything was half price in U.S. dollar terms. Hotels, restaurants, and shopping were very affordable. While I did not have much time to do any shopping, I knew my little shopper would love it when she came down. Also, since we traveled on a per-diem rate based on dollars, I could upgrade my hotel and take her to some fabulous dinners. The audit team and I were already enjoying some great dinners at night. As I noted before, the upper class of Mexico lived very, very well. Fine dining in Mexico City was available in some regions of the city. The better hotels were also very nice. The new hotel I picked out for Mary Ann's visit was exceptional. It had beautiful gardens, a fantastic pool area, and some great restaurants on the premises. The rooms were spacious and well-appointed, all well within my per-diem rate given their currency's devaluation. As it turned out, President Carter and his wife were staying there during their state visit that week.

I was missing Mary Ann, and I wanted her visit to be perfect. I also knew I would have to take her shopping, so I needed to scope out the best area for that as well. She arrived that Thursday, and I went to the airport to pick her up. I had already changed hotels, so upon arrival, we went to the new hotel. I knew she would need some time to unpack and get ready for dinner. After checking the menu at the fine-dining restaurant at the hotel, we decided to have dinner there. Mary Ann had gotten contact lenses for the first time that week. Back then, all contact lenses were hard lenses, and you had to take them out every night. She had only had them for a few days before she came to Mexico, so she was still getting used to them. As she was getting ready for dinner, I noticed that her eyes were a little red, and they were watering, almost like she was crying. She kept taking them out, putting them back into the solution, and then back into her eye. The heavy smog in the city was causing her some extra irritation, but she wanted to leave them in. As always, as she emerged from the bathroom, all set to go to dinner, she looked amazing. I escorted her to dinner, past the pool area and beautiful gardens. We saw them setting up for a luncheon around the garden area, where President and Mrs. Carter would host the next day.

As we entered the restaurant, the maître-d could not take his eyes off Mary Ann. As he took us to the table, he could see Mary Ann's eyes were tearing. He asked her if something was wrong and looked at me with some distaste as if I had done something to make her cry. Mary Ann said, "nothing is wrong. I am trying to get used to my new contact lenses."

With that, he brought over the menus and started to go through the specials for the night. Mary Ann is using the napkin he had handed her to wipe her eyes. The tearing was getting worse. He finished with the menu items and leaves the table. I can see him over Mary Ann's shoulder, talking to the headwaiter and pointing at the table. I start thinking this guy also thinks I have done something to make Mary Ann start crying.

We were ready to place our order, and I motioned to the headwaiter to come over to the table. He grabs a box of tissue paper and comes to the table. He hands Mary Ann the tissues and stares at me in disgust. I remember thinking, *Man, this is getting serious; I may not get out of this restaurant alive.* We order dinner. Much of it served table-side. As they brought our drinks to us, I noticed that the maître-d was standing there by our table well within earshot. It appeared that he was trying to hear if I was saying anything wrong to Mary Ann that was making her cry. As we talked about our little second honeymoon plans, Mary Ann's eyes, while red, were not still tearing. I told some jokes to get her laughing and calm the maître-d down. The salad chef had come to the table to prepare and serve our Caesar salads. As he starts his work tableside, he is also looking at me with much displeasure. At this point, I thought there might be a wanted poster of me in the kitchen titled "Bad Hombre." Mary Ann decided it was time to take her contacts out and use her glasses. I asked the waiter where the ladies' room was, and he kindly escorted Mary Ann to the ladies' room.

With that, the maître-d came over to me and said, "Sir, how can you be so cruel to such a lovely lady? Sometimes I do not understand you, American men. You should be ashamed of yourself."

I responded, "Please, sir, calm down. As my wife said, she had gotten new contacts this week. I do not appreciate you attacking me like this. The two of us are very much in love and have just recently married. She is down here for a second honeymoon while I am here on business. I appreciate you caring so much about my wife, but she is OK. Again, we are very much in love. You need to back off and leave us alone. Everything is fine."

With that, Mary Ann returns to the table, and dinner was served. This time it is Steak Diane, also served table-side. Mary Ann's eyes are dry but still a little red. As the chef prepared what was a delicious rendition of Steak Diane was, he could see we were both having a delightful time and were very much in love. After a great meal, we walked through the garden area and back to our room. I told her how cute it was that the entire restaurant staff had fallen in love with her. And that I was lucky to get out of there with my life! I also told her what the maître-d said to me while she was in the bathroom. We both laughed and paused for a quick hug by the pool.

The next couple of days were spent shopping with Mary Ann and with some quiet time together by the pool. The time went by too fast. Soon it was off to the airport on Monday to send my little angel back to Chicago without me. I wrapped the audit field work up and headed home three weeks later. As suspected, we did find evidence of fraud, and Rockwell had to write off an extra $6 million that quarter. José and the leadership were all changed out, and a few years later, they shut the entire operation down. It was too hard back then doing business in Mexico with all the corruption.

While the Mexico audit was painful for us, it did produce some positive results. I received a nice bonus and was promoted to Audit Manager. They also put me on the high-potential list at Rockwell. It was a formal process at Rockwell, and they even had staff that would regularly interact with you. They would sit with you and help you plan out your career path at Rockwell, helping you plan your next move organizationally and geographically. It gave both Mary Ann and me a feeling of control of where our next family journey would take us. It also allowed us to move up the date of starting a family. We would no longer have to rely on Mary Ann's salary to pay the mortgage. As we had both agreed, once we started a family, she would be a stay-at-home mother. It did call for some more frequent trips to St. Michael's to check in with the Lord to ask for his help and guidance. We knew we were on the clock given Mary Ann's surgery and our challenge even to have that first child. I remember thinking at the time, what happens if it's me that can't produce a child? How unfair would it be for Mary Ann to believe it was her fault? Trips to St. Michael's were always good for us. Dinner or brunch in the city after mass became special for us when we were living there. It gave us a great excuse to get back to the city and relive those early great times in our relationship. We took a walk to Lincoln Park and sat on that unique bench to add to our memories.

I could see Mary Ann getting anxious for that first child. When we would see couples in church, at restaurants, or in the park, our stares at them almost became embarrassing. My travels were reduced to a few days of checking in on my audit teams with the audit manager job. Many, like before, were local. Mary Ann was still enjoying her job at Inland. The commute was still working for her, and she got into reading books on her commute. Mary Ann always loved to read, and this gave her some quiet time to do that. We were far enough out that she always got a seat on her ride into work. It was still like it was on the bus ride to work on the way home: Someone would always offer her their seat for her ride home at night. If I were in town, I would usually get home before her. Then I would stare at the front door much as I did at the cashier desk at Inland, waiting for her to enter the house. We were both in a place in our lives that we wanted to be. We knew how lucky we were to meet each other. We would both say, unprompted, think, what would have happened if you went to college and if I did not go to Nebraska? The Lord had been good to us; now, we hoped that he would continue to do so.

We were making frequent trips to Tinley Park to see her family, becoming my family, golfing with her father, and Mary Ann hanging out with her mother, brother, and sister. We had many dinners with their extended family. I was so much feeling a part of the Lesin clan. While we missed hanging out with all our friends, this family time was well within our desired diet. Our larger friend group was still going through a period of getting married, some at this point having their first child. All were exciting and always a reason to get together. We had such a fantastic group of friends, and it was exciting to see how her friends became friends of my friends.

Exciting enough that I decided it was time for another "hat party." By now, we had furnished our house, so it looked like a home. At the last hat party, most people had to stand or sit on folding chairs. Now we had actual couches and real chairs. Most of our friends were currently married or at least engaged. The evening went late into the night as it did back then. If you had too much to drink or long drive home, you stayed the night. No eggs benedict the next morning, but coffee, eggs, and bloody Mary's were served.

Audit schedules were set out six to nine months in advance. That made sense because we had to give the sites some warning that we would be on site. They had to decide on our on-site visit. It also gave them the chance to perform whatever pre-audit would be appropriate. Our audit scope was increased in 1977, when the United States passed the Foreign Corrupt Practices Act. Any U.S. company now had to confirm that none of its foreign subsidiaries were involved in any form of illegal payoffs. It was now the normal process of selling in most countries outside of the United States. It was a massive piece of legislation. When fully implemented, the law would make U.S. companies non-competitive in specific markets around the world. It told U.S. companies that you cannot do business how 100% of its foreign competitors were doing business. That meant that we would have to do audits in all foreign countries where we did business, the problem for us was we did not have audit offices outside of the United States. We did have many foreign subsidiaries and foreign manufacturing locations, all in Western Europe. Thus, each regional office had to take on the responsibility for the audit. U.S. corporations had two years to audit all their foreign subsidiaries and fully comply with the new law. There were a standard eighteen questions that had to be answered, all by the most senior person in charge of the foreign subsidiary. It all had to be done in person with the corporate auditor in charge of the engagement. It was specific enough that we had to go to Pittsburgh to be trained on the entire process.

We had three subsidiaries that were considered high priority in the Central region: One in the UK, one in France, and one in Germany. Given my new position as Audit Manager, I oversaw all three audits. Given the auditors' shortage, I would also have to take the lead field audit role in one of the three audits. I chose the UK location as my field audit role and would manage the other two from that location.

It was now time to let Mary Ann know about my schedule change and the need to go to Europe. As a foreign audit assignment, we already knew about the travel home restriction. The audits were all scheduled for six weeks. The fourth week was set aside for R&R and a spousal visit. Mary Ann was not happy with the news. Life was good for us with my new manager role, and I had much more time in the office and evenings at home with her. We had gotten into a rather good routine and had already started the process of starting our family. That process was now going to be interrupted. Starting a family was already our number-one priority, and now that was going to be put on hold. As the reality of the trip to Europe was beginning to set in, we started trying to see the trip's positives. I had always wanted to visit the UK and, more importantly, Ireland. It was the ancestral home of my father's family. Between my dad and his brother Uncle Tom I heard many remarkable stories of Ireland. It was the country where their father was born before coming to the United States as a small child. Uncle Tom was the family patriarch. He kept in touch with the entire family tree. Much of our extended family was still in the Kansas City area. He would go out of his way to reach out to all aunts, uncles, and cousins. They would keep everyone informed on how each was doing.

Once a year, Tom would sponsor a picnic or gatherings for the extended family as well. I made a point to reach out to Uncle Tom to get all the facts I could on the Irish Manning Clan. For Mary Ann, the chance to see London was of interest to her. She had once traveled to Spain with her girlfriend Linda, so this would not be her first trip over the pond. We decided that she would come over sometime during the third week of the audit. We would spend time touring London. We would take off together to Ireland for our R&R. The plan gave us both something to be excited about. It made the unexpected trip to Europe more palatable to us. With that, we marked our calendars and spent as much time together as we could before I took off to Europe.

It was now time to head to Europe. I had to leave on a Saturday because going to London meant you landed on Sunday. With that, I took the train up to Preston, England, where I would spend most of the next six weeks. Preston was about a three-hour train ride from London. I did not know it at the time, but Preston was close to Manchester, England, where my grandfather was born. While Irish, his parents were living there when he was born. Preston is also close to Liverpool, where the Beatles started.

The company had booked us all a room at the Tickle Trout Hotel on the River Ribble. I got a big kick out of that name and could not wait to tell Mary Ann that she would be staying at the Tickle Trout Hotel, which was on the River Ribble. Aside from having a very English name, the hotel itself was quite lovely. It was only a short distance from the site we would be auditing. The other two auditors on my team had already arrived. They decided to come in early to get some sightseeing done in addition to having a chance to recover from jet lag before we started our audit on Monday. They were both single and thus more flexible in their schedules.

We started the audit first thing on Monday. The President of the subsidiary was on-site when we arrived. To kick off the audit, we did our usual round of introductions with the senior staff. By now, all the European press was having a field day with the passage of the Foreign Corrupt Practices Act, writing many stories of how U.S. companies would be losing all their business in most parts of Europe. While some of the countries, including England, had somewhat similar laws, it was never enforced. None of them went as far as the U.S. law on this. The President made it clear that he thought it was a stupid law and was not clear at how his division would compete going forward.

That is what had the President so upset. Later, when I did my one-on-one with him to take him through the now-famous eighteen questions, he told me, "Steve, do you realize we sell our products for 10% to 20% more over here in Europe than the team in the U.S. or Canada? The only reason that we can get such a premium for these machines is simple: It is because we give kickbacks to all the decision makers and government officials. Everybody does it. It's how business gets done in most parts of Europe, and I am sure in Asia."

I said, "I am sorry; I am not here to defend the new law. I do, however, need to take you through this questionnaire."

It was the first time I did this questionnaire since our training for it in Pittsburgh. This gentleman was upset. He was at least twenty-five years my senior, a highly successful executive in his own right, and likely a known leader in the publishing business in Europe. Now I had to cross-examine him with this questionnaire. Neither one of us was comfortable with the situation.

As the second week of the audit was winding down, I got excited about Mary Ann's visit. The weather for Mary Ann's visit was forecast to be dry but not too warm. Hoping she had studied the forecast before she finished packing, I made my way back to London. We were going to be renting a car in Ireland. Even though I warned her not to overpack for the trip, I knew she would. For some reason, her flight was into Gatwick airport, rather than Heathrow, where I landed. Not knowing the layout of Gatwick, I left early ahead of her arrival. As I stood in the arrival hall waiting for her, I decided to get some flowers at the floral shop there. I chose a big arrangement of beautiful yellow flowers. She always looked great in yellow. I knew she would like them.

As I saw her exiting customs, I noticed she had a little extra bounce in her step. I remember thinking that is good, and she must have gotten some good sleep on the flight over as she made her way through the crowd; pretty as ever, I went to embrace her. With that, she reached into her purse and pulled out a cigar. She stuck it into my mouth and said, "Congratulations, you are going to be a father!!"

I could hardly stay on my feet. I was anxious to be with my little angel, now finding out that we were on our way to starting a family. I still remember that moment some forty years later. I was squeezing her so hard with love and excitement. Then I realized I had to be more careful. My wonderful bride was now carrying our first child. We collected her luggage and, yes, a lot of baggage. Then we made our way to the train back to central London. I could not wait to hear the entire story. When did she find out she was pregnant? How far along was she? How and when did she tell her parents? Did she call mine as well to say to them? Also, had she had a chance to call her surgeon with the delightful news?

In her cutest and most loving voice, she said, "Stephen, of course not. I wanted you to be the first to know!"

That called for another big hug and kiss and a big thank you to the Lord. I knew she was tired from the long journey, but we could not stop talking on our way to London. I asked her if she had gotten any sleep on the airplane.

She said, "No, I was practicing on how I was going to give you the big news."

OK, there you go, another big hug and kiss. We were both so excited about the news. Then I asked when Mary Ann found out she was pregnant.

It turned out she had some suspicion before I left for London. Mary Ann was not sure, and she didn't want me to worry or cancel my trip. A little over a week after I left, she had gotten the news from her doctor. The unfortunate thing had to sit on the information for almost two weeks. I know that was hard for Mary Ann under normal circumstances. It was even bigger news. Mary Ann always had a tough time keeping a secret. I am sure this one was driving her crazy. No doubt she wanted to share the news with her mom and dad, along with her girlfriend, Linda. It was so cute sitting there watching her tell me the story as her joy increased with every word.

We had gotten to the hotel around noon. I found a unique hotel in London for us, above Hyde Park. London hotel rooms are not that spacious, and they are not cheap. Thankfully, this one was on the approved hotel list from Rockwell. Unfortunately, the daily per diem was not large enough to cover our dinners in London, especially not this one. We had something to celebrate that night. As we got to our room and started to unpack Mary Ann's two suitcases, I had to scold her for over-packing briefly again. Gently remind her that cars in Europe are generally small, and probably even smaller in Ireland. Later in our marriage, I would learn that these discussions were only to make me feel better. I found that it would not influence Mary Ann's future behavior. She pretty much ran the show and thank God for that. I could not be upset with her anyway. My little angel just flew across the ocean to deliver me the best news possible. We so much wanted this day to happen, and with the grace of God, it did.

I could see Mary Ann was getting tired. All the excitement of the trip and delivering such great news was fading. Jet lag and the effect of the time change was starting to set in. I suggested that she take a warm bath and catch a few hours of sleep. I had read before I came over that the best thing to do on international travel was to get yourself into the time zone you are in as soon as possible. Eat the appropriate meal for that time of day and go to bed when you would for the evening in your new time zone. She did not get much of a meal on the flight. I knew she was going to be hungry when dinnertime came along. I had also selected an excellent restaurant for our first meal together in London. I told her too that I would go for a walk while she napped. I wanted to find a chapel to say some thank-you prayers. Praying for a healthy baby was also going to be on the list. I suggested to her that I would be back around 5 p.m. That would give her time to get ready for our 7 p.m. dinner reservations.

Europeans take their dinners later, but at 8 p.m. seating would end up being too late for her on her first night. I was able to find a lovely chapel not too far from the hotel. The chapel was old like most buildings in London at the time but beautiful. It was not Catholic, but I was sure the Lord would hear my prayers as he would for all those who worshiped in that chapel. I sat in the chapel, thinking about how lucky we were. The two of us were very much in love. And now, in the footsteps of starting the family, we always wanted. We owed so much thanks to the surgeon who had operated on Mary Ann. I was sure when Mary Ann got back and told him the good news, he was going to be thrilled. We did not know it at the time, but our first child would grow up to be a doctor as well! It is amazing how certain things connect in our lives. I stayed in the chapel for a while. I stared at the altar and thought about all that had happened since going to Chicago and meeting Mary Ann; what a wonderful person she was and how lucky I was to be able to call her my wife. And now *the mother of my children.* I was sure that if we were able to have a healthy baby now, there would be more on the way.

Time almost got away from me. I needed to start my way back to the hotel. I stopped by the restaurant on the way back to the hotel. I wanted to let the maître-d know that we would be celebrating something special at dinner tonight. He was excited and promised me he would help make the celebration dinner special.

As I got back to the hotel, I entered the room. I knew Mary Ann was going to be in deep sleep after her journey. Not wanting to startle her, I softly kissed her on the cheek.

She slowly opened those beautiful eyes of hers and smiled. She said, "Stephen, I was really in a deep sleep. Please lie down and hold me while I try and wake up." It was an offer I could not pass up. As we lay there together, she said, "Stephen, I was having the most delightful dream. We were there together, and we were baptizing our baby. The problem was that the baby was all dressed in white, and I could not see if it was a boy or a girl."

I told her it would not matter; let us pray for a healthy baby, with more on the way. With that, another great hug and kiss. Unfortunately for Mary Ann, it was time to get up.

Which meant that, as a good husband, I needed to start tickling her. She was very ticklish but hated to be tickled. It usually ended with a punch in my stomach and another kiss. She was now awake and ready to start getting ready for dinner. I knew this would take a while, so I turned on the local news. Back then, there were only about three or four channels in the UK. It was the same throughout Europe at the time. Pretty boring TV. Maybe that is why the people read so many newspapers over there.

Mary Ann got ready. Although tired and jet-lagged, she looked special. Together we headed off to dinner. The dinner location was within walking distance of the hotel. We soon arrived for our dinner seating. Mary Ann and I grew up in the Midwest. As such, we were pretty much meat-and-potatoes eaters, much like our entire family. Fish in the Midwest were not great. With both of us being Catholic, we had memories of "Fish Fridays" during lent. It all put fish in a bad light for us all. With all my audit trips in the Midwest and having steak every night, I knew I needed to break the habit. While in the UK, I had gotten to enjoy their fish. Scottish salmon and Dover sole were becoming two of my go-to dinners. Knowing that this first night in the UK would call for a lighter dinner, I suggested she try one of those two dishes or find another more delicate dish. She studied the menu and asked more about the Dover sole and why I liked it so much. I said it was a light white fish, very mild. It was usually served broiled or sautéed in butter and cooked on the bone with the bone removed when they served it. The thought of being sautéed in butter caught her attention.

I am not sure if cooking in butter was a Dutch thing or not. Mary Ann's mother always used an unusual amount of butter when cooking at home. Mary Ann's mom wrote many recipes over the years for her. Had we digitized those recipes and searched for the word "butter," the search would have likely shut down the computer. The term "butter" was in every recipe. All those recipes were good; it just put too much butter into everything. Today, we still feature our Mary Ann recipe book every week at our family Sunday dinners, but we cut down the butter by half to two-thirds, and everything is always good.

She ordered the Dover sole, as did I. I wanted to order a special bottle of champagne to celebrate our special news like the one we had on the cruise. That was not going to happen. Once she found out she was pregnant, Mary Ann never had another alcoholic drink - not until she was through nursing the baby. The words *marry someone that you want to be the mother of your children* came to mind. The Dover sole came with capers. She had never had capers before. She asked, "what are these green things on my fish?"

I said, "capers."

"What are capers, and where do they come from?"

I said, "I am not sure, probably caper trees." I was sitting too far away for a punch in the stomach. I just got one of her stares, no kiss. We passed on dessert since it was getting late.

As we walked back to the hotel, I could not pass up the opportunity to rub her stomach. I held her, and I told her that I would do everything I could to make this child the most important thing in our life. She put her hand on mine while I rubbed her stomach. She said, "your hand is a little high, but our little child is in there somewhere." I did not want the night to end. Mary Ann was exhausted and could not wait to get back into bed. As I held her, I told her, and for the first time, my mother's words said to me: *Marry the girl you want to be the mother of your children.*

She said, "I love your mother. I have already started to read parenting books." She pointed to her suitcase. In there, she had four books on motherhood and childbirth. She said, "Stephen, I've got this. I won't let you or our children down."

She never did.

We both slept in the next morning. I knew Mary Ann was going to have some difficulties for the next few days. Jet lag is a challenging thing to overcome. You must give it a few days. She was afraid of having morning sickness on the trip, but the first week she did fine.

I took her out for brunch. She had her favorite eggs benedict, but this time no Bloody Mary. After brunch, we got a taxi and went to see some of the sites around London. The first stop was Buckingham Palace. It was a chilly but dry day in London. Unfortunately, we were too late to see the changing of the guard. You usually had to be in position for that by 10:30 a.m. I promised her we would get back for that the next day.

We then went off to see Parliament and London Bridge. There is so much incredible history to see in and around London, and Mary Ann loved her time there.

It was about 3 p.m., and I could see Mary Ann would need her second wind to get through the afternoon. I took her back to the hotel for a little nap.

One of the other audit teams was also in London for their break. I went to meet up with them while she napped. They gave me a briefing on how their audit was going. They also mentioned a high-quality restaurant in which they had dinner the night before. It sounded interesting, so I booked a table for us at 7:30 p.m. I wanted to give Mary Ann some good nap time. When I got back to the hotel, I went to the room to see how she was doing. A couple-hour nap is an effective way to get through the second-day jet lag.

She was already up. When I came into the room, she was reading one of the baby books she had brought over with her.

I said to her, "Looks like you are getting ready for motherhood." I then told her about my meeting. I told her the team found an exciting restaurant and that I'd made dinner reservations for the two of us at 7:30 p.m.

She said, "Stephen, what I would enjoy would be a McDonald's cheeseburger."

I said, "Mary Ann, we are in London. Why would you want to go to McDonald's?"

I imagined there was one somewhere around London; I just had not seen one here. As it turned out, McDonald's had opened their first restaurant in London a few years earlier. It had not caught on all that well yet. I was able to locate one a short cab ride from the hotel. I had heard that pregnant women do get cravings, and I think Mary Ann's was a McDonald's cheeseburger. If that is what my little angel was craving, then that would be on the dinner menu for the night. It would also take some pressure off the per-diem the company was offering, helping to cover the dinner bill from the night before.

The rain had set in, which is often the case in London. We borrowed an umbrella from the hotel and got a taxi to McDonald's. Taxi cabs in London are unique. They drive specially built taxi cabs that help them navigate some of the very narrow streets in London. London was built well over a thousand years ago, long before automobiles. The roads were designed for horses, chariots, and carriages. The London taxi cabs can turn on a dime, which helps them get through the very narrow streets and short turning areas.

What is also very neat about the taxi experience in London are the drivers. They are delightful and always up for a good chat with a tourist which London was full of, especially in the summertime. They are also very well trained. To be a taxi driver in London, you must take an apprenticeship for three years. They even must memorize the city map and the names of all the key businesses in the city. Part of the final exam is the examiner getting into the taxi and then telling the driver the business name - not the address, just the name of the business. The taxi driver must take you directly to that location without looking at a map. The journey must be on the most direct route possible. I was always amazed by this process.

Over the years, as I got to know London better, I never experienced a bad ride. London itself is not that big, but there were many businesses, hotels, and restaurants there. The good news for the taxi driver is that many had been at the same location for hundreds of years. Central London, thankfully, did not get bombed that much during World War II. The Germans had thought that they were striking London during their bombing raids. As it turned out, they had terrible coordinates. Most of the bombing happened east of the city, which saved all the city's main treasures. Areas east of London had heavily gotten damage. You can easily recognize the post-war buildings from the historic architecture of London when you travel there.

We got in the cab, and I said, "McDonald's restaurant." The taxi driver turned the meter on, and we were off, soon to arrive at our second dinner date in London, at a McDonald's. Mary Ann was pleased. I ordered up some cheeseburgers, French fries and splurged on two chocolate milkshakes.

When I got to the table, Mary Ann smiled and jokingly said, "Sweetheart, you certainly know how to spoil a woman." We finished dinner, took a walk with our umbrellas, and stopped by a pub not too far from the hotel—a glass of water for my bride and a pint of Guinness for me. I had to get ready for our trip to Ireland.

The next morning, we had to get an early start. I wanted to make sure Mary Ann saw the changing of the guard at Buckingham Palace. We also had to pack to catch the train to Preston later that day. We left our luggage with the porter at the hotel and took a taxi to the Palace. The crowds were large around the Palace. The taxi driver gave us some advice on where to stand to get the ceremony's best view. After viewing the ceremony, we made our way to Westminster Cathedral. There we took the tour and found a chapel area where we could both say a few prayers. We wanted to pray together, thanking the Lord again for helping us to start our family. We both knew how fortunate we were. Celebrating it together was very special that day.

We made our way back to the hotel, collected our luggage, and made our way to the train station. Preston was about a three-hour train ride from London. I loved riding the trains in England and usually bought first-class seating to make sure the coach was not too crowded. They had big windows, so I thought Mary Ann would enjoy the view of the English countryside. She loved every minute of it. She got a big kick out of the fact that we were staying at the Tickled Trout on the River Ribble in Preston. She said, "Where do they come up with these names?"

I told her I thought it was more of a British thing. She would see more examples of it in and around Preston.

We would be in Preston for three days and then would take our flight over to Ireland. I had to rent a car in Ireland. While it was against corporate policy for us to drive on foreign trips, this was personal travel. I was a little nervous about driving in Ireland. Like the UK, they all drove on the wrong side of the road, which, of course, I thought, was stupid. I knew Mary Ann was not going to be thrilled about this. She never was a big fan of my driving. She was a back-seat driver, one who always sat in the front passenger seat. There was an awful lot of Mary Ann-isms that came out of her while I was driving. I knew I would be getting a new set of driving instructions once we got to Ireland. All Great Britain countries, colonies, and former colonies adopted left-side driving. The countries included Australia, India, Singapore, Malaysia, New Zealand, South Africa, and the UK and Ireland. Canada used to drive on the left but changed to right-side driving in 1921. Even Japan adopted left-side driving. I later found out that this stemmed from the Japanese custom of walking on the road's left side due to the Samurai carrying their swords on their bodies' left side.

When we got to the Tickled Trout on the Ribble River, Mary Ann was reasonably impressed. The room had plenty of closet space and a large king-size bed, not overly appointed, but everything she needed and a bonus with the Ribble River off the hotel's back patio! They also had a lovely reading area off the restaurant that would give her some time to read her parenting books she had brought over for her trip. Giving her something to do while I was 9working that week. In Mary Ann's eyes, all was good.

By now, she was recovered from the jet lag, had her usual energy level, and getting into England's history. She was very excited about being so close to Liverpool. Mary Ann was a huge Beatles fan. Being that close to Liverpool was a post she would want to put in her baby book. Not having Facebook at the time meant you had to write something down somewhere. She did not keep a diary, so I told her, "Put it in your baby book." She kept an unbeliev-able complete set of baby books for our kids. Unfortunately, she did not have one of her own.

She still appreciated my attempt at humor. I had planned many different excursions for her while working that week and some special dinners for her. I had arranged for a tour company to pick her up every morning and give her a guided tour of the area. They had a list of the usual places of interest in the area. I told them, "As long as the first stop is Liverpool, then you will make her trip a success." They said, "No problem, that is a common request for us. We have a complete Beatles tour." She started day one with that.

I never liked eating at the hotel that I was staying. I thought hotels had a restaurant only because they had to offer breakfast to their customers. Customers were seldom there for lunch. They had to leverage their investment in a kitchen with dinners but usually nothing special. There were exceptions to this rule for me. I still have favorite restaurants at hotels that I have stayed in worldwide, but the Tickle Trout would not be one of them. Great people there, extremely helpful, and friendly.

There were so many neat places around the Preston area to eat. I could not wait to take her to one particular place where King James the First was so impressed with a cut of beef that he "knighted" it, making that cut of beef "Sir Loin" in 1617. You cannot make this stuff up. The restaurant started in the fifteen hundreds, maybe earlier. Mary Ann and I, being part of the "meat and potatoes" family of citizens, had to have dinner there. The history that you see in England is unbelievable. The restaurant, Hoghton Tower, was founded not that long after Christopher Columbus discovered North America. It was more than unique. There were many examples of this type of history. The restaurant was outside of Preston. The doors and ceilings in the restaurant were not large or tall. Mary Ann was five feet three inches tall, so it was not too much of a problem for her. I was a little over six feet tall. I think they dug out some of the original restaurant floorings to help make the ceilings taller. The population has all grown taller over the years. The average height back then may have been well under five feet. I am sure, like most first-time diners at Hoghton Tower, we ordered the sirloin steak.

The next day Mary Ann went off to Liverpool for her Beatles tour, and I went back to the audit. That evening, I asked my audit partner to join Mary Ann and me for dinner. He also happened to be a big Beatles fan and enjoyed hearing Mary Ann tell us about her day in Liverpool. We finished the week with more tours for Mary Ann.

We then made our way to Manchester airport for our flight to Dublin. We picked up the rental car at the Dublin airport and made our way to our hotel. While checking in, the gentleman at the front desk told us that there was a wedding that weekend in the hotel and said that we were invited to attend. Mary Ann and I looked at each other with some confusion. I asked the man why we would be invited to a wedding for a couple we did not know?

He said, "most hotel guests were there for the wedding, and you may as well attend. It will be loud, will go through the night, and you won't be able to sleep anyway."

As we were to find out, Irish weddings go on for days. They start with a dinner after the wedding for the invited guests. They then open the party to all friends and neighbors of the couple or the parents. The bar is left open, and the band continues to play Irish dance music. They continue to serve food. It is not as fancy as the main event's food, but enough food for balancing all the partygoers' alcohol content. The wedding party goes well into the wee hours of the morning. When they finish, people go home and get ready for day two of the wedding. That usually starts before noon the next day, and the process was repeated.

Thank God Mary Ann was over her jet lag. We decided to take in the wedding. We were not sure what we were in for, but we enjoyed the Irish song and dance. We were also very curious to see an Irish wedding. I had heard about them, but this would be a first for both of us. Mary Ann was always in for a good party and some dancing. She wouldn't be drinking, but she would be dancing. We went up to our room, unpacked, and got ready for the party.

Since the gentleman at the front desk said that there would be food served late, we decided to address Mary Ann's McDonald's craving. We found a McDonald's that had opened in Dublin and had a late lunch. It was not too far from our hotel. With that, we went back to the hotel to get ready for the wedding. We were planning for a casual trip to Ireland, so we didn't pack extra wedding clothes that didn't matter. All invited guests were well dressed for the occasion. The uninvited guests were dressed for a party, all in casual clothes. We blended in perfectly. Of course, Mary Ann stood out because she looked good in anything. The groom's parents quickly fell in love with Mary Ann, and they asked us to sit by their table. The invited guests and the uninvited guests could not have been nicer. The Irish music was to die for, and Irish music and great Irish ballads played through the night. All went out of their way to show us all the Irish dance routines. Mary Ann hardly left the dance floor. Everybody wanted to dance with her. As she danced, I would be telling anyone who would listen about my Irish heritage. I was hoping someone would be able to connect me with my Irish family tree. One of the guests said, "Go to the town where you think your family was born. Check with the local parish. They keep a record of all marriages and baptisms. They may be able to help." It was now getting exceptionally late. The clock was fast approaching 2 a.m. It was clear the party was not going to be ending soon. It was time for us to say our goodbyes. Our first introduction to my Irish home country and great culture was fantastic; such friendly and caring people. They took us into their hearts and family, and they could not have been more pleasant. For both of us, it was our first visit to Ireland, and we loved it.

I have since been back many times. It was the first trip I took after Mary Ann died. I went there with my brother. He took me there to help clear my head. He could see I was having an extremely challenging time after her death. He knew that Mary Ann and I had shared an unforgettable time in Ireland and knew I had some special memories of her there. Part of her soul still lives in those hillsides of green.

The next morning, we woke up to the sound of Irish music. Round two of the wedding had started. While we loved all the people we had met the night before, we had other things to see in Dublin. We got up and went to find a friendly Irish pub where we could have brunch. A good Irish breakfast always hits the spot. Mary Ann was picking at her food, which was not like her. I said, "Mary Ann, I know you are tired. Are you not feeling well?"

She said, "Stephen, I think I am getting morning sickness. I know that I am tired since we were up so late last night, but I don't feel that well."

Sure enough, morning sickness was setting in for my sweetheart.

We did some touring around Dublin, including a tour of the Guinness brewery in Dublin. The tour was quite informative. Guinness started brewing their beer in Dublin in 1759. The site was expanded many times, but for many years it was the only brewery for Guinness beer. It was often said that Guinness beer did not travel well and always tasted better in Ireland than anywhere else in the world. That week I found that to be true. I would occasionally have a pint of Guinness in Chicago, usually around St. Patrick's Day. It was good but not nearly as good as the Guinness I had in Ireland that week. Mary Ann was never a big Guinness fan but enjoyed seeing and hearing the history of the company. She enjoyed Dublin and looked forward to seeing the rest of Ireland.

We did not know it at the time, but some twenty-two years later, I would take the child that my wife was now carrying back to Dublin. We visited Trinity College in Dublin. It was for a research year after graduating Pre-Med at UCLA before going to Medical School.

We continued our tour of Ireland. The plan was to drive from Dublin across Ireland to Shannon. There we would fly back to London for Mary Ann's flight back to Chicago. Our tour took us to many unique Irish towns and villages, many of which my Uncle Tom had suggested may be home to some in our Irish family tree. He said the main cities were Cork, Tipperary, Galway, and Shannon. We went to them all. The problem with car travel in Ireland back then was that the roads were all very narrow and winding. There were no super-highways. To make it even more challenging, they had free ranges, which means there was no fencing on their farms. There are some hedgerows in some areas but no fences. You would often come up over a rise in the road and see sheep and cattle walking in the road. You had to stop; they had the right-of-way.

The roads were not heavily traveled, so for the most part making driving on the wrong side of the road much more manageable. There was seldom someone on the other side of the road - the side I should have been driving on anyway! The winding roads and the roads' up and down did not help Mary Ann's morning sickness. She was a champ as always but had a tough time with the travel. She hung in there, but we made many stops. The views of the rolling green Irish hills were amazing, and it is such a beautiful country. I was also able to get quite a few suggestions on my driving skills that week. Mary Ann was such a good back/front-seat driver, even when she was on the wrong side of the car.

We finally ended our visit in Shannon. On the last day, we took a tour of Bunratty Castle. It was close to Shannon and not too far from our hotel in

Limerick. It was a fun tour of a fifteenth-century Irish castle. They also had a version of the Blarney Stone. Folklore had it that if you kiss it, you get the Irish gift of gab. Mary Ann thought it appropriate that I kiss the stone. She suggested that I may have inherited my dad's art of storytelling. I laughed, giving her a kiss and a hug. I then kissed the Blarney Stone. Little did we know that the best storytelling I would do someday would be a story about her—the love of my life. And the best *mother of my children* I could ever have met.

We left the castle and stopped by a restaurant and pub attached to it. The castle and the restaurant were both busy. We were able to get a couple of seats at a large table. There were three or four couples at the table, all tourists. Mary Ann never met a stranger and quickly opened a conversation with the couple sitting next to us. She introduced us both to the couple, then asked where they both lived. The wife said they were from Dallas and here on vacation. The husband said, "We took a tour to Ireland before we caught up with our son, who is in Germany on an audit."

I said, "Really? I am over here on an audit as well. Mary Ann came over last week. The company allows spouses to visit midway through the audit."

The wife said, "Our son is not married. We came over to join him in London during his week off."

I said, "That is interesting. What company does your son work for?"

The husband said, "It's probably not a company you would know. Their headquarters are in Pittsburgh, but he works out of their Dallas office."

I said, "Could that company be Rockwell International?"

He said, "Yes, how did you know that?"

"Well, I work for that same company. I am managing all the audits for them this year in Europe. Is Craig your son? I met him in London last weekend. He is one of my best auditors over here."

Sure enough, that was their son. We all wondered how the world could be this small. A fifteenth-century castle and restaurant were full of tourists.

The same thing happened to Mary Ann and me about ten years later. We had checked into a hotel in Hong Kong. We were on vacation there with my brother and his wife. After we checked in, we went to the room to freshen up and unpack. Then we went down to meet with my brother and his wife for dinner. We went to the elevator, pushed the button to go down, the doors opened, and out walked one of our neighbors and our kids' soccer coach. We were shocked. How does this happen? It is an exceedingly small world we all live.

Mary Ann was still struggling with morning sickness. She hung in there to meet Craig's parents, but we did not stay for the Irish ballads and dancing. The next morning, we flew back to London, and then she connected with her flight to Chicago. It was so hard to see her off, but we both enjoyed our time together. I completed the audit and returned to Chicago two weeks later.

HAVING OUR FIRST CHILD

*M*ary Ann had already told her parents and good friend, Linda, by the time I had returned to Chicago. I waited until I got back to the United States before calling my family with the fantastic news. My mother was over the moon with the information. Our child would be the first grandchild for the family, and my parents had been waiting a long time for this special delivery. They already started planning their trip to Chicago for late December or early January.

Mary Ann continued to work through most of her pregnancy, religiously taking the train to work every morning. She used that commuting time to continue reading her books on motherhood and caring for a newborn. There was no doubt that she was going to be ready when our first child was born. The pregnancy was going well for Mary Ann and our child. Her doctor was in the city, so it was easy for her to get to her appointments. The doctor also had admittance rights to the hospital near our home. When the time came, he would be there to deliver our little angel into the world. While we were uninterested in knowing the sex of our first child, her doctor was betting on a boy. He said that the way she was carrying the baby, it was sure to be a boy. The science of predetermining the sex of a baby was suspect back then, and we didn't care to know - deliver us a healthy baby, and we would take it from there.

It was quickly moving into winter then. The snow came early and often, making Mary Ann's trips into the city more complicated. I feared she would slip on the ice on her walk to work. It was going to be one of the snowiest winters on record for the city. Mary Ann and I talked about how difficult it was getting for her to travel to work. Finally, we decided that she would take a leave of absence and finish her pregnancy at home. She was as tough as any young mother, but the weather was not our friend that year. Chicago set a record for snowfall. The record still stands today. From December to February that year, we got 80.6 inches of snow. The snowdrifts on the roads made travel almost impossible. In our area, some of the snowdrifts were over eight feet high. I flew into O'Hare one day and looked down on the city while we were landing. It looked like someone had taken a giant cookie cutter over the city to form the streets. It was amazing.

Our townhouse had a flat-roof garage. More than once, I had to climb onto the roof of the garage to shovel the snow off. I was afraid that it was getting too high, and the snow's weight may cause the roof to collapse. I still remember the last time I was up on the roof. I looked out over the incredible snowdrifts in the neighborhood, thinking we have got to get out of here. No one should have to live this way.

When I got back inside, Mary Ann asked how it went. I told her, "Sweetheart, we have got to move out West."

She said, "Where would we go?"

I told her I wasn't sure. "Maybe we should pull that snowblower we recently bought behind our car and drive west. We will not stop until someone asks us what that contraption tied behind the vehicle was; we can start looking at that point. We have lived in the snow belt all our lives, and I have had enough.

She said, "Stephen, calm down. We need to focus on bringing this baby into the world, and that time is coming soon."

Thanksgiving and Christmas had come and gone, and we shared both with Mary Ann's family and many relatives. All were excited for the special day that was quickly approaching but concerned about the constant blizzards. Radio and TV continued to blame the Mayor of Chicago for everything snow related. In part due to the snowstorm that winter, mayor Michael Bilandic, who had replaced Richard Daley upon his death, lost his re-election bid in April of 1979.

The doctor had told Mary Ann that she would be delivering our child sometime early to mid-January. We both had hoped that the snow would stop falling and make our trip to the hospital more manageable and safer after she started labor. Well, the snow did not stop falling, and her due date was fast approaching. The night before, Mary Ann was to go into labor, and we were watching the evening news. A reporter came on stating there was a heavy blizzard that evening, and a pregnant woman and her husband could not get to the hospital. It was the same hospital that we would be going to, which turned out to be the next night. The mother, with the help of the police, had to give birth in the car. Although they were close to the hospital, they could not get there in time for the delivery.

I looked fearfully at Mary Ann and said, "Mary Ann, I am not sure if I know enough about childbirth to be able to help you give birth. Do any of the books you bought talk about what we should do if we can't make it to the hospital?"

She said, "The one over there on the table talks a little bit about it, but let's pray that does not happen to us."

I got the book and started reading it feverishly, more than a little scared about the possibility. I could not sleep that night. I was worried that we would be put in the same position and deliver our first child in the car. I knew I would not be capable of doing that. *Who trains for something like that?* I knew Mary Ann had the same concerns.

The snow had stopped the next day, and the city could get the snow plowing out once again to clean the major streets. Local and neighborhood streets remained snow-packed. Being so close to her due date, I worked from home so I could be with her. That night she woke me up and said, "It's the time!"

She had everything already packed for the hospital, a quick shower, and we would be off, it was a little past midnight. It was dark, but the streets were well lit. The problem was, still, how to get through the neighborhood streets. Only the significant thoroughfares had been plowed. I had the two most important people in my life in the car, and I knew I had to be careful. I also knew I had to get her to the hospital to ensure safe delivery. The side roads were icy, and I could hear my tires spinning on the ice.

Mary Ann turned to me and grabbed my arm. She said, "Stephen, be careful and go slow; we still have time. My labor pains are not that frequent. Please just get to the main roads."

We drove past the location where the couple had to deliver their child in the car. Passing that location, I said a quick prayer asking for fast and safe passage to the emergency room.

We arrived safely, and I parked the car outside the emergency room entrance and took Mary Ann inside. The nurses knew what to do. They asked Mary Ann if this was her first birth, and when the labor had started. They then told me to park the car, get her belongings together, and go to the admitting desk in the hospital's front. They would have a room assigned for her in a brief time, and I could meet her up there.

By the time I got to her room, she had already gowned up and was resting in her bed. She looked so cute in her gown, with her big tummy and an even bigger smile. She was scared and anxious about what was about to take place for all three of us. The good news is she had a lot of confidence in her doctor. The admitting nurse told Mary Ann that she had a few hours before the baby would be born. Her doctor was notified, and he would be in around 6 a.m. that day to see her.

It was now approaching 3 a.m. We were both tired, and we tried to get some sleep. We were on the third floor of the hospital, and we both looked out the window and saw the snowdrifts on the roof. Mary Ann said, "Stephen, I can't tell you how worried I was that we would not get to the hospital in time. I didn't want to say anything, but I was worried all night after hearing that news report. Thankfully, with my guidance, we made it here safely!"

I told her that she was still the best backsSeat/front-seat driver that I had ever married. It's nice when you face danger, and you still have a chance to joke about it. She was now in the bed, and I was in the chair next to her, holding her hand, getting ready to start our family. The Lord was on our shoulders that night, and we knew it.

About 6:30 a.m., we were awakened by a knock on the door, and as her doctor walked in. Being the first time for us to meet, I shook his hand and introduced myself to him. He said hello to Mary Ann and asked how she was feeling. "How is your little son doing?" He was still convinced that we were going to have a boy.

She ignored the comment about a little boy and said, "We are both doing fine."

He did a quick exam to try to determine how far along she was. With that, he said, "You still have some time to go. Why don't you both get some breakfast, and I will stop back by in a couple of hours?"

We ordered breakfast, but I could see the labor pains were getting worse for Mary Ann, although she tried not to show it. By noon I went down the hall and asked her nurse to let the doctor know that the labor pains increased in intensity.

Finally, at 1:46 p.m. on January 19, 1979, Mary Ann gave birth. I was able to be in the delivery room, and as Mary Ann was giving birth, I heard the doctor say to her, "Look at the head on that boy. Look at the shoulders on that boy." He was still thinking we were going to have a boy.

Then he pulled the baby up, gave it a little spank on the butt, and handed the baby to my wife.

"Congratulations, Mary Ann, you have a nice healthy baby girl."

As Mary Ann was holding Kristina (Kristie) Marie Manning for the first time, I walked over to the bedside to see for myself. All of a sudden, the medical staff started to hurry around the room. They grabbed Kristie and took her to a room next to the birthing room; no one said a word to us. They were concerned about something, and now, so were we. I went over to the room they had taken Kristie to. I saw them trying to suck something out of her mouth and were trying to help her breathe. I panicked, thinking this can't be happening; all we wanted was a healthy baby. We had come too far for this special moment. Still, nobody told me what was going on. Thankfully, Mary Ann was still exhausted from birth, and as she lay in bed, she could not see what was going on.

I heard her calling my name, "Stephen, is something wrong with our baby?" I went back to her bedside and told her I thought they are just cleaning her up. She said, "But I don't hear her crying. Why isn't she crying? I want to hold her," with that, Kristie let out a big cry. Thank God she was breathing. Whatever the problem was, they seemed to have solved it. In a few minutes, they brought her back into the room and handed her to Mary Ann. Both of us could not hold back our tears of joy. It was such an extraordinary moment for us all. They started filling out the information for the birth certificate. They turned to us and asked, "What name have you picked out for your daughter?"

I thought about teasing the doctor and throwing a very masculine name out there. No need, Mary Ann beat me to it. She took my hand and proudly said, "Kristina Marie Manning. That's Kristina with a 'K.'

Mary Ann stayed in the hospital for three days. Enough time for me to go get some yellow paint. I needed to finish painting the baby room before we brought our new little treasure home.

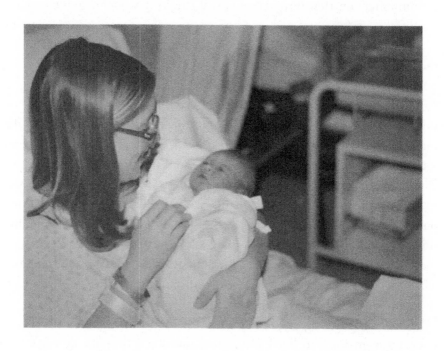

Once home with Kristie, Mary Ann quickly got into her new mother role. She wasted little time getting her room ready. All the new baby clothes got folded and put away. She set out multiple outfits for each day so she would always look clean and fresh. She also prepared her special place on our couch to hold and feed Kristie throughout the days ahead. I was so impressed with how well prepared she was for her new role as *mother of our children*. She would sit for hours just holding Kristie on that couch, singing to her, and just smiling. It was such a wonderful and peaceful thing to watch, and I think Kristie was smiling as much as Mary Ann. Her little eyes just sparkled when she looked at Mary Ann.

Kristie was an incredibly happy and pleasant baby. We took many pictures of her growing up. I held one aside, saying this will be on the book cover of "The Best Baby" book that I was sure she would someday star in it. Indeed, the experience with Kristie did not offer us any fear of having more children. For me, seeing how well Mary Ann handled and cared for our first child reaffirmed my choice of *Marrying the woman you want to be the mother of your children*.

With the holidays now behind us, the next big family gathering would be Kristie's baptism. That would happen later that February, about five weeks after she was born. Thankfully, the heavy snows of January had subsided, and the streets were back to normal. Mary Ann's extended family and my immediate family were all able to attend. My brother Mike and her sister Peggy were Kristie's godparents. Although Mike had to miss our wedding, he would not miss this opportunity to be godfather to our firstborn. My family stayed with us in Roselle, and all of Mary Ann's family drove up from Tinley Park that day to help us celebrate. Thankfully, the neighborhood we lived in had an entertainment center you could rent out for the day. The Lesin family did the catering, and again my dad and Uncle Bill handled the bar. This time they were on their best behavior. Both were under strict orders from their respective wives. The day was bright and sunny, and Mary Ann looked precious, holding Kristie in her all-white baby gown. The baby gown was made from Mary Ann's wedding gown, sewn together by one of Mary Ann's aunts. It was all such a special day and one we were able to enjoy with our extended families. My mother pulled me aside and again congratulated me on finding and marrying Mary Ann. She, like I, knew Mary Ann was going to make a perfect *Loving Mother.*

Our life certainly changed with having a baby. No more late nights out in the city. None of our friends had started their families yet, so we pretty much hung out at our house. Kristie was too young to leave with a babysitter. We would occasionally take her to Mary Ann's parents' house. They would watch her while we visited friends or had a short dinner date somewhere near her parent's house. Ray and Midge were good parents, and we knew they would be great grandparents and take loving care of our little treasure. They wanted as much time with Kristie as they could get. They understood our move out of the Chicago area was going to happen sometime in the future. I could tell early on that Mary Ann was trying to teach Kristie how to overpack, just like her mother. Every time we would travel with Kristie, Mary Ann would load the car with all of those 'just in case' items she always liked to pack. I am sure she thought the daughter must be like mother and required multiple changes of clothes. She wanted to make sure her little daughter looked perfect.

Kristie slowly started to get into a regular eating and sleeping routine. Like every new baby, it takes time for them to establish a familiar pattern. For the first few months, she was up almost every two hours at night. I felt so bad for Mary Ann. Mary Ann, like me, loved her sleep. She would just be getting into a deep sleep when Kristie would cry, and she would run to her room to hold or feed her. I was such a sound sleeper I would not always hear the crying or Mary Ann going to the room. I was still amazed at how Mary Ann could hear almost every movement in the crib her children made. Mary Ann had some hearing loss from a childhood illness. Often, she would have a challenging time hearing everything being spoken in a room. When it came to hearing her kids, however, she heard everything.

I could see all of this was making Mary Ann tired throughout the day. She hung in there, though, knowing that Kristie would someday get to at least a four-hour sleep schedule. I would occasionally put a robe on and join Mary Ann while she gave Kristie one of her late-night feedings. I often wondered how such a little baby could cry so loudly. It didn't bother Mary

Ann. She would calmly pick Kristie up, lay her on her shoulder and softly pat her on the back, singing lightly into her ear. Her calm, soft singing often put Kristie and I both to sleep.

Kristie grew up quickly, as all children do. She loved to play on her blanket in front of us at night. Always so busy with her little hands. While Mary Ann made dinner, I got my one-on-one time with her. Then after Mary Ann stopped nursing, I was able to help feed her. Although our social life was shrinking, our family life was growing in so many unique ways. When Kristie was a little over nine months old, we were all playing together on the floor in the family room. With that, Kristie pulled herself up to the couch, looked at both of us with a big smile, and took two or three steps towards us. She then just sat down, probably as surprised by the event as we were.

Mary Ann could not believe it. She said, "Did you see that? Our little girl just took her first steps! She was walking."

Mary Ann was always excited about any accomplishment our children had. Mary Ann would quickly pull out their baby book and make an entry and time-date it. Kristie took her first steps in November 1979, she wrote. That was even before Kristie was crawling. Unfortunately, we would not see her second attempt until she was well over one year old. Of course, Mary Ann would tell anybody who would listen that her daughter started walking at nine months. Our children still cherish the baby books that Mary Ann kept for them.

Moving to Pittsburgh and
Having Our Second Child

*A*s I mentioned earlier, Rockwell had a staff that would help manage
its high-potential employees' career path. We would meet with them
quarterly, either by phone or in person. They would check in on you to see
how you were progressing in your current role. Then they would discuss
possible next steps in your career and any feedback they had from management on your performance. They had excellent visibility to potential future
positions that might be opening in the corporation. With that, they would
make recommendations on which of those positions would be best for your
development. It was a very well-thought-out process and gave you the confidence that the company was willing to invest in your future at Rockwell.

A good guy named Greg ran that process for the company. Greg was
about eight years my senior. He was a good-looking guy, always well dressed,
and very professional. He was very well connected to the leadership group at
Rockwell and took his job very seriously.

It was time for my quarterly visit with Greg. As it so happened, Greg
was in the Chicago area, so he came by our offices there. Greg was very well
briefed on my internal audit activities and knew I had the General Auditor's
support. As our meeting got started, Greg said, "Steve, we think it is time for
you to take the next step in your development here at Rockwell." He went on
to suggest that the next best step for me was a move into Corporate Finance.
There was a new leadership team assembled at the Corporate Offices in
Pittsburgh. He thought a role in that new department would be best for both
the company and me. I thought, *Really, Pittsburgh, Pennsylvania?* While I was

not necessarily a world traveler, I pretty much knew I would not be getting rid of my snowblower in Pittsburgh. I said, "Greg, any chance this position could be based out of Rockwell's West Coast office in California?"

He pushed back and said, "No, not at this time. We are still developing our organizations out there. Besides, given your career path, you need to have your ticket punched at Corporate, and this is an appropriate time for you to do it." I trusted Greg, so I asked him for a few days to think about it and talk to my wife about the move.

I made sure I got home early that day. I wanted to be able to sit down with Mary Ann while things were quiet at home and before Kristie had gotten up from her afternoon nap. As we had previously discussed possible relocation out of Chicago, it was always in the abstract - No set timetable and no set destination. Therefore, it made the discussions far less immediate and impactful. Now the debate was going to be about reality and the fact that we would be moving our young family. I knew this was going to be a hard decision for Mary Ann. Moving the first granddaughter away from newly minted Chicago grandparents was going to be hard. Also, moving Mary Ann away from the safety net of family and friends would undoubtedly be on Mary Ann's mind. While I was not excited to be moving to Pittsburgh, Greg had convinced me that this would be the right move for me. Ron and Cheryl, my previous boss, and his wife when I joined Rockwell, had also recently moved to Pittsburgh as he took on a new role at Corporate. I had stayed in contact with Ron after his move. He told me that he and Cheryl were delighted with their decision. Now I needed to do my best sales job about the move with Mary Ann.

As I entered the house, Mary Ann was a little surprised by my early arrival home that day. She said, "Stephen, is everything OK? Why are you home so early today?"

Not wanting to worry my beautiful bride, I said, "Everything is fine, sweetheart. How is Kristie doing?"

Mary Ann said, "Fine. She was a little fussy earlier and was late getting down for her nap. Everything is pretty quiet right now."

I said, "Good. Let's sit down. I have something that I want to talk to you about."

I think Mary Ann had been expecting this discussion for a while. She looked at me with concerned eyes and asked, "Stephen, is this serious?"

I held her hand and said, "Yes, it is, but I think we can handle it." I told her about my conversation with Greg that day and the offer he put on the table for me. It was another one of those times that Mary Ann would want to take some time to digest the news. She sat back on the couch and put her hands over her face. She took some deep breaths and said, "Stephen, our life here is going so well. We have a new daughter that we both love. I am getting into a good routine as a new mother, and I love being so close to my family. Are you sure we need to do this?" Not only had Mary Ann grown into being a wonderful *mother of our children*, she also was a loving and supporting wife. I knew we could have an excellent conversation about this.

While it would be a difficult one for Mary Ann, we together would weigh all the pros and cons of the offer. She rightly asked what the alternatives were that we had to this offer. I told her I could probably stay on for a little while in my current role. However, if I turned this one down, I would be taken off the high-potential list. Therefore, the next move would likely not be a promotion but could still involve a relocation. I told her I was not ready to leave Rockwell at this point in my career. I was learning too much at this company, and they were investing in my career.

I said, "You know, Ron and Cheryl really like Pittsburgh, and we could make sure we live somewhere close to them. That way, you wouldn't be alone."

She said, "Mr. Manning, sometimes you're a hard man to love. Help me start fixing dinner. Kristie will be getting up from her nap soon. I need more time to think about this."

With that, I gave her a big hug and said, "no worries, sweetheart, we have a few days to decide. I know this is a big decision for the entire family. We don't want to get this one wrong."

As we started fixing dinner, we heard Kristie beginning to wake up from her nap. I thought this would be an appropriate time to leave Mary Ann alone and process her thoughts about relocating to Pittsburgh.

With that, I took a bottle up to Kristie and got her up from her nap. It would give Kristie and I some alone time together. I held Kristie on the couch and offered her some formula from her bottle. She had had a good nap; her eyes were bright, as was her smile. I started to tell her about our pending move to Pittsburgh, knowing she would not understand what I was telling her. I told her that her mother and I would make this decision together. I told her we would never do anything to hurt her, and if someday she wanted to return to Chicago, she could.

As it turns out, she did exactly that some twenty-two years later, to go to Medical School. She was accepted to and graduated from the University of Chicago Medical School. She then decided to stay in Chicago to do her residency at Northwestern Hospital. Coincidentally, that was part of the same hospital system she was born.

Soon Mary Ann came up to see how we were doing and let me know dinner was ready. During dinner, I could see Mary Ann was still processing the thought of moving to Pittsburgh. I knew this was a more challenging decision for her, and she would need more time. I quickly changed the subject to one of her favorite ones. "Tell me again how Kristie was doing today?" I asked.

She lit up with excitement. "I think Kristie is trying to talk! When I say mommy or daddy to her, I think she knows what I am saying. Kristie reaches out to me with her little arms, smiles, and seems to try and repeat my words. I know she is close to talking. I hope it happens when you are at home." With that, she turned to Kristie, and with a lovingly soft, stern voice, she said to Kristie, "Say daddy, say, mommy."

Kristie then gave us that big smile, waved her little arms up in the air, and kicked her tiny feet. She was getting ready for that baby book moment, and I hoped with all my heart that her first word would be "mommy."

The next day I got a call from the firm that Rockwell used to relocate their executives. The firm specialized in this, and due to Rockwell's size, we were one of their largest clients. The lady gave me a quick overview of the program and told me HR would be sending me a packet on Rockwell's relocation policy. She assured me that the program Rockwell had put together with them would make the entire process extremely easy. More importantly, there would be no out-of-pocket expense for the executive and their family. She also offered to send me information on Pittsburgh itself and current real estate listings. Given the cost of living in Pittsburgh, she suggested that we could buy a lot more house for the same money there.

When I got home from work, Mary Ann was ready to talk. She wanted to know more about the new role I would have in Pittsburgh and if there would be any travel involved. She said, "Stephen if you are going to take us to Pittsburgh and then jump on a bunch of airplanes and travel, I am not up for this. You can't take me to a new city and just leave me home alone to raise Kristie."

I told her that would not be the case. The new position would involve financial analysis of internal and external investments by the company, mostly capital investments at our factories and possibly some acquisition work. Any travel would be in and out the same day, using its corporate fleet of aircraft. One of the divisions of Rockwell built corporate jets, so we had easy access to that fleet.

She then asked how long we would be in Pittsburgh and about my desire to move out West.

I told her that I would have to commit to at least two years in Pittsburgh. Then Greg promised to get me a shot at a position somewhere in Rockwell's West Coast operations, probably in the Los Angeles area.

She then said, "I know you warned me about this possibility, and I thank you for that. It is just now that it is a reality; I am nervous. You have to hold to your promise to Kristie and me that you will not be traveling all over the place in this new role."

I gave her a big hug and thanked her for being such a good wife and mother. I promised her again about the travel ban and told her I would work hard to make this transition as easy as possible for her. Hopefully, we could find the house we wanted and a good neighborhood with many kids and stay-at-home mothers.

I started the new job a few weeks later. The relocation firm was excellent. They even asked to interview Mary Ann to do whatever they needed to make this as easy as possible for her and our child. It was Mary Ann's first interview with anybody after she stopped working after Kristie was born. It made Mary Ann proud that she was going to be part of the process.

Mary Ann came out a few weeks later for our house hunting visit and to see Pittsburgh. They assigned an agent full time that week to show Mary Ann around all the neighborhoods of Pittsburgh. We knew what we could afford to spend on a house, and we gave that information to the agent. I told Mary Ann that the location and home would be entirely her choice and take the time necessary to get comfortable with that decision.

Mary Ann found a neighborhood she liked and a home that would be more than sufficient for our young family. It was a five-bedroom, two-story home on a lovely lot at the bottom of a hill. I was not sure why we needed a five-bedroom house, but it was the one that Mary Ann had picked out, so it was to be. I think she was buying the neighborhood more than the house itself. Behind the home was a protected wooded area that led into a small lake attached to the neighborhood park. More importantly, it was a neighborhood full of kids and stay-at-home mothers. Most of our neighbors were six to ten years older than us. Most had kids at home, with some in high school. The agent was great. Once Mary Ann was sure that this was the home for us, she took her around to meet all our new neighbors. Mary Ann felt amazingly comfortable with the neighbors and Pittsburgh in general.

The people of Pittsburgh could not have been nicer people. They were very friendly and welcomed families from out-of-state. Pittsburgh, in 1981 was the second-largest corporate headquarter city in the United States. The city was used to having executives move in and out. Our local community developed programs to help quickly orient new families to their new neighborhoods. It sponsored a program Mary Ann grew to love called "Mother's Day Out." It was a program where a young mother could drop their kids off for free daycare for one or two days a week. It was usually at a church or community center staffed by licensed daycare personnel. They would let you drop off your children for up to three or four hours. That would give a young mother enough time to have appointments, go shopping, or just chill out with some alone time. It was just *what the doctor ordered* for Mary Ann. She took full advantage of this program.

Also notable for Mary Ann were the neighbors across the street, Lauretta and Jack Broderick. They were older than us and had two lovely daughters, Kim, and Michele. They would soon become our go-to babysitters while we were in Pittsburgh. The first non-family babysitters that Mary Ann would trust. Kristie was one-and-a-half at the time and never had a non-family babysitter. Mary Ann was undoubtedly protective of her first child. Lauretta took Mary Ann under her wing from day one. Lauretta treated Mary Ann like her younger sister and could not do enough for her. The neighborhood, like all neighborhoods in Pittsburgh, was close. You never really felt like you needed to lock your doors. If you ever run out of anything, you could quickly go next door and borrow whatever you needed. Every month one of the couples on the street would sponsor a dinner party. It was an excellent way to meet all the neighbors. Although Mary Ann dearly missed her family, she felt that she had an extended family in Pittsburgh.

My new job was going well. The team at work was easy to get along with and particularly good at what they did. Many were recent transplants, as there was a new CEO in place, and he was bringing in a lot of his team from around the country. The good news for Mary Ann was that I was not traveling much at all. If I did, I was always home at night.

My commute to work was not great, as the streets of Pittsburgh were not great back then. However, I could carpool with a coworker who had just moved into the neighborhood from Dallas with his family. The house we bought, while lovely from the outside, needed a lot of work inside. The house itself was about fifteen years old. It still had all the original paint on the walls and dated tile and carpeting. That meant the first six or seven weeks I would spend all weekends painting and laying new tile in the kitchen and bathrooms. I was not handy at all, but at least I knew how to paint. I later learned how to lay tile. While needed, we would not replace the carpet. It was necessary for sure, but just not in our budget.

First, of course, was to get Kristie's room ready, then attack the down-stairs rooms, and then work my way back up to the other four bedrooms upstairs. Mary Ann had picked up some color paint charts on one of her Mother's Day Out ventures and started picking out colors for all the rooms. I did not ask for any input on her choices, just a kindly nod occasionally to confirm her selections. That was OK; I was a painter, and she was the decorator in the family. We were going from darker colors to lighter colors, so I was worried about how much paint they would take to cover the walls. I was more concerned about the time it would take to paint the walls, not really about the cost of the paint itself. Sears had just released its "Guaranteed One Coat" paint product at the time. I thought, "Great, this product is for us." I went down to the local Sears store to procure all the things necessary; paintbrushes, masking tape, drop cloths, ladders, etc. I had nothing needed to make any home improvement. Sears quickly became my go-to place for everything. Knowing that we would be spending some serious money on this project, I even opened a Sears credit card account. I measured all the walls in each room to figure out how many gallons I would need for each paint color. With all supplies in hand, I was ready to start my project.

Kristie was getting big now, crawling everywhere and getting into everything. We had to keep an eye on her when she was not napping. As Kristie was getting older, the nap time was getting shorter. She did become very fond of a bounce chair that Mary Ann's mother had brought her before we left Chicago. She could play in that chair for hours. That was fortunate because Mary Ann had her own set of chores to help get our house in order the way we wanted it. So, what we did was put Kristie and her bounce chair in the room I was painting. That way, I could keep an eye on her while I painted. It also allowed me to teach her the art of painting walls. I finished Kristie's room, cleaned up, and took all my tools downstairs to start prepping the living room. That would be my Sunday project. I had finished early enough in the day to ensure the paint would be dry by the time we put Kristie down for bed. Mary Ann and I were both exhausted from our first day of remodeling.

After dinner, I took Kristie up for her bath, and Mary Ann cleaned up the kitchen. After putting our little angel to bed, we both sat on the couch, happy that day was done.

The next morning, we were awakened by Kristie, ready to start her day. Thankfully, she had slept through the night, Mary Ann and I needed a good night's sleep. Mary Ann went to get Kristie up, and with that, came back into our bedroom and said, "Steve, you need to come into Kristie's room. The paint on her walls is not right."

I went into her room, and sure enough, the Sears' "Guaranteed One Coat" did not work. You could still see the darker colors underneath the newly painted walls. I thought, "this can't be right." No way am I going to paint every room twice. This project is going to take forever.

I got up, got dressed, and drove down to the Sears where I had bought their famous One Coat paint. I took my empty paint cans over to the paint department and told the salesperson what just happened with my paint job the day before. All he could say was, "Sorry, sir, most times it only takes one coat. It looks like you are trying to paint over too dark of a color and you will need two coats of paint. The good news is we stand behind our guarantee. Here are three more gallons of paint on us!"

Paint every wall twice. That is the last thing I wanted to hear. Plus, I would have to wait for the first coat to dry before applying the second coat. Five bedrooms, a living room, dining room and kitchen. This project was going to take months to finish. Kristie was going to have a PhD in the art of painting by the time I was done. I knew I had no choice. Mary Ann wanted all the walls repainted and would not be happy until it was done. I thought, *alright, get on with it. You're the one that uprooted your wife and baby to Pittsburgh.*

Many more weeks of painting the walls ensued. I had gotten all the downstairs done and new tile in the kitchen laid. While exhausting, Mary Ann's color choices were perfect, and the house was taking shape. It was time for our favorite Saturday night date, dinner together at home consisting of steaks off the grill with a nice bottle of wine. I brought the steaks in; Mary Ann had made a nice salad with some fresh corn on the cob. As I sat down and started to pour the wine, Mary Ann asked, "What room are you going to paint tomorrow?"

"I thought the room next to Kristie's would be next."

Mary Ann said, "Maybe you should hold off on that one. I am not sure what color we should make that baby room." I thought that was weird, as she had never referred to that room as a baby room before. With that, I went to pour her a glass of wine. She looked at me and said with a smile, "no, I better not; I think I am done with wine for a while."

"Oh my God, you're pregnant! When did you find out?

She said, "The doctor just called earlier to confirm. It looks like I am due in January again."

We could not have been happier - well settled into Pittsburgh, Mary Ann loving the neighborhood, and Pittsburgh itself. Our house was coming together as she wanted it, as well as our family. Prayers to God would be made the next day at church. We would be praying in the cry room together with another child someday soon. When Mary Ann saw how happy I was, she just started crying with happiness. We were both where we wanted to be and with the person we wanted to be with. Instead of three, we would soon be four. Neither of us cared if it was a boy or another girl—just a healthy baby.

Mary Ann's pregnancy with our second child went well. She had found a doctor close by that she trusted, and I am sure that was with the help of our lovely neighbor Lorretta. Kristie was now fifteen months, starting to talk, always smiling, and now walking. Mary Ann had gotten into a good routine with Kristie. When the weather permitted, they would both go to the park behind our house. Their favorite activity was to walk to the park and feed the ducks in the pond. It wasn't a big pond, but there were plenty of ducks to keep them busy. Given Kristie's infatuation with ducks, Mary Ann had bought plenty of duck toys and outfits for her with ducks on them. Of course, there were always a few floating duck toys in the bath for her. Bath time was still my favorite one-on-one time with the kids as they were growing up. They all loved the water and, of course, the bubbles in the water and Kristie's ducks.

With all the remodeling on our new house done, we spent more time together over the weekends and at night after Kristie was in bed. Mary Ann loved her TV shows at night. It gave her time to relax from being a very attentive mother throughout the day. We both had our favorite spots on the couch, and she always controlled the TV remote. Fortunately, we enjoyed the same TV shows, and if there were ones I did not, I would at least pretend to. At the time, we only had one TV in the house, so I had little choice. The good news was that Mary Ann enjoyed sports. That year, both the Pittsburgh Pirates and the Pittsburgh Steelers were extremely competitive. Willie Stargell's Pirates won the World Series in 1979. Terry Bradshaw's Steelers completed their dynasty by winning their fourth Super Bowl in January 1980. Pittsburgh was a great sports town, and all wore black and gold. So, if either were on TV at night, she would usually give up the remote, and we would both watch the game together. The only TV series that would override a Pittsburgh football or baseball game would be the TV series "Dallas." It was a top-rated TV series, and Mary Ann would never miss a new episode or re-run.

When the holidays came that year, Mary Ann was too far into her pregnancy to want to travel. Thanksgiving was always a time we both wanted to be around family, but it would not happen that year. The good news was that our wonderful neighbors, the Brodericks, invited us into their home for Thanksgiving. Mary Ann offered to bake the pies, and Loretta and Jack handled everything else. Everything was perfect, and while not with direct family, we enjoyed being with our new Pittsburgh family that year. Jack was kind enough to let us all watch the traditional Thanksgiving Day Nebraska-Oklahoma football game before dinner. Back then, it was a college football tradition that Nebraska would play Oklahoma on Thanksgiving Day. Both teams were college football powerhouses, and the winner of that game often had a realistic shot at the national championship. Unfortunately, Nebraska lost that close game twenty-one to seventeen and finished ten and two following an earlier loss to Florida State. They finished number seven in the final AP polling that year.

With Thanksgiving over, we started getting ready for Christmas. It would be Kristie's second Christmas, and the first time she would know what was going on. Mary Ann took her to see Santa as soon as she heard Santa was at the mall, the Monday after Thanksgiving. She couldn't wait to see her smiling little angel in Santa's lap. We had also heard from Mary Ann's parents that they would be coming out for Christmas. They were not going to miss a chance to see their little granddaughter opening her Christmas presents. It would also be a chance for Ray Lesin to see our new house and to explore Pittsburgh. Midge had already been out to help Mary Ann get the house in order after we had moved in. Knowing that her parents were coming out for Christmas, Mary Ann was in full decoration mode. Not having to decorate such a big house before, there was a lot of decoration-buying that had to take place. Of course, Mary Ann loved to shop, and with her Mother's Day Out babysitting support, she was able to find ample time to get her Christmas shopping done. With all the decoration-buying and Christmas gifts for Kristie, we agreed to go light on buying each other gifts that year. The only thing Mary Ann wanted was a VCR so that she could record her TV shows. That technology was released a few years earlier for the first time, and it soon became a must-have product, especially for Mary Ann. My shopping that year for Mary Ann was effortless: Buy and wrap up a VCR and plenty of extra tapes to go along with it.

Mary Ann's parents arrived about a week before Christmas. There was snow on the ground, so no golf for Ray and me, but an excellent chance to get in some bowling while he was out. Mary Ann was able to drive them around the Pittsburgh area to show off our new town. Being in the manufacturing business, Ray was excited to see Pittsburgh. It wasn't the steel town; it historically had been as many of the steel mills were closed or significantly downsized. My office was in the U.S. Steel building in downtown Pittsburgh. It was on the fifty-first floor, so it had an excellent view of Pittsburgh and the three rivers that flowed through the city and surrounding areas. Mary Ann brought her parents by the office along with Kristie. The company allowed you to host them in the executive dining room for unique visitors, which I did. It was a very well-appointed dining room with an excellent menu. I was seldom able to eat in it, but it was quiet in the office that week. Many of the executives had already started their Christmas holiday and were out of the office. My only hope was that Kristie would be on her normal good behavior during lunch. Of course, she was, and many of my co-workers enjoyed meeting her and Mary Ann, some for the first time.

The Christmas holiday season was getting off to a good start for us - good family time for all and a chance for Mary Ann's parents to meet all the neighbors. We were hosting the monthly neighborhood dinner party that month for our first time. Mary Ann was nervous and wanted everything perfect for the event. Fortunately, her mother was there to help her prepare the meal. As I mentioned earlier, Midge was an excellent cook. Mary Ann was slowly learning her mother's cooking skills, but it was not yet a priority for her. She was more focused on being *a mother* than a good cook, which was more than fine with me. It would not be long before she mastered the cooking part of being a great wife *and mother*. The holiday neighborhood dinner went off without a hitch, and everyone enjoyed meeting Mary Ann's parents.

Christmas morning was so much fun. We had bought a beautiful tree and set it up in the living room, with plenty of gifts under the tree for Kristie. There was also a note from Santa thanking her for the cookies and milk for himself and his reindeer. Kristie let us sleep in a little bit that Christmas morning, which everyone appreciated. I had my camera out taking pictures of Kristie's every move. Mary Ann had her dressed in a red pajama set with a white bow on her head as she came down the stairs. Midge, Ray, and I could hardly hold back our excitement for this Christmas moment for her. With some lovely Christmas music playing in the background, Kristie quickly went to her pile of presents. I do not think she understood why she was getting them. It took little time for her to start ripping into her first present. From there, she went from one gift to another, stopping only to give an occasional smile and kisses to her grandma and papa. When she finished, we moved into the dining room for a special Christmas breakfast that Midge had prepared. After breakfast, we took the little red sled that we had gotten Kristie and pulled her on her new sled around the backyard. Christmas dinner was my job, so I started to prepare the prime rib we would all enjoy later that evening. Ray and Midge stayed through New Year's Day and then headed back to Chicago. As always, it was hard to see them go. Kristie gave them both big grandma and papa hugs, and I drove them to the airport. Midge knew she would be back in a few weeks to help Mary Ann after she had our second child.

The doctor had confirmed to Mary Ann that her due date would be late January, probably not too many days after Kristie's second birthday on January 19th. We, as before, could care less about having a boy or girl. We were only praying at church for a healthy baby. That would be number two for us. We knew if God let us, we would have more. Mary Ann already gave us some room for the outcome by postponing my new baby room painting.

As it got closer to Mary Ann's due date, I decided to work from home. As every year in January, it was snowy with some ice. Nothing like the snow we got in Chicago before Kristie was born, but enough snow to be an issue. As I mentioned, we lived at the bottom of a reasonably hilly street. If there were any ice mixed with the snow, it would often be a problem getting up the hill on either side of the house. I would often have to back up as far as I could on the street to give me a running start to get up the hill if it was icy. Sometimes I made it, and sometimes I just could not get out of the neighborhood.

Going out the other side of the neighborhood was somewhat more manageable since it was not as steep. The good news was that was the direction of the hospital. However, given our experience with Kristie's birth night, we were still concerned. Also, given it was Mary Ann's second birth, her labor would likely be somewhat shorter. I did not want to get a call from Mary Ann at work saying it was time for her to go to the hospital and get home from work to get her to the hospital. Sure enough, around 4 p.m. on Tuesday, Mary Ann told me it was time. I called Lorretta and asked if she could watch Kristie while I took Mary Ann to the hospital. She knew she was on call for this and was more than ready to comply with the request. I also called Midge and told her to start packing her bags for a return trip to Pittsburgh.

We were quickly off to the hospital. Mary Ann always had everything packed that she needed and plenty of "just in case" clothing. She also had a complete list for Lorretta of everything Kristie might need while in the hospital. Of course, she made a second list for me for when I returned from our second child's birth. Mary Ann made lists for everything, but in this case, it was not a terrible thing. I knew I would have my hands full taking care of Kristie as well as her mother did. I also knew Kristie was old enough to see if I could not do what her mother always did for her. Our little jewel was a smart baby.

The trip to the hospital turned out to be easy. The roads were cleared earlier in the day, and the hospital itself was close. We pulled up to the front door by the admitting station. I got a wheelchair and took Mary Ann in to get registered and examined. Like with Kristie, I parked the car as they checked Mary Ann in. As I returned to the admitting room, I could see Mary Ann talking with one of the doctors. I walked over and introduced myself to her admitting doctor. He said, "Congratulations on having your second child. It looks like labor has started, but it will be a few hours until your baby will be ready for birth. We are going to take Mary Ann up to her room as soon as it is ready, and you can join her there." I waited with Mary Ann until they took us both up to her room.

The admitting room staff was typical Pittsburgh: friendly, helpful, and very encouraging on our next step in building our family. They could tell we were nervous and went out of their way to calm both Mary Ann and me down. Mary Ann could not help but ask the staff if there would be a TV in her room. A new episode of "Dallas" was airing that night, and she was hoping to watch it as we waited for our new little treasure to arrive. All birthing rooms at the hospital were private rooms, so we knew we would be able to enjoy our time together alone. It would also give us a chance to see the episode of "Dallas" without interruption.

As we waited for Mary Ann to give birth, she pulled out her list of possible names we had been discussing. There was one list for boys' names and another in case we had another girl. We were OK with having either, but I was betting on a boy. I just figured the odds would be a boy this time since we had just had a little girl. We had agreed to a top three list of names for either outcome, although I knew Mary Ann would get the deciding vote. After a few hours, Mary Ann's labor started to increase, and it would soon be time for her to deliver our second child.

The hospital was again one of those that allowed the father to be in the delivery room. Today that is standard practice, but back then, it was selective and at the call of the delivering doctor and the hospital. As we moved into the delivery room, I could see Mary Ann was starting to have some painful labor pains. As she started doing her deep breathing, the doctor checked her out and said, "OK, Mary Ann, it looks like you are ready to deliver your little angel."

From there, things started to move fast, and I took my position behind the doctor with eyes on my lovely bride. It was becoming a challenging delivery for Mary Ann, and I could see the pain in Mary Ann's eyes. As our baby started to deliver, I could see a lot of blood coming from Mary Ann. The doctor was moving fast, wanting to get the delivery done so the medical staff could address Mary Ann's bleeding. Not knowing what was going on, I was again worried about our second child's birth and getting faint with the sight of all the bleeding. Seeing that I was getting a little faint, a nurse moved over next to me to catch me if I fainted. With that, the doctor pulled back with our new baby in hand and said, "Congratulations, Mary Ann, on the birth of your new little daughter!" The doctor gave her a little spank on the butt, and she gave out a big cry. Even today, I think I may have seen our little girl throw a left hook at the doctor after he spanked her on the butt. Her personality was already starting to show up.

After delivery, the nurses took our baby girl to clean up and told me to follow them. The medical staff had some work to do to stop Mary Ann's bleeding and wanted both of us out of the room for that effort. I wouldn't see Mary Ann for another hour or so while she recovered from the birth and the repair work, they needed to do on her. We would find out later that this would be her last natural childbirth. If we were to have more children, they would have to be delivered by cesarean section. I decided to stop by the chapel to say some prayers of thanks to the Lord for a healthy baby and pray for my wife's quick recovery. The delivery nurse figured out that I would likely have gone to the chapel. She was kind enough to come to find me. She wanted to give me an update on both Mary Ann and our new baby. Our little girl checked out fine and was asleep in the nursery. Mary Ann was still recovering. I thanked her for her thoughtfulness and kindness and took a walk to the nursery to see our new little girl.

Since Mary Ann had not announced to the medical staff or me our baby's new name, her crib's pink card just said, Baby Manning. It was so precious to see our new little girl quietly sleeping in her crib. The nurse in the nursery saw me looking at my little girl and was kind enough to tilt her crib up so I could see her more clearly. I knew when Mary Ann got back to the room, they would bring her to us, and I would get a chance to hold her for the first time. I then went back to the room and waited for Mary Ann to return. They finally brought her back to the room. She had lost a lot of blood, so they were still transfusing some blood back into her body. She was exhausted and needed to get some sleep, as did I. Even though tired when they asked her if she wanted to hold her new daughter, there was no hesitation.

"Yes, please bring her to me."

As they rolled her into the room, I saw Mary Ann's eyes light up. She was more than ready to start raising our second daughter. She held her for a few minutes and then smiled at me and said, "Stephen, would you like to hold your new daughter? Please meet Karie Lynn Manning!"

I was OK with all three of the names we had down selected, but I must admit, Karie Lynn was my favorite. I was hoping that was the one that Mary Ann would choose. We both took turns holding Karie for the first time, but it was late, and we both needed some sleep. Mary Ann said, "Stephen, I need some sleep now. Why don't you go home and get some sleep as well? Later in the morning, you can call our parents and let them know we have a new little girl, and her name is Karie Lynn, born on January 24th, 1981, two years and five days after Kristie was born." I kissed both Mary Ann and Karie and went home to get some much-needed sleep.

Mary Ann's mom had already booked her flight to Pittsburgh. She would arrive later that night. I would certainly welcome her help with Kristie. Because of Mary Ann's bleeding with the birth of Karie, she would be staying at least an extra day in the hospital. I am not sure what I would have done without the help of Loretta and Midge. Of course, Mary Ann would have been able to handle it, but I was not sure at all if I could. Midge helped me get everything ready for Mary Ann and Karie's homecoming, which came four days after Karie's birth. That gave me time to get her new bedroom painted in the right colors, to Mary Ann's great satisfaction. With everyone now home, we quickly got into the rotation of having two babies in diapers.

Kristie was not sure what just happened. She had the house and her mommy and daddy all to herself, and now she had to share. Kristie was very curious about who this new visitor was to her little castle. Little did she realize at the time that Karie was more than just a visitor to her castle.

Mary Ann was always good at splitting time with her children. She had developed a schedule that would allow her to spend some one-on-one time with each of our kids. She knew that they all had different personalities, and all needed special attention.

Karie had a little different personality than Kristie. Things were a bit quieter when it was just Kristie at home. Of course, she had everything to herself for a couple of years, so everything came easy to her. Now she had to share with her sister. Karie, on the other hand, knew nothing about that peacefulness. From the very beginning, Karie was louder than Kristie and was never afraid to show her displeasure when things did not quite go her way. Mary Ann handled it all beautifully. Although Karie was too young to talk, Mary Ann always knew somehow what was upsetting her. I was helpless, only knowing that she seemed to cry a lot. Karie also smiled a lot, still showing her emotions.

It was fun seeing our two little girls growing up together. Mary Ann enjoyed buying the girls matching outfits. She would dress them up to perfection and then take them on walks. Kristie would walk to the park with her, and Karie was in her stroller. There were many trips to the park to see the ducks in the afternoon and then back home in time to welcome daddy home from work. Mary Ann would always gather the kids when she heard the garage door open when I came home from work. As soon as I opened the door, she would have all the kids there ready to greet me with smiles and kisses. To help top off the day, I would also get a nice welcome-home kiss from my lovely bride as well.

A few months after Karie was born, I had gotten a call from Greg. He wanted to tell me about a position that was going to open in Anaheim, California. It was a financial management role within Rockwell's defense electronics business unit. I had not had much exposure to the defense electronics business unit at the time, but the fact that it was in California had me interested. That night when I got home, I told Mary Ann about the call from Greg. Mary Ann was less than enthusiastic about the news. She had become delighted with our life in Pittsburgh and all the friends and neighbors she had met. Karie was still very much a baby, and she was getting into a good routine with both girls. Long term, we both had eyes on the West Coast, but she was not convinced it was time for yet another move.

I suggested that I go out to meet the management team out there and see if the position would be a good fit for me. A few of my former audit team members had already moved to the West Coast with Rockwell. I was able to reach out to them to get some additional information on the position from them. Generally, the feedback was all positive. Greg had also told me that due to Rockwell's work for the government at this site, I would need to get a top-secret security clearance. That would take a few months to complete, so he wanted to get the process started as soon as possible. I went out to Los Angeles that following week.

I had only been to Los Angeles once before, with a college friend on a road trip there after graduation. We had taken off from Lincoln, stopped in Denver, and then dead-headed to Las Vegas for a few days. After Vegas, we headed to Los Angeles. I remember arriving at UCLA and looking out over the campus thinking, *are you kidding me? I could have spent my last four years on this campus instead of Nebraska??* The atmosphere was terrific, and the campus was beautiful. The next time I would be on that campus would be some twenty years later, moving our oldest daughter Kristie into the freshman dorm.

My interview trip to Anaheim took the entire week, the longest I had been away from Mary Ann and the girls since we moved to Pittsburgh. I wanted to get a good feel for the management team that I would be working with and quickly look at the area's real estate market. Rockwell had set me up with one of their relocation experts in the area, so I set aside a day and a half for that part of the visit. I also received a quick non-classified briefing on Rockwell's defense electronics business model. That business unit dealt with electronic systems that supported several powerful weapons and space systems. Most were significant aircraft systems, from the F-111 fighter to the upcoming B-1 bomber, along with the MX missile. They had been heavily involved in the Apollo space systems and were working on the upcoming Space Shuttle. There were other classified systems that I would find out about later. Overall, the product portfolio was impressive.

The real estate side of the visit was far less impressive. There was almost no way to compare real estate prices between Pittsburgh and Anaheim. Houses were smaller, lot sizes were smaller, and the space between houses was smaller. The only thing more significant on the West Coast was the price per square foot you had to pay for a home. I knew Mary Ann was not going to like this fact. Although Rockwell would be giving me a cost-of-living adjustment and a raise for the new position, it would not be easy.

I gathered all the information on the new position and the real estate market and headed back to Pittsburgh that Friday. I needed to be as transparent as possible with Mary Ann. Given the timing, we would have to make the go/no-go decision before she had a chance to visit the area.

Mary Ann had pretty much blocked out the weekend to discuss the possibility of moving to California. She was trying to have an open mind about the West Coast's move but wanted to hear all the facts in detail that weekend. She had also had a busy week with the girls and looked forward to some parenting help that weekend. I got back late Friday night, so we planned to take the girls to the park the next morning. Kristie showed Karie how to feed the ducks, and we started a long weekend discussion. Knowing that Mary Ann would be the most interested in the housing elements related to our move to California, we started there. I had collected some of the listing information of the houses I saw that week and some general overview materials on the area. It was clear from the outset that there would be no five-bedroom home in our future, but we did not need something that big at the time anyway. The other thing that was hard to explain to Mary Ann was the mix of neighborhoods you get in California. Finding a home as close to the ocean as possible was of interest to both of us. We also wanted something close to parks where the girls could play and good schools and daycare.

This discussion was not going well. Mary Ann was pleased with our life in Pittsburgh, and the thought of moving was not sitting well with her. We had the house the way we wanted it, and she loved the neighbors and the neighborhood. I didn't particularly appreciate seeing the frown on my lovely bride's face as we had the discussion. While she was always willing to have the conversation, she wanted to make sure she had full input to any decision that would affect the family. Mary Ann also did not like change.

The affordability index of Pittsburgh could not be matched anywhere in California. On the plane ride back, I did some calculations on how much house we could afford. The raise and the cost-of-living adjustment that I would be getting took some of the stings out of what we saw on home prices. It was still going to be a compromise. We then talked about the job itself and if there would be any travel involved. Thankfully, this was a no-travel job, which made Mary Ann happy. She was a little taken aback because I would need to get a top-secret security clearance, thinking there would be some level of danger in the new role. I told her not to worry; everybody on the senior staff had to get that only due to the nature of the government contracting work that unit did. We would be developing weapon and space systems that might not even come into production for five or six years. Many of the systems Rockwell was involved with later became known as President Ronald Reagan's "Star Wars" program.

We continued to talk through the weekend, weighing all the pros and cons of such a move. Finally, Mary Ann turned to me and asked, "Stephen, from a career point of view, what do you think this move is going to do for you? It can't just be a move to sunny California."

I told her that what interested me most about the new role would be getting closer to computer technology. It was an area that I thought would get a lot more interesting in the future, and all of that would be happening on the West Coast.

She thought about it for a few minutes and then turned to me and said, "OK, Mr. Manning, this moving thing is going to get old soon, so you had better be right this time."

This was going to be the most challenging move of our life together. Taking her away from the home and neighborhood she found was going to be difficult. I was just hoping we could see the same situation in Southern California. I was not so attached to Pittsburgh, but Mary Ann was more than happy there. With that, I called Greg on Monday and told him that I would take the job in Anaheim.

Moving to California

ithin two weeks, I was at my new desk in Anaheim. I met my new team that was made up of six direct reports and a great secretary. All were long-term Southern California residents, and most had been with the company for at least five years. That was a good thing since they had an in-depth knowledge of doing business for the Defense Department and other agencies. Doing direct business with the government and its agencies had specific rules. My staff was more than helpful in keeping me on point with these new rules. How they ordered the product, how we had to report on development costs, how they defined direct cost and indirect cost were crucial factors in our financial reporting. When you have products that only one customer could buy, the entire business model changes, which was ultimately why I did not like the defense contracting business. Basically, we were a paid Research and Development site for the U. S. Government. It was interesting work, and what then-President Reagan was doing with "Star Wars" gave us some fantastic programs. Many involved some awe-inspiring advanced technologies, and we were involved with a lot of them. However, it was a great technology that only had one customer, the U. S. Government. I missed the marketing and strategy efforts needed to address a larger, more dynamic marketplace. I benefited from the exposure to all that technology later in my career as I moved into the commercial electronics market.

I was not in love with my new boss. It was the first time in my career that I would not be able to build a relationship with my boss. It also was the first time my boss was not a mentor or teacher. While I was fortunate to have had bosses, who were both in all my previous positions, this guy was a dictator.

He took no time to tell me what he was looking for or how he wanted to see it. As I learned from my staff and my secretary, his direct reports' washout rate was significant. I eventually called Greg to see if he thought I was doing something wrong. He said, "No, Steve, we were hoping you could help turn him around. No worries, we are aware of this issue. Hang in there; his boss knows we have a problem with him."

I chose not to share these issues with Mary Ann. I knew that situation would be addressed. As I said before, I trusted Greg.

It was fast approaching Mary Ann's time to come to visit the area on her one-week house-hunting trip. That meant I had to stay every other weekend in Southern California to find the right locations for our house search. I hated being away from Mary Ann and the girls every other weekend, but I knew this was a critical mission I was on. We thought it would take a month or two, but it took over three months. Those were the loneliest months that I would ever have, driving all around the area to find a neighborhood that Mary Ann would be happy. Orange County covered all the places that would be a reasonable commute area to where I was working. I was having difficulty finding a home that we could afford and that she would be happy with. There were some genuinely nice developments, like Mission Viejo, that were perfect for us, planned communities that were very well thought out. Unfortunately, it was just above what we could afford at the time. I did finally find some areas that would meet Mary Ann's desires, and not too far from where I was working.

One thing that helped bring home pricing down to more reasonable levels back then was home mortgage interest rates. They had skyrocketed in the early eighties due to the runaway inflation that I had studied back in college. As my economic model had predicted, compounding energy inflation would prove to be a ticking time bomb. Mortgage interest rates rose to slightly over 18%. It was like buying a home on a credit card. As interest rates rose, the price of homes went down, since fewer people could qualify for a mortgage. That caused a supply/demand imbalance in the housing market. We were able to benefit from that since the Rockwell relocation package would buy your mortgage interest rate down for four years to match the interest rate you had on the home you were selling. In our case, that meant we would effectively keep our rate at 10.5%. Any monthly mortgage payments above that rate would be rebated by the company. This was a significant benefit to us as; without this program, we would have had to rent our home.

Mary Ann came out for the week. We had already accepted an offer on our home so we knew how much we could afford to spend on our new home. I had planned the entire week for her. We would spend the daytime looking at a selection of homes I had picked out for her and then drive through the areas of Orange County in the afternoon. I wanted to make certain she was comfortable with the neighborhoods that I had targeted. I also got a hotel close to the ocean. I knew she would quickly fall in love with Southern California if we could find a home that would suit her. I planned all our dinners at restaurants that looked over the ocean and had access to the beaches in the area. It was both romantic and relaxing for us, and I knew she would be having stress the entire week.

We finally found a three-bedroom home that she was OK with us in Anaheim Hills. It was close to my office and not too far from Disneyland. I knew she was already thinking of how much fun it was going to be to take our little girls to the Magic Kingdom someday soon. In keeping with Kristie's love for ducks, she and Karie would soon be meeting Donald Duck. With our mission accomplished we flew back to Pittsburgh, both looking forward to kissing and hugging our two little treasures who were waiting for our return.

The move to California was uneventful. Rockwell's relocation company did their normal excellent job and we barely had to lift a finger. Since it took the movers three days to deliver our household goods, we took full advantage of the time. We got ourselves a room at one of the Disneyland hotels. It would be the first of many visits with our girls to the Magic Kingdom. The good news was our new home had been recently painted and re-carpeted so our weekends would be free to explore the area and the beaches with the girls. We found a beach that Mary Ann and the girls loved and would go there most weekends. Mary Ann would pack a lunch for everyone, gather the girls' beach toys, and we were off. The girls would play just outside the waterline of the waves, and when the water was warm enough, Mary Ann and I would take the girls into the ocean. It was always a fun and relaxing day at the beach with the girls and my lovely bride.

Mary Ann was able to locate one Mother's Day Out program at the local church in our neighborhood. Unfortunately for her, it only operated one day a week. While it gave her a little break during the week, she had to plan carefully around that schedule. We also had difficulty locating a babysitter for the girls when we wanted to go out. What depressed Mary Ann about the new neighborhood was the lack of stay-at-home moms and other young kids our kids could have playdates. Mary Ann would often put the girls in a twin stroller and walk with the girls around the neighborhood. This would generally be a magnet for other young mothers in the community who also wanted to find young kids to play with their kids, but not here. I am sure this was a problem in many neighborhoods in the area. With the high cost of housing in Southern California, both parents had to work.

Also, the commute times were generally extended in Southern California, so parents usually arrive home well after 6:30 p.m. This did not leave much time for the kids to have play time with their neighbors. It made for a very lonely time for Mary Ann. Trips to the park sometimes paid off, but far too often, the parks were empty during the day. Mary Ann was trying her best to be a good sport about our new life in Southern California, but I could tell she was disenchanted with our new life there. Often when I would get home from work, she would start talking at a hundred miles an hour, touching every topic under the sun. I told her once, "Please just slow down, and I can't listen as fast as you are talking." She stopped talking and started to cry. Then she said, "Stephen, I am sorry. I just need an adult to talk to occasionally. I love our girls, but eight hours a day of baby talk is driving me crazy."

I felt so badly for her. At the time, I did not know what to do. I just hoped that a new neighbor might finally show up with some little kids close to the girls' ages. That was all going on simultaneously, and I was having problems with my new boss. So, there we both sat, frustrated with our decision to move out West.

The girls were keeping Mary Ann busy. Kristie was getting old enough to give Mary Ann some help with things. While still an infant, Karie was also getting more active and crawling all over the house and patio. We had to keep an eye on her when she was out on the patio. When you live in Southern California, you are always going to get snails in your garden. Karie decided any snail in our garden had to end up in her mouth. If you left her for more than a few minutes, she would find a snail, and she always did. You could never take your eye off her when she was in the backyard. Kristie would just shake her head and sometimes point and yell "SNAIL" to alert us. To this day, escargot is still one of Karie's favorite appetizers. Mary Ann was never a huge fan of escargot; I think it had something to do with how many times she had to pull snails out of Karie's mouth when she was younger.

Fortunately, winter started to set in, and the holidays were just around the corner. When you live out West, and your friends and family live in the Midwest, you get plenty of visitors during the winter, and of course, for family, our doors were always open. Both of our parents made their way out to see us and thankfully made extended stays with us. It helped Mary Ann and the girls. It offered the girls multiple trips to Disneyland with the grandparents to where we bought a family season pass to the Magic Kingdom.

However, after the holiday season passed, we were back to dealing with the realities of our new life. Mary Ann was still lonely during the day, and I still had problems with my boss.

One day I got a call from Mike Haltom. Mike was a good friend who had previously worked with Ron Sanderson on the Dallas audit staff. At the same time, we were both in Pittsburgh and was working for the President of Commercial Electronics Operations at Rockwell. His boss Paul was a highly successful executive at IBM earlier in his career. When Paul left Rockwell to become President of the Burroughs Corporation, Paul took Mike with him. Mike and I did not keep in touch as much as I would have liked, so it was good to hear his voice again.

After getting caught up on his new role with Paul and my new position at Rockwell, Mike said, "Steve, I have a position that I would like you to consider. As you may have read, Burroughs just acquired Memorex in Santa

Clara, California. Paul and I are going to be out there next week, and I think you should come out to meet with us."

Burroughs, at the time, was based in Detroit, Michigan. When Paul and Mike took their new positions, Mike had reached out to see if I would be interested in joining them there, and I declined. I let him know that I desired to move out West. I reminded Mike that I had no desire to move back to the Snowbelt. He told me, "No worries, this position would be in Santa Clara, California, and would be reporting to me." Mike was going to head up the integration team for Burroughs as they consolidated Memorex into Burroughs. I told him I would have to talk to Mary Ann about this and call him back in a couple of days. I trusted Mike and respected Paul, so I thought it might be a solution to our dilemma with our current situation if the job is right. I got home that night and started the discussion with Mary Ann. The timing was right. All Mary Ann said was that if we were going to move again, it better be to a neighborhood of kids and stay-at-home mothers.

The next week I went up to see Mike and learn more about Memorex and the opportunity there. I had a chance to meet most of the senior staff and learn much about Memorex's history and why Burroughs acquired them. One of my most interesting interviews was with the Chairman of Memorex, Clancy Spangle. Clancy was one of the most respected industry executives, known for his integrity and strategic thinking. I would soon come to respect and admire Clancy as well.

There is one story about Clancy that spoke volumes to me. The technology groups in Silicon Valley had quite a few Associations that we all belonged to. When there would be high-level meetings of the Associations, I would often go to them with Clancy. All his CEO peers would be in the room together. When Clancy would enter the room, he was the only CEO who would get standing applause as he entered. It was quite impressive. Before Memorex, he was Chairman of Honeywell's Information Systems business. While at Honeywell, Clancy was the one who pushed the U.S. Government to sue IBM for their business practices around their introduction of the IBM 360 line of computers. It was a massive lawsuit at the time and took years to resolve.

Clancy and I would grow to be great friends, and he was a great mentor to me. My first interview with him was classic Clancy Spangle. It started with him giving me a brief background on his career, and then he asked me to describe mine. As I took him through my time at Inland Steel and Rockwell, he stopped me and said, "I don't know what it is about you young executives. Look at how great Rockwell is treating you; why do you now want to leave them?"

I said, "excuse me, Mr. Spangle; you guys are the ones that asked me to come to see you. I currently don't have any plans on leaving Rockwell. It was just out of respect for Mike and Paul that I accepted the requested interview."

With that, he excused me from his office. As I left Clancy's office area, Mike pulled me aside and asked how my interview with Clancy went. I told him I did not think very well and told him what Clancy said. He told me, "no worries. Paul has already told him that we were going to hire you. Now go down and see the head of HR; he is preparing an offer for you and wants to take you through it."

Knowing Mike and Paul, I knew it would be a generous offer, and it was. I thanked everybody for the opportunity and told Mike I would go over the offer with Mary Ann and get an answer back to him by Monday. Mike knew and respected Mary Ann and knew I would not decide without her approval.

With an offer in hand, I flew back to Orange County to discuss the next steps with Mary Ann. Mary Ann, God, I love her, was getting used to these discussions. The good news was she was not happy and thought a change might be good for the family and her mental health if we did it right this time. I agreed and told her this time, like with our move to Pittsburgh, she would get the final vote on the neighborhood. Given her approval on the move, I called Mike and resigned from Rockwell the next day. It was hard, Clancy was right; Rockwell had been exceptionally good to our family and me.

As Mary Ann and I got ready for yet another move, we wanted to take full advantage of all the things we liked about living in Southern California. There were indeed downsides to our time there, but there were also some positives. We spent time at our favorite beach and at Disneyland. We knew we would miss both in the Bay Area. Karie was also getting a little older and getting to the age where she could enjoy it more. When Karie was happy, her smile would knock you over. She always showed her emotions, but when she smiled, she lit up everyone around her. She was undoubtedly a cutie. I was so lucky to have these three women around me, and I knew it was all about how Mary Ann was *raising my children.*

I started at Memorex in August 1982, two weeks after I had resigned from Rockwell. My routine would be to fly up Monday morning to San Jose. This area, in general, was referred to as 'Silicon Valley.' The Bay Area referred to the entire area from slightly North of San Francisco all the way South and East of the city, any place within twenty to twenty-five miles from San Francisco Bay. The San Jose airport was at Silicon Valley's heart and only a few miles from my new office and the apartment I was renting. Every other weekend I would stay in the Bay Area to get a feel for the neighborhoods. To my surprise, the housing prices were higher in the Bay Area than in Orange County. I figured at the time that the only higher-priced housing in the United States would have been in New York City. It was an error not to check this out before I accepted the job and salary at Memorex. At this point, it was water under the bridge, and we would have to deal with it. What it did mean, however, was there would-be neighborhoods closer to the office that would be too expensive even to bother looking at.

The relocation company gave me a real estate map of the Bay Area. I wanted better to focus my weekend house-hunting ventures in more afford-able communities. I could see that to get something that we could afford, my commute to work was going to be close to forty-five minutes to an hour in rush-hour traffic. I figured if that is what it took to get Mary Ann and the girls into a neighborhood that they liked, then it would be worth it. I would just leave a little earlier in the morning and chill out on the drive home at night. Through my research, I found two communities that I thought Mary Ann and the girls would like. Pleasanton was a long-distance drive for me, but not as heavy traffic as Almaden south of San Jose. Almaden was a shorter drive but had heavier traffic so both commutes would be about the same time. Both areas had good schools and housing that looked affordable by

Bay Area standards. They both also had a country club that I thought we would be able to afford at some point. Both clubs were very family-oriented, with two good golf courses, tennis courts, and a pool area. Pleasanton had more new construction going on at the time and seemed to have more of a bedroom community feel to it. I gathered data on both and took it home for Mary Ann to review before making her house hunting trip up to the Bay Area.

As Mary Ann was going through the information, I had gathered for her; I could see she was getting nervous about the move. As I did, she could see that the housing costs were more than either one of us had anticipated, in some areas substantially more. These were all very desirable areas, and all much closer to where I would be working. I told her not to worry about the commute time. Like we did in Pittsburgh, we just needed to focus on the neighborhood and find the most affordable house we can. Given the housing cost surprise of the Bay Area, I thought it would take more time to do the housing search. I suggested that she have her mom and dad come out to watch the kids and that she should plan her house-hunting trip for two weeks instead of one. That way, she would have plenty of time to make the right decision. With that plan in place, we flew her parents out, and she came with me the following week for her two-week visit.

The relocation company assigned her a separate realtor for each area since the areas were so different pricewise. I wanted her to see all the communities in the area, even those neighborhoods that I thought were well out of our price range so that she would have a feel for the Bay Area. She started on the west side of the bay from Palo Alto down through Los Gatos and Saratoga. These were lovely areas and good for her to see, but there was zero chance that she would find anything that was going to work for us. After day two of her house hunting, she was very depressed and could not get comfortable with housing prices in the Bay Area. She said with sadness, "Stephen, how did you miss so badly on Bay Area housing prices? What I have seen over the last two days is just ridiculous. I didn't see anything worth living in that we can afford."

I told her not to worry, "What you saw was where CEOs, lawyers, and doctors live. There were more appropriate areas in the Bay Area that would work for us. The only thing we would have to give up on was how long my commute was going to be."

She calmed down a bit, and I took her to a nice dinner, and we had some excellent alone time together. We couldn't do too many dinner dates down south because we never had a regular babysitter. It was a lovely night out, so we decided to walk back to the hotel. I put my arm around her and held her tight while we walked. I was confident that we would find a place that worked for her and the girls, and hopefully, we would live there for many years to come. This relocation thing was getting way too complicated, and I knew Mary Ann had had all she could take of it.

The next day Mary Ann and another realtor went to the South Bay. They visited homes as far south as Gilroy, California, and North up through Almaden, California. I knew she would find more reasonable home prices in that area and some attractive new development homes in Gilroy. When I met with her that evening at the hotel, she was in much higher spirits. She said, "Stephen, I am much more encouraged with the home values I saw today. I didn't find a neighborhood that excited me, but at least I saw some homes we could afford that could work for us." I was so relieved with that statement, and that twinkle was starting to come back into my bride's beautiful eyes. Mary Ann was such a strong person. She put up with all this moving around the country because she knew we were doing things that would make our family stronger. She would have lived in the snows of Chicago forever if she thought that would have made our family stronger.

It was never about money for Mary Ann, just about what it took to have the best, most successful, and happy family that we could build together. I loved her so much for this and wanted to make sure I didn't do anything to screw that vision up.

The next day she visited homes in the East Bay, starting with Fremont, California, and further north to Pleasanton. Fremont would be closer to my office, but I knew the prices were about 15% to 20% higher there at the time. I also thought that she would fall in love with the town of Pleasanton.

It was a small town at the time and had a much stronger family feel to it. There was also some new construction in the north part of Pleasanton, just a few miles from downtown, that I thought she might find interesting. Home prices would still be at the high end of our affordability limits; I figured if she liked something there, we would be able to make it work.

When I saw her later that day, she was in a much better mood. She told me that she thought that Pleasanton was her top choice from everything she saw, followed by the Almaden area south of San Jose. She liked the town's feel and said she saw plenty of mothers with their children in and around the neighborhoods and at the parks. She was just worried about the commute I would have to the office. Pleasanton was about thirty-five miles from my office. I told her not to worry; if Pleasanton worked out for her, I would deal with the commute. I suggested that she take one more day to check out the neighborhoods south of San Jose since they were her second choice. If she was still convinced that Pleasanton would work for us, I would take the next couple of days off, and we would find a home there. I reminded her, "your instincts were right in Pittsburgh, and you loved it there. I trust your judgment this time as well. I want to make this move work for all of us."

The second visit to Almaden wasn't that necessary, but we had the time, and I wanted her to be sure. When we got back together later that day, Mary Ann reconfirmed that Pleasanton was her final choice. She said, "I like the small-town feel of Pleasanton and felt a sense of community there today."

I was so happy to hear that from Mary Ann. I said, "Sweetheart, I knew from the moment I saw Pleasanton that you were going to like it there. Let's take the next two or three days together and find our new home." We both hoped that this would be the last home search for many years to come.

Pleasanton was a small community by Bay Area standards back in 1982, with less than 36 thousand residents. The town only had one stoplight back then, and it had good schools, friendly parks, and a lovely downtown area. Pleasanton had resisted the growth that was happening all over the Bay Area in the late seventies and early eighties. The city council had voted for little or few growth policies for many years but started to open itself up to new development. In the early eighties, a commercial real estate developer convinced the city council to build a large business park at the north end of the city.

Along with the building permit, the developer agreed to widen the streets and install additional stoplights. He also built a vast sports park and another fire station. Other monies were also set aside for some new schools. On the northwest side of town, a major shopping center, Stoneridge Mall, was also built. The sleepy city of Pleasanton was on its way to seeing some major growth.

As a result of Pleasanton's long history of slow growth, quite a large mix of older homes in the area sprinkled in with some more recent construction. Mary Ann had visited both on her prior visit. We spent the next two days going through everything that was on the market at the time. Although prices from our perspective were high, in Bay Area terms, the prices had been depressed by the high mortgage interest rates that were still prevailing at the time. A standard thirty-year mortgage with 20% down was 18.5%. Existing homes were sitting on the market for extended periods.

The builders of new homes were struggling to move their inventory. I favored the new-construction homes in the area. They had suitable lot sizes and all the modern appliances; most new construction were two-story homes. The existing homes were a mix of one-story and two-story homes, but their styles and appliances were often dated. I knew if we could find a home that we liked, I would negotiate with the builder, given their inventory buildup. On our third day, we decided to focus on a new community built just north of town called Country Fair. It was developed by a local builder called Ponderosa Homes. As it turned out later, the owner of Ponderosa Homes, Kile Morgan, became a good friend and occasional golf partner of mine. They had an excellent reputation for building quality, good-value homes, so we were not afraid of buying one of their products.

As we were driving around that neighborhood, we turned the corner, and out in front of one of the new homes were three little girls playing in the front yard. The youngest one appeared to be the same age as Kristie. Mary Ann turned to me and said, "Stop the car."

She scared me, as I was afraid that maybe one of the little girls had gone out into the street, so I stopped immediately.

Mary Ann waved to the little girls and their mother, who was out front watching them play. She then saw that the house across the street was for sale and simply said, "buy that house!"

I said, "Don't you think we should look at it first? Besides, sweetheart, it's their five-bedroom model. We don't need a five-bedroom house again."

She said, "I don't care, let us get back to the sales office and buy that house before someone else does. This is the neighborhood that I was looking for."

As ordered, I turned the car around, drove back to the sales office, and negotiated a deal to buy that house. While they did the paperwork, we got the keys to the home so we could at least walk through it before we signed all the papers. Mary Ann's instincts were correct again. The family living across the street with the three girls was the Reidy family. Mike, Kathie, and their daughters, Erin, Mary Frances, and Meagan, became lifelong friends. Over the fifteen years we owned that house, we shared many holidays and family events. Kristie and Meagan, who were the same age, went all the way through high school together. Both families remain close even today.

Mary Ann was anxious to get moved into our new home. We were fortunate enough that the house had been finished for a few months. To make it move-in ready, the builder agreed to do some painting for us and install all the window coverings as part of the deal. That was good because the house was way at the top of our affordability index, so we had little money to complete all this work on our own. Part of the deal included front yard landscaping as well, but we had to handle the backyard. All that work would have to come another day, but it would have to be done soon with two small girls. There was no way Mary Ann would let her kids play out in the front yard with all the construction traffic. New homes were being built all down the street as Kile was finishing out his Country Fair development. We also knew we had to get the backyard landscaping done before the winter rains came.

We settled into the house within a month, and Mary Ann could not have been happier. She said, "Stephen, this all feels so right for us. I think we have found our home."

Soon the interest rates started to fall back to more reasonable levels, and County Fair began filling up. Kids and stay-at-home mothers were everywhere. The couple that moved in next door, Dennis, and Kathy Praske, had two children as well, Karen and Steve, and Karen was also Kristie's age. Mary Ann also joined the Pleasanton Newcomers Club. The club planned events throughout the year, including dinner parties every month, much like in Pittsburgh. Mary Ann was on the Board of the Newcomers Club and eventually took on President's role for a couple of years. She knew how consequential these types of organizations were for new families in the community, and she wanted to do her part to support it. We met many new friends through this organization, many with kids the same age as ours. Playdates for our kids would no longer be a problem in our new community of Pleasanton. We were quickly settling into Pleasanton, and most importantly, Mary Ann was happy again.

Kristie and Karie were growing up fast. At first, there were not that many little girls Karie's age in our new neighborhood, which frustrated Mary Ann. Every time she saw a moving van pull into the community, she would pray for a little girl Karie's age. Kristie would sometimes include Karie when she, Karen, and Meagan would play together, but not always. It did not make Mary Ann happy, so when the girls played at our house, the rule was Karie must be included in all games. The neighborhood families quickly learned that no one messes with Mary Ann's children. To ensure that most playtimes be done at our house, Mary Ann always made sure we had the best treats in the neighborhood. Mary Ann also had a full VCR library of children's movies and cartoons. Mary Ann was *a loving mother,* and everybody in the community knew it.

She still lined the kids up when she heard the garage door open as I returned from work every day. Those drives home always ended with hugs and kisses from the kids and a hug from my lovely bride. We had to get used to later dinners because of my commute, but there was still time for me to play with the kids before dinner. After dinner, when I would give them their baths, Mary Ann would always lay out their pajamas, so once I had them shiny clean, I would get them in their pajamas, and we would take them to bed. We would each take a book and one of the girls and read them a story before putting them to bed, a routine we enjoyed! Once the kids were in bed, it was Mary Ann and Steve's time. One night I remember well, we sat down to relax after the girls were in bed. I sat on the couch with Mary Ann, hugged her, and said, "Mary Ann, I can't believe how good a mother you have become. You have everything so well organized. The girls are so happy, and I see it in them every time I come home from work. You are everything I ever hoped you would be in a wife and a *loving mother of my children.*"

She snuggled close to me and gave me a kiss on my cheek. She said, "Stephen, this journey has not been easy, but I think we are where we need to be as a family. Trust me, and I was apprehensive about where this all was headed last year in Southern California. I knew that life was not what we wanted. I know all families go through that at times, but we are where we need to be now. I love you, and I know that our family is always at the top of your mind. We are doing this together; I couldn't be happier with our life and our family right now. Please don't do something crazy and make us move again. It's not too late to try and get you that boy I know you want, and I want to!"

I held her tight and quietly thanked God for allowing me even to meet this special young lady, let alone marry her. Life always throws you many curveballs, but I got this one right down the middle and hit it out of the park!

Thank God the minivan was invented. With two little ones and the hope of additional children on the way, Mary Ann needed a new car. The 'Green Pea' was well past its "use-by" date, and it was time to go car shopping. Mary Ann had always done all the research on minivans and had decided on the model that she wanted. She had some colors in mind, and I asked that she stay away from the color green this time—to no avail, since green was her favorite color. As we got to the dealer, the salesman spent all his time selling to Mary Ann. I am sure they were told, "Always sell the minivan to the mother." Once we decided on the model and color we wanted, I told Mary Ann, "Please go into the waiting room." I wanted to take Mary Ann out of the negotiations. She was thrilled with the thought of having a minivan for the girls. Price for her was no longer going to matter, and the salesperson knew that. I reminded Mary Ann that I use to sell cars and sometimes negotiations aren't that easy to watch. I am not sure she was happy with that response, but I gathered the girls and went into the waiting room. I told the salesperson that my wife's favorite color was green and that we would like to buy a green minivan - not a dark green one, but something in a lighter green. He said, "sir, we don't offer that color in this model year. Are you sure she will only buy a green one?"

I said, "wow, that is a problem; she really likes green. But she is ready to buy." With that, he went to see his manager. The manager quickly came out to see how he could help solve this issue. He told me, "Sir, we don't even have a green minivan on the lot. There is a nice light blue one here and has all the upgrades on it. It's only $3,000 more than the standard unit."

I answered, "while personally, I hate the color green, I just can't get my wife past that color. It's the color car her dad first bought her. If you can sell me that blue one at the same price as the standard model, I will try my best to convince her that this is her only option today. Mind you, and this will not be easy."

Luckily, it worked, and we soon drove off with Mary Ann's new blue minivan, the girls safely belted into their baby seats. Minivans back then were the best things for anybody with a family. We owned five over the early life of our family; the blue one was the first.

When we first moved to Pleasanton, we were told that there were plans for a Catholic School system from first grade through junior high, though likely not a high school. Mary Ann and I both went through high school in the Catholic School system and were very much looking forward to our kids doing the same thing. As the girls started school, we were disappointed to find out that the Diocese of Oakland scrapped their plans for a Catholic School system in town. They had owned all the land needed for this but decided to sell it all off to developers. The public school system in Pleasanton was highly ranked. While disappointed that there would not be a Catholic school system, we were okay with the situation. The kids' grade school would be remarkably close to our house - Not walking distance, but indeed a comfortable bike ride. When Kristie entered first grade, Mary Ann signed up as a part-time classroom volunteer, as she did with all our children. That helped her get to know who the better teachers were, and she always made sure our children got the best teachers available for their grade level. We also signed the kids up for every sport we could: soccer, swim team, tennis, softball/baseball, and gymnastics. We thought that the kids who play sports would be a better group for ours to hang out with. As it turned out, many were from the neighborhood as well, so carpooling to and from games would make things easier, especially when you had kids playing games at the same time at different locations in town.

Having Our Third Child

My job at Memorex was going well. Part of my responsibilities was to look for a startup or small private companies developing technologies that might be complementary to Memorex's products. If they had some promising technology, we would consider investing in them. Silicon Valley was flush with new startup companies pursuing developing technologies. Even back then, everybody knew someone who hit it big with a startup, either by getting acquired by a larger company or going public, a neighbor, relative, classmate, or friend of a friend. That had quite a few good scientists, engineers, marketing, and salespeople, leaving more established companies to join a startup. Silicon Valley was full of venture capitalists with plenty of money to invest in high-tech startup phenomena. Their investment model was to invest in the ten most promising startups, knowing that only three would likely make it to a liquidity event, either as an IPO or bought by a larger company. The valuation model, which still works today, assumes that out of ten investments, three successes would pay for the five that failed and the other two that only grew to cash break-even. The high returns on the three paid for everything else and offered the venture capital fund a very substantial return. No one ever talked about the seven that did not go public, only the three that did.

All companies in Silicon Valley were losing good people to these startups, and Memorex was not excluded from this brain drain. To protect our market position, we decided that we would invest in some of these startups - certainly not the ones that were hiring our key engineers, just the ones that were developing complementary technologies to ours, not copying ours. Typically, we would take a 10% to 20% position in that company and get at least one seat on the board. The Memorex executive that sponsored the investment would usually become our board member. It was a complicated process, so we decided to limit this to no more than ten companies. This initiative was well thought out and developed by Clancy Spangle. My staff had to vet all these investments. That meant proving the strategic connection and affirming the technology connected to our strategic/product plan, and then doing the investments' financial due diligence. To help with all of this, I was able to bring in another former auditor and good friend from my Rockwell years, John Pelka. John wanted to get to the West Coast and was interested in what Mike Haltom and I were doing. Like Mary Ann and I, he and his wife Chris moved from Chicago to Pittsburgh with Rockwell. They were great friends, and John was a great resource at Rockwell. When I knew I needed to expand my staff at Memorex, he was one of the first people I called.

One of the business groups that I became close to at Memorex was their Communications Group. That group developed communication devices for the IBM enterprise computing environment, essentially printers, controllers and terminals that communicated with the IBM mainframe. It was a large and growing market at the time, but we only had a small market share in it. I felt that we were missing an opportunity in this market. I thought that a better focus on the product might lead to a significant increase in sales. Our European sales team had achieved far higher sales in this product area and came to me with an idea. They had identified a small private company in the UK that had developed some exciting terminal products for the non-IBM enterprise market. They felt that if we worked with that team, we could use some of our technology to launch comparable products into the IBM enterprise market. Our terminal products at the time were dated and costly, well behind some new products recently introduced by IBM and one other competitor.

This idea fits our investment model, so I agreed to fly over to the UK and meet with that company, Future Computers Ltd. The company was venture capital-funded in the UK and located in East Croydon, about ten miles south of the London center. The founder was a gentleman by the name of Brian. Brian was a sound engineer, but his greatest strength was identifying, recruiting, and managing strong engineering talent. I respected Brian, and we later would become close friends and business associates. I spent the better part of the week with the Future Computers team and was immediately impressed by how strong the engineering team was. They had a great can-do attitude. They had already been briefed by my European colleagues and showed me a mockup of a unit that could work for this project. The unit had a very futuristic design and was less than half the price of our current product. It also offered a color screen version, which our team had been working on for over a year and a half. Satisfied that they had something that would work for us, I flew back home and suggested to Clancy that we move forward with Future Computers. I also suggested that we make an equity investment in the company and put someone on their Board.

Clancy loved the UK. He had spent several years living in London while he was running Honeywell Information Systems European business. He said, "I am planning to be in Europe next month, get more details around this project, and then you and I can go meet the team while I am over there next month. You have the most passion for this project, so I want you to lead on this. Go ahead and start your due diligence process on the investment. If all looks good and we make the investment, I want you to take the Board seat."

Board meetings were every six weeks, so I knew that it would mean frequent trips to the UK. I also knew I had better get this information in front of Mary Ann to make sure she would be OK with it. I decided to wait until the weekend before telling Mary Ann about the potential for me to make frequent visits to the UK. While I had to do some limited travel in my new role, it would be a short one- or two-day trips domestically and just once a quarter to Europe or Asia for regional business reviews.

That weekend was quiet. We had recently joined the Castlewood Country Club, and we were enjoying some family time around the pool there. Kristie was already a good swimmer, and Karie, who loved the water, could float around the pool on her baby inner tube. There was also a large baby pool that they both loved to play in. The Reidy's were also members, and Meagan joined us there as well. We were well into our second year at our new home in Pleasanton, and Mary Ann could not have been happier. We were well settled in, with plenty of kids and mothers to befriend in the neighborhood. She had also met many new friends through her work with the Newcomers Club.

As we lay in the shade by the pool, I decided to tell Mary Ann about my discussions with Clancy and our planned next visit to London. Mary Ann never liked it when I traveled but was reasonably comfortable if I was only out for a few days. After I told her about the plan and the possibility that I might join the Future Board, she was not happy. She said, "Stephen, don't ever think that we are moving this family out of the United States, for one. Secondly, why do they have board meetings every six weeks? Aren't board meetings usually once a quarter?"

I told her that in most cases, that is true. "I think the investors are trying to keep a closer eye on the team. It's a young company, and I think the investors aren't yet sure if the management team is fully capable of managing the company's growth. Also, investors in the UK are very conservative people by their very nature. I have not met any of the investors, so I can only speculate. And oh, by the way, we are not leaving California, let alone the United States. It is only a board seat; I will still have my day job back here."

She responded, "OK, Mr. Manning, but no weekend travel, and please don't take the whole week to have a one-day board meeting in London. No reason you can't leave on a Monday and be back home by Thursday."

I told her, "That should be doable; the board schedule will be set far in advance, so you will always know my travel schedule on this. Maybe at some point, you can join me on some of these trips. Our time together in London is still one of my fondest memories."

She said, "We will see about that, but you know I don't like being away from my girls."

Mary Ann was so in love with being a mother. Everything she did was always around being the *best mother* possible to our children. Mary Ann arranged playdates for them and made sure they had enough friends to play with, and took them to every child event she could find. She put many miles on her minivans over the years, driving the kids to where they had to be.

I flew over to London that next month with Clancy. On the way over, he asked me, "Steve, how many of these new terminals do you think we can sell? I want to get a better feel for how big of a deal you think this is for us."

I answered, "Clancy, all the financial assumptions suggest we can sell up to 30 thousand of these over the next three years. It's a big market, but we only have a small share of it."

He said, "OK, I am going to hold you accountable to that number. Anything less than that will not be acceptable."

We did the deal and started to develop the product along with the Future team. Once we had completed testing, we were comfortable with the product performing up to our customers' expectations. We launched it in North America, Europe, and Japan. Before we shipped our first units, we had a backlog of 70 thousand units. It was an enormous success, and we gained market share in all our key markets. Six months later, we released our color screen version of the unit. It was even more successful. With that success, Clancy appointed me President of the Memorex Communications group. At age thirty-three, it made me the youngest Group President in Memorex's history or their parent, Burroughs. What was also remarkable was that Mike Haltom had been promoted to the President of the Storage and Tape Group of Memorex, the largest group at Memorex. He and I managed over 70% of the company now, although I will admit that his job was much more difficult. His products were far more complex than the technology my group was dealing with, both from a development and manufacturing point of view.

When I got home to tell Mary Ann about my promotion, I couldn't wait to hold her. I told her about my new position and said, "Sweetheart, you helped make this happen. You were with me every step of the way and made many sacrifices along the way. I want to make this a celebration for both of us. With all my trips to London, I have a ton of mileage credits. Let's take a ski trip to Switzerland to celebrate this. Our relationship started with a ski trip. Let's celebrate that. I will get my parents to come out to watch the kids for two weeks." Mary Ann and the kids loved my parents, and they were still living in the snows of Nebraska, so a trip to California would be great for them. She finally agreed to a vacation away from the girls.

We made plans to fly to Switzerland, ski the Swiss Alps, and enjoy our time together. No bus this time. We booked first-class air tickets to Zurich, Switzerland, and a train to Davos. We had planned a couple of days in Zurich to recover from our jet lag. Mary Ann thoroughly deserved this vacation. Once she got over the fact that she would be away from her girls for two weeks, she got overly excited about it. Back then, international first-class across the Atlantic was to die for. Excellent seating, fine wines, appetizers, and outstanding dinners. The wine and dinners would feature destination-famous selections, and all were unbelievably delicious.

Back then, there were no direct flights to Zurich, so we had to stop and change planes in New York's JFK airport. It's not one of my favorite airports, but it was necessary to connect to Zurich. San Francisco's flight to New York was extremely comfortable and was Mary Ann's first experience flying first class. It was a domestic first class, so I knew she would be in for even more of a treat when we took our next leg across the Atlantic. As we taxied to take off from JFK to Zurich, I looked over to Mary Ann. I smiled and thought how appropriate this was for her to be treated like the princess she was. She had put up with so much from me. Now it looked like we were getting to a place where we could be happy and raise that family we always wanted. We were so lucky to achieve what we always wanted. I turned to her and said, "I wouldn't mind having that same hug you gave me on the Inland Steel ski trip right now."

With that beautiful smile, she grabbed me and said, "Mr. Manning, you are sometimes a pain in the ass, but I love you. I know you are always trying to do the right thing for our family. Sometimes it is simply hard to keep up with you. This will be our time together, and I am so looking forward to it. By the way, when we land, we need to call home and see how the girls are doing." Classic Mary Ann, the *Loving Mother* who I was fortunate enough to have married.

We flew Swiss Air to Zurich, and the food and service could not have been better. Upon arrival, we checked into the Hilton Hotel in central Zurich. It was late in the evening when we got settled, so we decided to take a short walk around the city. We already had a nice dinner on the flight over, so we were pretty much ready for bed after our walk. Mary Ann was not used to dealing with jet lag, and I wanted to make sure she had a good night's sleep on our first night in Switzerland. Zurich is a beautiful city with many sightseeing opportunities. We spent the next day visiting some of them and enjoyed a special dinner that night. Mary Ann loved fondue, so I asked the concierge to arrange a 6:30 p.m. reservation for us at one of the city's better fondue restaurants. It was within walking distance of the hotel. I wasn't a big fondue fan, but I was a huge fan of keeping my sweetheart happy. As we walked to dinner that night, Mary Ann said, "Stephen, I am so excited about our ski trip. I have such fond memories of our first ski trip together. Let's take the time to make this one special. I just hope I get over this jet lag before we hit the slopes."

A 6:30 dinner reservation by European standards is considered early. I knew the restaurant would be mostly empty that early in the evening. However, I wanted to make sure Mary Ann enjoyed the evening and dinner before her jet lag began settling in. Fondue is a delicious meal if you wish to take your time, have plenty of conversation, and enjoy the dipping, which is what we did. About mid-way through the dinner, Mary Ann looked at me and said, "Steve, I think it's time for us to try for that boy I know you want. The girls are growing up, and they are both out of diapers and much easier to manage now. Our life has settled down for the most part, and we are both delighted with our life in Pleasanton. Let's try and fill one of those empty bedrooms we have open upstairs. Kristie will soon be at the age where she can be my little helper with our next baby."

I said, "Sweetheart, you are such a *loving mother* to the girls. I know it's not effortless, but you are so organized with them you make it look so easy. I would love to see our family grow as we had always dreamed. Another little one in the family sounds great."

I reached across the table, took her hand, and said, "Let's take the next step with that plan. Who knows how long it might take this time?" We finished the fondue, and I looked at her and asked, "Any room for a nice Swiss chocolate dessert?"

She smiled and said, "Is the Pope Catholic? Of course, I saved room for that!" My little bride loved her chocolates. The evening was cold but beautiful. After dessert, we walked back to the hotel, holding each other tight all the way back to the room.

The next day was going to be short for us. We had to repack our bags and prepare for our train ride up the Swiss Alps to Davos. We would stay that week in Davos, ski there, and the area in and around St. Moritz. Both were lovely alpine cities and world-famous for their skiing and hospitality. After lunch, we made our way to the train station. It's about a two-and-a-half-hour train ride from Zurich to Davos. We planned to get there in time to check into the hotel, check out the city and find a wonderful place for our dinner that night. We got to the train station in plenty of time and checked out the train bound for Davos. I saw that the first-class cabins had large windows, which I thought would give us breathtaking views of the Swiss Alps along our journey. The trains themselves were classic. They reminded both Mary Ann and me of something you would have seen in the "Sound of Music," one of her favorite movies. We couldn't wait to board the train and start our journey. We bought tickets in the first-class cabin, checked in our luggage, and made our way to our seats.

The skies were clear blue that day, so we knew we would have some great sightseeing along our journey. A large group of vacationers near us on the train were from New York, not surprisingly, loud and boisterous. We could not help but overhear them talking about the forecast ski conditions at Davos and St. Moritz's. I interrupted one of them and asked, "What have you heard about the ski conditions for this week?"

He turned to me and said, "Haven't you heard? Switzerland is having a drought, and this year they have had the worst ski conditions in the last twenty-five years. Not much snow, and the slopes are icy. They don't normally need, or have, the snow-making capability we have in the States, so it's going to be dicey this year. We all come over here every year about this same time. We love skiing here and the nightlife, but this year will be pretty much a bust for us. Is this your first time over?"

I responded, "Yes, it is; we never thought we would have to worry about having snow in the Swiss Alps, didn't even bother to check it out. I am not sure if we would have changed our plans or anything like that. It's just unfortunate."

Mary Ann and I just looked at each other with some disappointment, but still happy that we would have this time together. We knew we would find a way to make the best of the snow and certainly enjoy seeing the Swiss Alps for the first time together.

As the train made its way up and through the Swiss Alps, the scenery was amazing. We could tell that there was not that much snow on the ground, especially at the lower elevations. But the little villages and chalets we saw along the way were fantastic. Mary Ann looked out the window and started humming the "Sound of Music." I could tell my little princess was in an incredibly happy place.

We arrived at our ski lodge midafternoon. The lodge was quaint and very well appointed. It was owned and managed by a Swiss couple that told us it had been in the family for three generations. They were too excited to hear we had come all the way over from California and quickly apologized for the ski conditions. If we checked with them every morning, they would help point us in the right direction for better snow conditions. The Davos ski area was massive, so we had plenty of ski runs to choose from. The couple could not have been more helpful. They told us our package included ski tickets and family-style servings at breakfast and lunch. At dinner, we could order off the menu. The dining room was a decent size, with long tables that you would share with other guests. There was also a spa on the property with a sauna, steam room, and a dipping pool. I wasn't sure what a dipping pool was, but I was a huge fan of saunas and steam baths, especially after skiing. Mary Ann, however, was not, and I was sure I would not be able to get her to join me there. The porter had taken our luggage to the room, so we went up to unpack. Afterward, we walked into town and rented our ski equipment for the week. We had chosen not to haul all our ski gear across the Atlantic and instead just rent the equipment there.

When we got back to the hotel, we stopped by the restaurant to see what they had on the menu for dinner. Our original plan was to dine out somewhere in town, but the menu looked appetizing, so we decided to dine in that night. Mary Ann wasn't too excited about sharing the dinner table with strangers and worried we would be seated with guests who did not speak English. Notwithstanding those fears, we decided we would give it a try the first night. After she freshened up, we made our way down for dinner. As we entered the dining room, you could see that many of the guests had already grouped up with others at their tables. One couple was a little older than us, sitting by themselves at one of the tables. You could tell that they were European, and I hope they could speak and understand English. The dinner hostess escorted us to that open table where that couple was seated. Hoping for an English response, I introduced Mary Ann and myself to them. Thankfully, with a German accent but in English, they introduced themselves. The couple was about eight to ten years older than us, from Frankfurt, Germany, and seemed genuinely friendly. Even though Mary Ann could be a bit shy, she was always very curious and enjoyed meeting new people. Mary Ann immediately turned to the wife and asked her where they were from and if they had any children. It turned out they had three, two girls and a boy ranging from eight to sixteen years old, with the boy being their youngest. From there, the ice was broken, and the ladies began a long chat about kids.

The husband finally turned to me and said, "Steve, what business are you in, and what brings you all the way over from California?" I told him about my role at Memorex and then told them how Mary Ann and I had met on a ski trip, now almost ten years ago. They both got a kick out of the story, and both knew how special this trip was going to be for us. He was in the chemical business in Germany. He had worked out of the company's New York office for a few years, where they had perfected their English. It was their third trip to Davos and, of course, all their previous trips had better skiing conditions. We would become good friends with this couple and shared most meals with them that week. Mary Ann exchanged Christmas cards with them for many years to follow.

After dinner, I tried to get Mary Ann to join me at the spa but to no avail. I was anxious to try it out and find out what a dipping pool was. I got into my bathing suit and robe and went down to the spa. The steam room was a decent size and had four seating levels to it. You could either sit or lay on one level, and there might be someone else above you. The room was not well lit, and there was plenty of steam in the air. So even if someone was close to you, you couldn't see them that well. When I arrived at the steam room, it was empty and turned down. I increased the temperature and laid down on the first level. As it heated up, I would go in and out of the room and take a cold shower to cool down between sessions. On my second session, I heard a couple enter, and they took their positions a level above me. Then another couple entered. The second couple was on the same level as I was. As I got up to take another cold shower, I noticed that no one was wearing any clothes: no towel, no bathing suit, nothing.

When I came back in, the first couple got up and went through a door in the back of the room. Then I heard some splashing and laughter before both reappeared. Next, the second couple got up and did the same thing. I was inquisitive. After both had left, I got up and went to the back door and opened it. What I saw was a reasonably deep pool - Not a big pool, but deep with icy water running into it. I decided that I needed to try it. I jumped into the pool, and as I got deeper into the pool, the water became almost frigid; I felt my feet going numb. It was a shock to the body, but I felt incredibly refreshed after I got out of the pool. I now knew what a dipping pool was, and it was delightful. I visited it every night after that.

When I got back to the room, I had to let Mary Ann know about the steam room, the dipping pool, and the fact that nobody had any towels or suits. All she could say was, "You are not getting me to go there; that's just disgusting. Are you telling me everyone was naked?" I had to tell her the story because I knew that she would never have gone for that.

With the help of the ski lodge owners, we were able to find some decent ski areas that week. Every morning they would check with the ski patrol and point us to the right location. There were many choices once you got to the top of the mountain, and they gave us a map to help guide us. One route they sent us on took us to the backside of the mountain. By the time we got through skiing for the day, we had to take a train back to Davos. Some of the ski areas were icy, but we found some decent snow-packed slopes - No fresh powder, but outstanding views and friendly people to enjoy along the way.

We spent the last two days in St. Moritz, one day to sightsee and another to do some skiing. After a beautiful week in Davos and St. Moritz, we took the train to Geneva. Our flight back to San Francisco would depart from Geneva and connect through New York's JFK airport. We looked forward to spending a few days in Geneva, another beautiful city in Switzerland. We planned to do some touring in and around the Geneva area.

The train ride to Geneva was as breathtaking as Zurich's one to Davos, but about twice as long. That would get us into the hotel before dinner with some time to freshen up. I always liked riding the train, mostly when the views were so fantastic. Mary Ann was a real bookworm, and this gave her some time to relax and enjoy one of the many books she had brought on our trip. She wanted to call home and see how the girls were getting along with Grandma and Grandpa. A cell phone would have been nice to have, but this was still a world without cell phones. We would be able to call home when we got to the hotel in Geneva. International long distance was not cheap back then, but we both knew it would be money well spent.

As soon as we got to the hotel, Mary Ann was on the phone seeing how everything was going. My mom and dad were having a ball with the girls, but I am sure they were ready for our return home. We had planned to spend three full days in Geneva. After talking to my parents and the girls' Mary Ann turned to me and said, "Stephen, this has been a great vacation for both of us, and I have loved our trip together, but I can't wait to get back to our girls. Is there any way we can catch an earlier flight home"?

I told her that I would contact the airlines to see if we could move our flight up. Since we were flying two different airlines home, Swiss Air to New York's JFK and TWA home, it might be difficult, but I would try. Both airlines had ticket offices in Geneva, so I went to see them the next day and was able to pull our flight home in by one day. We still had time to see the essential parts of Geneva and enjoy the last couple of days of our ski date alone and together. Mary Ann also wanted to have one final fondue dinner before we headed home. Wanting to make this last dinner special for Mary Ann, I asked the front desk to recommend the best fondue restaurant in Geneva and to make reservations for us that night for dinner. It was too far away from the hotel to walk, so we took a taxi.

The restaurant was in a beautiful part of the city in an older but well-maintained building. The restaurant had two levels to it, the main floor and a basement seating area. We were seated on the main level, which was very crowded. Later, we found out that the lower level was closed off for a large senior-level U.S. delegation having a formal dinner. They had all been in Geneva preparing for an important meeting between President Reagan and President Gorbachev of Russia. The meeting happened later that year and was called the 'Geneva Summit.' It would prove to be a hugely historic meeting. It was the first of three significant meetings that Reagan and Gorbachev would have to try to end the Cold War and the arms race.

When we got to the restaurant, we noticed quite a bit of security outside the restaurant but did not think much about it. As the group from downstairs started to leave the restaurant, even more security appeared; we knew something was up. After the group filed out of the restaurant, I asked our waiter who all those people were, and he told us they were people from the US government, and the group included three or four U.S. Senators. He said we were lucky to get a table tonight; they were full all night.

Mary Ann was impressed. She knew the restaurant was unique, and our dinner was excellent, but later we would find out we saw some real history. The next day we packed with anticipation of seeing our girls and made our way home.

The flight home was long, partially because we had to stop in New York to change planes. JFK is always busy, and flights often delayed, which was the case for us. On the way home, Mary Ann could hardly hide her excitement about seeing the girls, and unfortunately, she slept poorly. We finally pulled into the driveway around 6 p.m. My mom and dad did an excellent job watching the kids, but I am sure they were happy to see our faces as we entered the house. The girls were always well-behaved, but my parents were older, and two little ones are a lot to handle, especially for two weeks. They had already given the girls their baths, and they were in their jammies when they saw us, Mary Ann, and the girls' faces lit up like a Christmas tree. Many hugs and kisses were to follow for the whole family.

I took all the bags upstairs while Mary Ann was briefed about the girls and my parents together. I knew it would be a long time before I would get Mary Ann to go on a vacation again without the kids. My parents stayed for a couple of more days before flying back to Lincoln, Nebraska. That was helpful and gave Mary Ann a chance to get over her jet lag from the trip. Fortunately, we returned on a Friday, so I had a chance before going back to work on Monday. Things were getting back to normal at home, and the girls were back into their routine with Mary Ann. Dinners were always a little crazy, as the girls were becoming fussy eaters, and they took way too long to finish their supper.

One night, about a month after we had gotten back from Switzerland, I could tell Mary Ann was anxious to get the girls through dinner and their baths. She always laid the jammies out in the downstairs bath, and after dinner, I gave the girls their bath. They were both chatty that night, so the bath was taking longer than usual. With that, I heard Mary Ann yell from the kitchen, "Stephen, please hurry up with the girls' baths, it's getting late, and I want to get them into bed." I got them out of the bath and into their jammies and told them to "go kiss your mommy good night." We then both took them upstairs to bed and tucked them in.

As we got back downstairs to relax for the evening on the couch, Mary Ann said, "Stephen, I am sorry I rushed us all through dinner and the girls' baths so quickly, but I have some news for you. It looks like you are going to be a father again. Our next child is due some time in December."

I said, "My God, that happened fast. We just talked about that while we were in Switzerland. Sweetheart, don't get me wrong; I am happy about this. I always think about how we were so worried about having kids, I thought it would take much longer. How are you feeling?"

She said, "Actually, I am feeling better now, but after we got back from Switzerland, I just thought I had extended jet lag. It turns out I was having morning sickness!"

I quickly took her into my arms and gave her a big hug. Both of us could not have been happier with the news. This time I wished for a boy, indeed above all a healthy baby, but a boy, nonetheless. Mary Ann was of the same mindset, but we would do nothing more than hope for those results and wait for the birth to find out the sex of the baby. That's the way our parents and their parents before them did it, and we were both happy with that process. Mary Ann found a baby doctor who she loved and trusted in Pleasanton. We knew that our time for natural childbirth had passed. She let her doctor know about her delivery issues with Karie, so he was very prepared.

Our life was about to get remarkably interesting again with the upcoming birth of our third child. The girls were getting old enough that Mary Ann knew she could handle another child in diapers. Kristie was now six and a half, and Karie four and a half; so, they were aware of what was soon to come to our loving home in Pleasanton. I was busy at work but not traveling too much other than my London trips for the Future board meetings every six weeks. Business was good, and the Future-designed terminals were still a tremendous success for us at Memorex. With the growth of that business, our revenues had almost doubled. Our arrangement with Future was that we paid them a royalty for each unit shipped, generating a lot of cash for Future. The Future investors were happy with this arrangement but started to get concerned about how Future might invest these dollars in the business.

Brian had his engineering team working on a new product family, specifically a personal PC product line. After an earlier failed attempt to develop a stand-alone PC product, IBM had initially announced its first PC product in August 1981. Indeed, by today's standards, it was a very low-powered device, and at the time, few useful applications were available to run on it. That changed as the product became more popular. Brian's team had targeted that product and were working on a plug-compatible version of the IBM PC. As I mentioned earlier, Brian was an excellent technical manager. He knew how to hire and motivate high-energy engineers, both software and hardware. He assembled two small teams, one software, and one hardware-focused. The design they were working on looked very promising, but Future itself was too small to take that product to market independently. Brian's plan was to private label the product to larger companies, like Memorex and others, to rebrand the product under their own branding. They would then use their distribution channels to take that product to market.

At the March 1985 board meeting, Brian presented that plan to the Board, which included five different venture capital firms. The Board was uneasy about the project. They felt that it was putting a significant amount of the cash at risk that the company had collected through the Memorex deal. After the board meeting, the investors asked me to stay behind for a private session with them. They again expressed their concerns about the plan and wanted to know if I had seen it before the meeting. I told them that I had not seen the project itself but had been following the product's development through various meetings with Brian and his team. They then said that they were uncomfortable with where the company was going and wanted to make some leadership changes. Then asked if I would be willing to take over the CEO role at Future and recruit a new Chairman for the company. This discussion caught me off guard, and I told them that I was not ready to leave Memorex while I was incredibly supportive of the company and its success. I told them that my future there was bright, in part because of the remarkable success of the products Brian and his team had developed for us. They asked me not to dismiss the offer out of hand. They wanted to put together something formal for me, including an equity position in the company. They also asked me to put together a potential list of candidates who I would recommend for the Chairmanship role at Future.

After the meeting ended, I headed back to the hotel and prepared for my trip back to San Francisco the next day. I had a lot to think about on the flight home. I was not sure what the offer was going to be from the Board. It was a large Board and for what was still a small company. I liked the development team and Brian's leadership. They did not have all the technical capability for the full product line I was managing at Memorex, but what they did do for us was significant and delivered the products for us on-time, every time. The PC product that Brian was developing was not squarely in our product roadmap at the time. However, it did have some interest to me long term as more business applications were becoming available.

When I got home that Thursday, I pondered whether to tell Mary Ann about the opportunity the Board had presented to me. Not knowing its details, I thought it best not to worry Mary Ann about a job change.

We shared everything necessary in our family life, but unless the offer was substantial, I was likely going to turn it down anyway. As I waited for the offer, I started to compile the list of names that I would recommend to the Board of potential Chairman candidates. One name that quickly went to the top of my list was Clancy Spangle. Clancy was getting ready to retire from Memorex, and I thought he would be interested in this position. It would be a non-Executive Chairman's role so would not have to devote full time to this position. I knew his leadership on the Board would make a significant difference for the company and that he would have the investors' full support.

I reached out to Clancy to see if he was interested in that role at Future. We decided to get together for a golf game at one of the clubs Clancy belonged to that weekend to discuss the matter. Clancy belonged to several excellent golf clubs. San Francisco Golf Club, Menlo Park Country Club, Monterey Bay (Carmel Valley Ranch), in California, John's Island in Florida, Pine Valley in Pennsylvania, and Sunningdale outside of London. I would often tease Clancy about being a member of so many golf clubs. I reminded him that there was a USGA fourteen-club limit in golf. During that round of golf and at lunch afterward, we discussed the Future opportunity for us both. He wasn't keen on seeing me leave Memorex, but he knew that my group would eventually be sold off as Burroughs restructured itself. That happened the following year. Clancy finally said, "Steve, if you are going to take the CEO role at Future, then I would be more than happy to join the Board. If not, I would have no interest in that role."

I thanked him for his support and told him I would let him know my decision as soon as I saw the board's offer. After golf and lunch with Clancy, I headed home, knowing I had to let Mary Ann know what was going on.

Mary Ann's pregnancy was going well, and the girls were getting excited about having a new baby in the house. Mary Ann had bought them both new dolls, and they pretended their new dolls were our new child. It was cute to see them carrying the dolls around the house and talking to the dolls all the time. They were getting into being big sisters to our new little treasure that was to arrive in about five months. Mary Ann was also getting the room upstairs ready. The two girls had rooms upstairs toward the front of the house. Our new arrival was going to be in the room next to us in the back of the house. Mary Ann had all the walls in the house painted to neutral colors so that, depending on whether we had a boy or girl, we could paint the room in appropriate colors with bedspreads and pictures on the wall. As always, she was planning ahead, and we would be ready when the time came to bring our new treasure home.

As we talked about her due date, I told her I had some things I wanted to speak to her. I suggested that we get a baby-sitter that weekend and enjoy a nice dinner at the club on Saturday. Castlewood had a lovely dining area with views over the golf course and the pool, and massive old oak trees that lined the fairways. It was spring, so the hills were still green from the winter rains and the setting was beautiful.

We enjoyed our dinners there, with good service and great food at very reasonable prices. We didn't go out that often; Mary Ann loved getting dressed up for our little dinner dates. She would always do a fantastic job of getting the kids all ready for the babysitter. She would have their meals all ready and still appear fully decked out in a lovely outfit, hair, and makeup perfect. This night was no exception. She wore a very spring-like flowered dress and her precious smile, all of which lit up the room when she came downstairs. Once again, she reaffirmed how lucky I was! The girls weren't typically crazy about us going out, but they did enjoy the babysitter. When the babysitter appeared, we kissed the girls, said our goodnights headed for the club for our dinner date.

It was a beautiful evening, and we decided to take a seat in the lounge to have a drink before dinner and enjoy the views and the setting sun on the golf course and hillside. Mary Ann had her iced tea, and I had my usual. After the drinks were served, Mary Ann turned to me and asked, "What is the news this time, Mr. Manning? Is something up at work?" Jokingly, she added, "Do you still have a job?"

I laughed and said, "Everything is OK at work; it's just something that came up at the Future Board meeting. I wanted to discuss this with you. The Board has approached me with an offer to take on the CEO job at Future. They also want me to help them recruit a new Chairman. Nothing is official yet, and I haven't seen the offer. If I decide to do this, I will help them bring Clancy on as the non-executive Chairman." Mary Ann thought the world of Clancy, so I knew she would be OK with that part of the story. But she was taken back by all of this and said, "Stephen, you're doing so well at Memorex. You have only been there for three years, why would you want to leave, and don't you dare tell me we are moving to London!"

I said, "Don't worry, we are not moving to London, and I am not sure I want to do this anyway. If I did do this, I would set up an office here. The way they are headed technology-wise, Future needs a larger presence in Silicon Valley." As I had said before, Mary Ann did not like change, and I could see that she was uncomfortable with the discussion.

Since I did not yet have an offer, I thought it best to move on to other topics. To brighten her mood, I asked Mary Ann if she had signed the girls up for swim lessons yet. The club had a great pool with a big shallow area for the kids, and summer was fast approaching. Mary Ann liked the water, and she had been right about getting the girls into swim lessons from an incredibly early age. She said, "Actually, I was thinking about signing Kristie up this year for the swim team at the local neighborhood pool." Karie was still too young for the swim team, but Kristie's age group had a team. Both girls would eventually be on the same swim team, and both were extremely competitive swimmers. The only problem with the swim team was that the Saturday swim meets lasted the entire day. The kids might only be in two or three events for the day, but they would have to stand by after each event until they worked through all the age groups into the next event. The mornings were OK, maybe a little chilly, but the afternoon sun at pools without shade could be brutal. Mary Ann's rule was always if our kids were competing in any sporting event; our presence was mandatory, which I agreed. Changing the topic that night at dinner was a success, and we had a lovely dinner and a much better conversation.

On the way home, Mary Ann asked, "When do you think you are going to see this offer from the Board? Please don't do anything until we have a chance to talk again about this move."

I said, "Sweetheart, I would never make this kind of decision until we had a chance to talk about it. Let's see what comes about, and then we can talk about it together. It is a decision that will affect the entire family, and we always make those decisions together."

A few days after our dinner, the offer did come from the Board. It was a reasonable offer, including a stock grant of 10% of the company, full benefits, and a company car. Company cars were always a big deal with the Europeans, so I was not surprised that they included that in the offer. I thought they were a waste of money, but I guess when in Rome, do what the Romans do.

After getting the offer, I came home to discuss it with Mary Ann. I was still unsure if this was the right move for us, and I wanted to hear Mary Ann's thoughts. She always had a good perspective on any decision we were trying to make. As we sat down, one of Mary Ann's significant concerns was medical insurance. One, she wanted to make sure the offer included health insurance, and two, she wanted to make sure she would not have to change doctors when we changed medical plans. That was a crucial point that I had not thought of, so I was more than glad she had brought it up. Thankfully, I was able to get us on the same insurance plan with the same doctors. She was also concerned about my travel schedule and asked again why I wanted to leave Memorex. I told her I would plan to follow the same travel as I had done with the board meeting schedule, but I would likely return on Friday versus the Thursday return.

After a few days to think about the new position, Mary Ann said, "Stephen, if you want to do this, I will support your decision. Just please make sure you believe this is the right thing for you and the family."

I told her, "I am still a little bit on the fence about which way to go, but I appreciate your willingness to let me give it a try. If it weren't for the fact that my group was likely to get spun out of Burroughs, I would stay put." After a few more days of thought, I told Mary Ann that I decided to move on to Future and take the CEO role there. Luckily, Clancy agreed to join us as Chairman.

We were well into summer now, and the girls were enjoying their swimming, with Kristie on the swim team and Karie still enjoying the baby pool. I used to love taking them to the club to go swimming and seeing them dive off the diving board and into my arms. Karie was fearless and always smiling as she dived off the board and into my arms. She would then paddle back to the stairs with Kristie swimming behind her like a good big sister to safely make sure she got there. The family got into a routine that summer. I would get up early on Saturdays and head to the club around 6 a.m. There I would join other young fathers with kids to get in a quick early round of golf. I would then join the family at the pool around 11. We would hang out together at the pool, have lunch, swim, and relax until around 3 p.m. Mary Ann and I would play in the pool with the kids. Soon they would get bored with us and join their friends. Mary Ann and I would grab some shade with other couples that we had met at the club, and we would all watch our kids enjoy their summer together. Mary Ann always loved our time together as a family. Those Saturdays were stress-free, other than my early morning golf, and were the picture of family life we were both hoping to build.

One Saturday after we got back from the club, Mary Ann pulled me close to her, put her arms around my neck, and hugged me. She said, "Mr. Manning, don't screw this up with your new job. This is the family life you and I had always talked about. The girls are great, and they are happy. We have another child on the way. We need to keep making this work, and we are so lucky to be where we are as a family. I know you love your golf, and if you play early on the weekends, I am OK with that—Saturdays at the pool work for us. If you want to play on Sundays, it's OK, but you need to be home in time to take us to our usual 10:30 a.m. mass at St. Augustine's. I am OK getting the girls ready, and you don't need to be here to make us breakfast as long as we can stop for donuts on the way home."

That is when I learned Mary Ann's art of bribing! It is also where I realized that I was not always the best breakfast cook! Before that, I only played golf on Saturdays and was usually the breakfast cook on Sundays. I would get up early, read the Sunday papers, and get breakfast ready when I heard Mary Ann and the girls getting up. As the kids were getting older and staying up later on the weekends, they all tended to get up later. Mary Ann loved her sleep, so she was more than happy to let the girls sleep in on the weekends. Mary Ann needed time to get the girls all ready for mass on Sunday, so there was little time for a decent breakfast anyway. Karie loved her pancakes in the morning, but I think Mary Ann and Kristie loved their sleep more.

Like Mary Ann and Kristie, Karie also liked her donuts, and we had a great donut shop right by our house. The Sunday routine was that I would be home by 10 a.m., Mary Ann would have the girls all ready for church by that time, and we would head off to St. Augustine's. Mary Ann would dress the girls every Sunday. They were as beautiful as she was. Everything matched nice dress shoes and often with matching bows in their hair. I was so proud to walk into church with my lovely family. We were way past the cry room, where we had spent so many years as the girls grew up, and now able to hear the full sermon every Sunday. The girls would sit between us, Karie standing on the pew, and Kristie on the kneeler, so they could both see the altar. I would often look at them all and then up to the cross to thank the man hanging on that cross for his great kindness in letting me be part of this great family. The 10:30 mass was a long one, and the girls would often become restless as all kids do in church. After my lesson on bribing from Mary Ann, I decided to enforce a new rule. Any misbehaving in Church on Sunday would eliminate the trip to the donut shop on the way home. This rule was not well received by either the girls or Mary Ann. To bring peace to the family and make sure I was not evicted from the house, I delegated the donut/no donut and decision to Mary Ann. Amazingly enough, after that delegation, we never missed another donut stop after church. I must say the girls did perform better in church, knowing the threat was always out there. At least that's my story, and I am sticking to it. No matter how the kids behaved, I never ended a mass without thanking the Lord for the family he allowed us to have.

I started my new role in July. My arrangement with the Board was that I would open a U.S. office in the Pleasanton area. That office would be responsible for sales, marketing, program management, and production management. The offices outside of London would focus on engineering/development and product support. That is what the UK team did best, and I did not want to disrupt them in any way. Production was performed in Asia which could easily be managed from Northern California. It would be a while before we staffed the U.S. office, so I decided to work from home. The fifth bedroom was downstairs, so I made it into my office. I quickly learned that the Manning household was not conducive to a home office. Mary Ann did not like it when I shut the door and still wanted to keep the kid's toy box in the room. She wasn't happy that I could not babysit during the day when she had to run errands. Early morning calls to and from Europe were also not well received. I finally decided to pack up the office and get a serviced office near the Stoneridge Mall, an expense not budgeted for but worth keeping peace in the family for sure.

Mary Ann was now well into her pregnancy, and everything was going fine. The girls were getting excited about the new arrival. Kristie was getting ready for first grade and Karie for pre-kindergarten. I remember telling Mary Ann how I felt happy and sad about how fast the girls were growing up. Kristie was starting to ride a bike, and Karie was quickly behind her on her tricycle. The only problem with our lovely home in Pleasanton was that it was not on a cul-de-sac. While traffic was not heavy on the street in front of our house, there was enough traffic that we would always have to be out front when the girls were out riding. Mary Ann would still be sitting on the front porch with her glass of iced tea, keeping a close eye on our two loved ones. The ritual would follow over the years, to include roller skates, skateboards, and later roller blades.

It was time for Kristie's first day of school for the first grade. I remember it like it was yesterday. We all packed into Mary Ann's minivan and headed off to Walnut Grove, the grade school not too far from our house. Mary Ann had already signed up for various sessions as a teacher's aide. She would drop Karie off in the morning for pre-kindergarten, which was only a half-day. Then she would help in Kristie's class until she had to pick Karie up and drive her home. All our kids would go to Walnut Grove for their elementary grades, and we did the first day of class ritual with them all. It was a good school and close to our neighborhood. When I drive by there even today, I can picture each one of them on their first day of school. There would always be a tear in Mary Ann's eye that first day of school, knowing that her little ones were no longer babies. Mary Ann was still excellent at asking the children what they learned in school. She would then make sure they had their homework done before going outside to play. She never went to college, but she was going to make damn sure her children did. All the kids did well in school, and all graduated college on-time. I was always immensely proud of the way Mary Ann instilled the importance of education to our children. She still did the vital work of *a loving mother.*

The fall was upon us as we got ready for Thanksgiving. Mary Ann's parents were to join us that year, and my parents would follow with their visit at Christmas. Mary Ann was in full bloom with our third child. We were only a few weeks away from its birth. Still, Mary Ann ran around the house, putting out all the holiday decorations and preparing for the big meal on Thanksgiving. As always, she wanted the holidays to be precisely right for the family and her parents. They arrived the weekend before Thanksgiving. We had converted my short-lived home office into a guest room so Midge and Ray could stay there. The girls loved it when the grandparents came to town and would always be found on their laps. Midge would read them books, and Ray would tell them stories of their mom growing up. Kristie asked plenty of questions about her first day of school in first grade and what she liked about school. Karie was not shy and chimed in on her pre-kindergarten experiences. I could tell Midge and Ray were as proud as I as Mary Ann continued to develop into *a loving mother.* The night before Thanksgiving, Midge and Mary Ann were busy getting things ready for the big meal. Ray and I hung out with the girls; Ray couldn't get enough of Kristie and Karie time.

Mary Ann then came out of the kitchen and asked, "Stephen, I know I have to ask. What time is the Nebraska/Oklahoma game tomorrow? I don't want you running in and out of the room to watch the game. Plus, you must make the gravy and cut the bird, so we need a plan."

At the time, Nebraska was number two, with only one loss to Florida State, which was a close game. Nebraska also had the highest-scoring offense behind Tom Rathman and junior I-back Doug DuBose. The team was on fire. Oklahoma was rated number five at the time, so I thought it would be champagne time and wanted to make sure we all saw the game. I had already gotten Red Shirts for everyone, although I knew that I would never get

Midge into one. I wasn't sure about Ray, but I had them for Mary Ann and the girls. The good news was the game would kick-off at 11 a.m. California time, so there would be plenty of time before Thanksgiving dinner to watch the game.

The next morning Mary Ann and Midge got breakfast ready, and I got ready for the big Thanksgiving Day match between Nebraska and Oklahoma. The game was played in Norman, Oklahoma, which gave the Sooners a substantial home-field advantage. I was nervous as I always was when Nebraska was playing a big game, but confident given Nebraska's high scoring offense that year and their number two ranking going into the game. Mary Ann realized that she would not have to stay standing until the first score since we were watching from home! I did, however, suggest that to her just before kickoff. With that, I got one of those, "Oh Stephen, I am not going to do that!" That was a good thing since Nebraska did not score until late into the second half of the game. At half time I heard Mary Ann telling Midge, *Thank God we are not at that game, we would still be standing!!* The game was a huge disappointment; the Oklahoma defense was too strong, and Nebraska only scored once, and that touchdown was a defensive touchdown. Nebraska went on to lose the game, and with a nine and three record, ended up eleventh in the nation. Michigan finished number one that year, and Oklahoma number two. I was not on my best behavior during the game but calmed down by dinnertime.

Dinner was excellent, Mary Ann did her typical excellent job, and Midge made her famous liver stuffing for the bird. Mary Ann and I loved Thanksgiving and always made it a unique family tradition. It later became even more impressive when the kids went off to college. The Thanksgiving holiday would still be the first time we would see the kids after their fall semester started. It would always be their homecoming since all went away to college to UCLA, Arizona State, or San Diego State. None of the campuses were that far away, but it would be our first chance to see their smiley faces after school started each year. For Mary Ann, Thanksgiving break could never come soon enough.

With Thanksgiving now behind us and Midge and Ray headed back to Chicago, Mary Ann started to get the house ready for Christmas. Away went all the Thanksgiving decorations, and in came the Christmas ones. Mary Ann loved decorating the home for the holidays and always did a fantastic job. I still, today, with a tear in my eye, pull out her favorite Christmas decorations. I spread them around the house, as she would, for our children and our children's children to enjoy. Christmas of 1985 was going to be a memorable and busy time for us. Our third child was due on or about December 15th. This time the delivery date was going to be a bit more precise. Mary Ann was going to deliver through a cesarean section due to her injury when Karie was born. My parents were due to arrive on December 20th, since it was their turn to celebrate Christmas with us that year. They were more than excited to be with us and meet their new grandchild. That would now be their sixth grandchild, as my brother and his wife had three girls to go along with our two.

The Manning family was growing nicely, but so far, there were no signs that the Manning name would continue our branch of the family tree. Mary Ann was amazing. Even though she was almost nine months pregnant, she showed no signs of slowing down as she prepared the house for Christmas and my parents' visit.

It was almost time for our journey to Valley Memorial Hospital. Mary Ann started to feel her labor pains, so we called her doctor and told us to make our way to the hospital. The hospital was in Livermore, the next town over from Pleasanton. It was a short drive from our house, and we made it there in less than twenty minutes. We were less rushed than before but still anxious for a smooth delivery and a healthy baby. I pulled up to the admitting portion of the hospital, got a wheelchair for Mary Ann, and we were quickly admitted and in the room within a few minutes. Her doctor was not yet on-site, so we waited patiently for his arrival.

While we were waiting, Mary Ann pulled out her list of names we discussed for our new arrival. Again, we had three finalists for a girl's name and three for a boy. I think we were both wanting a boy just to try to round out the family a bit. We also wanted to make sure we would extend the Manning family tree one more generation.

Indeed, a healthy baby was our number one priority, and there were no signs that this would be an issue. The hospital and doctor also allowed the father to be in the birthing room, so I was getting ready for that. I knew this birth would be given the plans for a C-section delivery. Mary Ann was trying to keep with the "K" naming convention for our kids. I never really asked where that thought came from, but there were plenty of "K's" on her list. On the boys' list of names, I favored Ryan Patrick to deliver our first boy. The baby naming convention that we were using was simple. The first name would be a little random and not related to any family name. The middle name would always be a family name. Kristie "Marie" was in honor of Mary Ann. Karie "Lynn" was in honor of one of Mary Ann's favorite cousins. In the case of Ryan "Patrick," it was a common Manning family name.

We were going over all the names when the doctor entered the room. It was my first chance to meet him, and I knew Mary Ann was amazingly comfortable with him. After I introduced myself to him, he started to take us through the procedure we were about to witness. The doctor said all signs indicate that both baby and mother are doing fine, and did not foresee any delivery complications. As he wrapped up the overview of what was about to come, he suggested that Mary Ann would likely be ready to deliver in a few hours. He was close with his earlier prediction that our baby would be born on or around December 15th. It was now December 17th and just eight days before Christmas. We were about to get our Christmas present early that year. Later, Mary Ann would always worry that our third child would lose out on its birthday because it was so close to Christmas. She would always ensure that this day remained special for our child. As delivery time was near, the nurses collected Mary Ann and gave me a gown to wear in the delivery room. We were both too excited, and as Mary Ann left the room, she blew me a kiss.

The nurse took me to the delivery room after they had Mary Ann fully prepped for the procedure. From there, everything started to happen quickly. I stood back and looked away while the doctor cut open Mary Ann, readying her for her C-Section. I already knew that I could be faint at the sight of blood, and I wanted to make sure I was standing and alert for the delivery. When I could see the doctor starting to deliver our baby, I looked excitedly and curiously for a healthy baby and to see if it was a boy or girl. The doctor held up our new child and said, "Congratulations, you have a healthy baby boy to take home to your family!"

Mary Ann and I both had tears of joy in our eyes. Mary Ann then turned to me and said, "Congratulations, Mr. Manning. Please meet Ryan Patrick Manning!!" The look on Mary Ann's face as she introduced me to Ryan Patrick could not have been more memorable. I know she was as happy as I was to deliver a boy, but the look of accomplishment on her face was precious.

The nurse handed Ryan to me while they stitched Mary Ann up. I was so excited to hold him. I had to sit down. I waited there for them to take Mary Ann back to the room. After getting Mary Ann settled, I stopped by the chapel at the hospital to say a prayer of thanks for a healthy baby and, of course, our first boy. Ryan was a big baby weighing nine pounds and four ounces at birth. He was born with a lot of hair and the two most prominent blue eyes you could imagine. When Mary Ann or I would take him shopping with us, people would often just stop the grocery cart so they could see his big blue eyes.

Mary Ann's recovery was fast, and I took Mary Ann and Ryan home on the 20th and then went to the airport to pick up my mom and dad for their Christmas visit. The girls were excited and there to help Mary Ann with whatever they could. They wanted to hold Ryan as soon as I got them home, so we each sat on the couch, and I placed Ryan on their little laps. They bonded with Ryan from the first day home. That 1985 Christmas was hectic, but we got through it. My parents stayed through New Year's. That helped get Mary Ann and Ryan settled and Mary Ann into her new role as a *loving mother* of three little ones.

KYLE RAYMOND MANNING IS BORN

*H*aving three little ones in the house took some time to get used to. Not only did we now have three, but one was a boy. We soon found out that having a boy is different from having little girls. Little boys, at least for us, were different. They are far more active and curious, and they climb on anything. Even Kristie and Karie would sit on the couch and watch with amazement as Ryan would get into everything like trying to climb up the bookcase in the family room. They were both Mary Ann's watchdogs with Ryan when she was in the kitchen cooking dinner before I got home from work. They would often be yelling *Mom, Ryan's doing this or doing* that as they watched over him.

Ryan was a good hugger, though. Once I got home and said hi to Mary Ann and the girls, I would hold Ryan until we sat down for dinner, and sometimes even through dinner. Mary Ann would also get her Ryan time. Ryan was a very deep sleeper, and it would take him a while to wake up after naps. Mary Ann would go to get him up from his naps or in the morning, and she would sit and rock him in his bedroom for at least twenty or thirty minutes. When he needed to wake up, Mary Ann needed to hold him for 10 or 15 minutes. Mary Ann was so good about carving out some time every day for her time alone with our children. She always knew what they needed and would take that alone time to service those needs. Even when they were younger and not yet talking, she knew exactly what they needed or what they were trying to say when they would get restless. It was hard for her to get them all on the same schedule, given that from youngest to oldest, there was a seven-year age difference. It made it even harder when I was traveling, which was increasing with my new job, mostly internationally. While I was usually home on weekends, I felt like I was in a constant state of jet lag. Mary Ann's sister Peggy had recently moved out to Pleasanton, which provided some help and companionship for her. When she first moved out, she lived with us and soon took a job at Future Computers and eventually settled into her apartment in town.

All this travel was putting stress on my relationship with Mary Ann. She was starting to think she was quickly becoming a single mother. So many family matters were falling on her shoulders, and that was not what she had wanted. She was exhausted as much as I was as she tried to keep the house together and raise our children. We started having arguments over stupid trivial things. The discussions were becoming more frequent and more intense. We both knew we had to do something different, and our life of "Camelot" was starting to come apart. That delightful feeling that we had for each other in Switzerland, not that long ago, now seemed like a lifetime ago. I knew this was something that I had to solve, but I did not immediately have all the answers. We were understaffed for what we were trying to accomplish at Future, much like any typical start-up. We were also getting ready to launch our new PC. We developed in the UK, production in Asia, and customers and prospects in North America and Europe. I knew I needed to bring in more senior managers to take over some of the load.

Mary Ann and I saw too many of the couples we met in the Newcomers Club fall apart with their marriages. Stress caused by the prohibitive cost of living in the bay area and the pressures of work can tear a family apart if they cannot find a solution. My family was my highest priority, and I knew it was Mary Ann's too. To get things back on track, I suggested to Mary Ann that we get a babysitter and get away together for a long weekend in the Napa wine country. Close enough to home, but far enough away that we could positively work through our issues together. After thinking about it for a few weeks, Mary Ann agreed to get a babysitter if we got home before the kids went to bed Sunday night. Her delay in agreeing to the weekend getaway started to worry me. Frankly, I was concerned that her reluctance to get away with me might not be because she didn't want to leave the kids; possibly, she didn't want to be anywhere alone with me. After she agreed, I booked us a room in the Napa Valley at a lovely small hotel and spa. We drove up Friday afternoon.

On the way up to Napa, I started the conversation about how different I felt our relationship was and how I wanted us to get back to where we were with it. I told her *that I would do whatever I had to do to be a better husband to her and father to our children.* She seemed to stiffen up when I started the conversation and was quiet. I was not sure if she was prepared for that conversation, so I encouraged her to respond. She still sat there silent. I began to think that this trip was a bad idea and maybe we should turn around.

Finally, with a tear in her eye, she turned to me and said, "Stephen, I am not sure you are capable of changing. You seem so dedicated to your job and career that it is getting ridiculous. You take off, fly all around the world, and when you get home, you are too tired to do anything. I don't want our family to live this way. We are not living the dream that we had, and I simply can't do this anymore."

That was a harsh response to my opening comments, but Mary Ann was never afraid to say what she thought. I told her, "Mary Ann, I know it's not been easy for us, but we are way too invested in this. That is why I wanted to get away, just the two of us. Let's take advantage of our time together this weekend and figure out what we need to do to get us back to our "Camelot." The relationship we have together, and with our kids, is too important not to try and fix things. I know I am the most to blame here, and I promise you I will do the things necessary to make things better. You and the kids mean the world to me. I do not want a life that does not include you and the family. Please, help me get better."

Mary Ann seemed to be calming down as we drove into Napa. I think it was important to her to know that I knew things were not right with us. I am not sure if she was at a point of changing the locks on the doors at home, but I think she may have been close.

As we pulled into the hotel and spa, I parked the car. I then turned to her and said, "Sweetheart, let's take the time this weekend to understand exactly what it is going to take to get things right. I love you too much not to make things better for you. I know we can do this."

With that, I got our bags together, and we went to check-in for what I was hoping was a relationship-changing weekend with my bride. The weather was warm, and the days were still long. The hotel setting was striking and was surrounded by vineyards on all sides. The lobby was small, but it opened to a beautiful patio area with a small pool and spa area. It was clearly designed for a couple's getaway: All the tables were set up and arranged for a party of two. After we got checked in, we walked towards the patio area that was a lovely area that just drew you in. Standing just outside the patio doors and putting my arm around Mary Ann, I said, "Sweetheart, why don't we cancel our dinner reservations for tonight. After we get unpacked, I will get some wine, cheese, bread, and some cold cuts, and we can have dinner out here. I so much want to continue our conversation, and this looks like the best spot for it." She agreed, and I could see she was getting more relaxed about things. I also knew once we started this conversation, Mary Ann would want to complete it.

We went to the room and got her settled, and I went to the store to get some local wine and all the fixings for our impromptu "dinner picnic." To make it official, I also got a nice picnic basket and a blanket. I knew this would be an important weekend, and I wanted to make everything perfect for Mary Ann. When I got back to the hotel, I could see Mary Ann was already out on the patio. I could see her staring over the vineyards and into the hills that surround Napa. I wasn't sure what she was thinking about, but she was clearly in deep thought. As I approached her, I put my hand on her shoulder and said, "Sweetheart, how about we throw a blanket on the lawn enjoy our picnic dinner there? I almost hated to interrupt you; you looked so peaceful. Would you care to tell me what you were thinking so deeply about?"

She said, "Stephen, I was just thinking of what you said and how we got here. I agree; let's spend the next couple of days seeing if we can really get things back on track with our relationship. I don't want to be like some of our friends who let their relationships and families fall apart. I am certainly willing to give it a try if you can make some significant changes."

We indeed weren't there yet, but it was a crucial step for us. I spread the blanket on the lawn, still with a lovely view of the vineyards and the hills beyond. I opened a bottle of wine, and Mary Ann spread out the cheese, bread, cold cuts, and some fruit, and we started to talk. It was an open and honest discussion about what was bothering us about our current relationship. Not a lot of significant issues, other than my travel schedule. But several smaller issues were accumulating. I think every couple has these types of problems, and if left unchecked, the accumulation of these can cause stress in the relationship. The evening was going well, good wine, tasty food, and a very heartfelt discussion. The sky was getting dark, and the stars were starting to appear. The stars were bright, much brighter than you see closer to the city at night. It was a perfect setting to have the discussion we needed to have. We covered a lot of ground that evening, but we did not address my travel schedule's most giant elephant in the room. That was going to be a more extended and more complicated discussion, and we decided to leave that for Saturday.

The next morning, we slept in and went for a brunch later that morning. I had arranged for some wine tours after brunch, and we wanted to make sure we did that with a full stomach. There were three wineries we enjoyed that we wanted to visit. We then planned to go back to the hotel for a swim before we went to dinner. There are some fabulous four- and five-star restaurants in the Napa Valley, and last-minute bookings are difficult. Since we planned this trip on short notice, I could not book any of the five-star restaurants, but I did find a nice four-star. Mary Ann seemed to be in a better mood that morning, and as we started our brunch, I started the discussion about my travel schedule. We had a lot to cover on this topic, and I wanted to get through the conversation before heading home the next day. I told her *how much I hated the travel I was doing. Constantly jet-lagged and exhausted. Waking up every morning and figuring out what country I was in by the accent or language of the person giving me the wake-up call—always missing her and the kids.* Traveling was difficult back then, no cell phones or email, so it was hard to stay in touch. I told her *it was awful, and I hated it.*

She said, "Stephen, please look at this from my perspective. You are hardly ever home. We have three kids at home now. I must get them all up for breakfast, take the girls to school or soccer or swim practice, and still make sure Ryan gets his naps. At night I must get their dinner ready, give them their baths, and clean up the kitchen. I am basically a single mother. I can't keep doing this. I know I still love you, and I think we have made a lot of progress this weekend, but I am not sure how much longer I can be doing this "single mother" thing unless things change. Please tell me how you are going to make things better. I want to hear those words this weekend and see the actions that follow those words. Please, for the family and us, you need to fix this!"

I told her *I had been thinking about this a lot and wanted to go over some possible options as we went on our wine tours.* Somehow, between this critical discussion and the next, we could finish brunch and make our way to the first winery.

As we started our first tour, we continued the discussion. I told her, "Mary Ann, I have already talked to Brian about my desire to reduce my travel. We agreed that he would handle the customers in Europe until we hired a salesperson over there. He would also handle all product planning and development issues in the UK and report back to me every week. He would also put one of his product engineering managers in charge of production in Asia until we hired someone for that role. That would leave us with one customer in Florida I would have to keep an eye on, and all the rest were in Silicon Valley. I have already hired a CFO who will be based in Pleasanton. I will soon hire a North American salesperson and a production manager in the Pleasanton office. It will all take some time, but the plan is in place. Please trust me and show me a little patience. I want what you want, and I will get this done over the next three or four months. I have already talked to Clancy about this, and I have his full support. I know if Clancy buys off on this, the board will soon follow."

These were the words that Mary Ann wanted to hear, and quite frankly, the words that she deserved to hear. Thank God, she still trusted me, so we were again walking hand-in-hand by the third winery. We went back to the hotel and took a swim. I knew Mary Ann was happy with the discussion when she swam up and gave me one of her famous swimming-pool hugs: her hands around my neck, and her legs around my hips, and a great big kiss on my lips.

With that, she whispered in my ear, "Steve, I want to thank you for putting this weekend together. We covered a lot of important ground, and I trust that you will follow through with your commitments to the family and me. I know it won't be easy, but you seem committed, and I trust you."

I knew we had our chance to get back to "Camelot," but there was a lot of important work ahead of us. We had a wonderful dinner that night. I am sure the food and wine were great, but all I can remember was the feeling of being back in touch with my bride that night. We committed to each other that we would do everything in our power not to miss this opportunity. We headed home to Pleasanton that next afternoon, with smiles on our faces and a real sense that we had accomplished what we needed to on that special weekend in the wine country of the Napa Valley.

The kids were happy to see their mommy and daddy home that Sunday. Of course, the girls had to tell their mommy of all the mischief Ryan had gotten into over the weekend. Nothing serious, just crawling around and getting into everything. He was still not walking, but that did not slow him down one bit. I started Monday rearranging my travel schedule. I canceled all my upcoming international trips other than my every six-week trip for the board meetings. I also started recruiting a North American salesperson and a production manager, both of whom would be based in Pleasanton's offices. Mary Ann was thrilled to see me following through so quickly with my commitments to her and the family.

A little over a month following our weekend in the wine country, Mary Ann and I were lying in bed getting ready for a good night's sleep when she rolled over to me to give me what I thought was our usual good-night kiss. But instead, she stopped and said, "Stephen, I have something to tell you, and I hope you are not mad about it."

I said, "Sweetheart, what is it, is everything OK?"

She said, "Well, I think I am about to find out. What I want to tell you is that I am pregnant."

I was utterly taken by surprise with this news, and she could tell. I said, "Mary Ann, we have never discussed more children since Ryan was born.

Ryan is not even a year old. Please don't get me wrong, and it's not that I am upset, just surprised by the news."

She said, "I know, honey, this was all a major surprise to me as well. I guess we got more done than I thought about our trip to Napa!"

I asked, "How are you going to handle two little ones in diapers?"

She said, "Don't worry, I can handle it, but I am going to need a lot of help from you and the girls."

I am not sure if either one of us got much sleep that night.

The next few weeks were calm after finding out about our little surprise that would join us next spring. Mary Ann had her normal morning sickness, but nothing too extreme. Ryan was still crawling and climbing everywhere, and the girls were still in awe over how he got into everything. Mary Ann turned to me once and said, "What are we going to do when Ryan starts walking? I am not sure I can keep up with him!" A few months later, we would find out. Our young boy just had more energy than our nice little quiet girls. The girls still treated Ryan as the dolls Mary Ann had bought for them before he was born. They would continuously dress him up in some of their baby clothes and put little skirts on him. I am not sure if they did that to please themselves or to tease me. Either way, they enjoyed it, and I think Ryan loved all the attention. The Reidy's also adopted Ryan, and the Reidy girls would enjoy joining Kristie and Karie, dressing up Ryan in their old skirts.

For some reason, Ryan became infatuated with garbage trucks when he was little. If he heard the garbage truck in the neighborhood during their weekly pick-up, Mary Ann would take him out on the front porch so he could watch with some amazement as they did their job of picking up the trash. He was *so* into it that Mary Ann would often put him in his baby seat in her minivan and follow the truck around the neighborhood. Ryan was quickly becoming our family garbage man. Mike Reidy would get into the act as well, and every time Mike made a run to the dump, he would always take Ryan with him. When Ryan got a little older and started talking, I once asked him what he wanted to be when he grew up. He gave me a straightforward answer with a big smile on his face: "Garbage man."

Ryan still needed his time to wake up after his naps or in the morning. Unfortunately, as Mary Ann was getting closer to having our fourth child, it was getting harder for her to hold Ryan on her lap.

When it started to get closer to our fourth child's birth, Mary Ann and I began to discuss how we would arrange the bedroom situation with our fourth. The girls enjoyed having their own rooms, which would be fine if we had another boy. If we had a boy, we were just going to put them both in the room Ryan was currently occupying. If we had another girl, we weren't quite sure what to do. Mary Ann wanted all the kids on the second floor, near our room. She didn't feel comfortable moving Kristie downstairs on her own, but also did not want to make the girls share a room. Bunk beds for the girls were a possibility, but if it was a boy, bunk beds for them in Ryan's room would also work. Either way, we knew we would need another crib. We had enough space in the master bath area for at least the first six months that would work in any case. With both girls back in school, she put Ryan in her minivan, went shopping for another crib, and looked at bunk beds options. I set up the crib in the master bath that night as Mary Ann described what our choices for bunk beds would likely be. I was always so impressed with how well-prepared Mary Ann was when she figured out the best ways of raising our children. She would think about our kids and their reactions to each situation during the day, inevitably making it all run smoothly for the whole family.

As we finished setting up the crib, she turned to me and said, "Stephen, having another boy would make all of this a lot easier. They can share Ryan's room; you get your second son, and the girls get to keep their rooms upstairs. I know you, and I have always said; Lord, give us a healthy baby, but I am just saying...."

I put my arms around her and said, "Sweetheart, the Lord has been very good to us, and while we can't take anything ever for granted, I am sure everything will work out." We were so busy putting the crib together and talking about what was next for us, and we didn't even realize that the girls and Ryan had come up to watch their daddy assemble the crib. Even though they were young, they already knew I was no mechanic and wanted to see if I could pull it off. Thank God it was a simple assembly, and there were no foul words spoken! The girls were quick, though, to let their mommy know that they did not want to share rooms!! Mary Ann gathered all the kids and took them downstairs as she started to get dinner ready. I packed away my tools, took another look at the crib, and thought, *man now I know why we ended up in a five-bedroom home.* Who would have ever known?

The holidays came and went quickly. It was my parents' turn for Thanksgiving and Mary Ann's parents' turn for Christmas. Mary Ann had done an excellent job of decorating the house for both holidays and served two delicious holiday dinners. The weather was exceptional that holiday season and both parents enjoyed their time out of the snow. Both grandfathers were getting older, and I started to worry about them at their ages shoveling the snow back in the Midwest. Both Lincoln and Chicago would get heavy wet snows, and neither one of them had snow blowers at the time. Ray Lesin had a friendly neighbor who would get out early and shovel his driveway for him when the snows were bad. My dad was not so lucky, and I knew he could not afford to hire someone to do it every time it snowed. My brother and I would eventually move our parents to Sun City West, Arizona, after my mom stopped working. We both had the opportunity to help them into their retirement and take them away from the snows in Nebraska.

Mary Ann was anxious for our fourth child to enter the world after nearly nine months of carrying it. We were planning to have dinner that night with a group of our Newcomer friends. Mary Ann asked me to suggest we go to a new Mexican restaurant that had opened north of town. She had read that having a nice spicy meal would help induce labor, and she was more than ready for all that to happen. I was not sure there was any merit to the theory, but I loved Mexican food, so I made reservations that night for the four couples. They all wanted to try the new restaurant, so they were more than happy with Mary Ann's choice. Mary Ann did not love spicy food, but as we were having dinner, I could see her putting on more salsa than usual on her enchiladas.

After a great meal and conversation with our friends, we headed home. Sure enough, I could see Mary Ann was uncomfortable with all the spicy food at dinner, but she was committed to playing out her theory that night. We went to bed around 11 that night, and around 3 a.m., she woke me up and said, "It's time; looks like my plan worked." With a smile on her face, she started getting her bags ready for the hospital.

We headed out to the same hospital where she had delivered Ryan only some sixteen months earlier. This time the delivery went quickly, and we had our fourth child and our second boy, Kyle Raymond Manning, born April 12, 1987. I am still unsure if Mary Ann's spicy food theory had any merit, but Kyle, like me, was a huge fan of spicy food as he got older. For him, the spicier, the better.

We had already decided that four children would complete our dreams for a family. After the delivery, Mary Ann had the doctor make sure there were no more surprise babies in our future. Kyle was a surprise for us, but he was also a treasure we quickly came to enjoy and love. Our house was now full. Kristie and Karie were able to keep their rooms, and Ryan and Kyle would share the bedroom next to us. The grandparents' bedroom down-stairs was full of many visits from both parents over the years, and we loved each one of them. Although the grandparents lived far away, the kids grew remarkably close to all four of them with their frequent visits.

Kyle started his life off in the crib in our master bedroom. Kyle was a very docile baby and was easy to care for. Mary Ann quickly got him into a nap schedule close to Ryan's, so she had some free time to spend with the girls. While they were older, she still knew they needed their special time alone with her, and she enjoyed every minute of it. While Kyle was calmer than Ryan, he also liked to climb the bookcase in the family room. He would always wait until someone was in the room to watch his climb. It was almost like he wanted everyone to know he was no less a boy than Ryan. Over the years, that would become more difficult in sports; Ryan had a special gift for sports like football, baseball, golf, tennis, and hockey. The girls were also great athletes and enjoyed success at soccer, tennis, and swimming. Kyle fought hard to find his unique sport and finally found lacrosse. Kyle was our only child to play lacrosse. He played it very well, which helped Kyle find his self-esteem and self-confidence. He grew nicely from that experience.

Mary Ann Loses Her Father,
Our First Family Tragedy

I always thought it was amazing how different the kids' personalities were. Same mother, same father, but all the kids were unique. Still, they all got along very well. The girls took on their role as big sisters and often helped Mary Ann with the boys. Mary Ann always had her hands full with four at home.

Shortly after Kyle was born, her dad started to have serious medical issues. First, he had a heart attack but worked hard to recover from that. His recovery seemed to be going well, but then he had a stroke. The stroke was severe, and Ray was unable to walk and had a tough time talking. We went back often to Chicago to check in on him, but he was not getting any better. Midge was struggling to take care of Ray, which became a full-time job.

It was late 1988, and I traveled to Germany, trying to get back to Pleasanton before Christmas. I had one stop left after Germany before I could get home; I needed to be in Salt Lake City for a meeting on December 22, 1988. I needed to complete my meetings in Berlin so I could get to London to connect to my flight there. The schedule was going to be tight, so I booked two return flights, one connecting through Chicago to Salt Lake early on December 21st and, as a backup, the last Pan Am flight out of London to New York, Pan Am flight 103. It was a popular flight since it was the last flight of the day out of London to the United States. I needed the insurance of that backup flight because the meetings in Berlin were not progressing very well. On the evening of December 19, I decided to leave

Berlin the next morning and then spend the night in London to ensure I made the earlier flight I had initially planned.

I canceled the backup flight. The connection got me into Salt Lake late in the evening on the 21st. I was exhausted and jet-lagged, so I went to the hotel and to bed. When I got up the next morning, I turned on the news. As the picture came on, I saw a picture of the nose of a Pan Am 747 lying in a field. Clearly, there had been some sort of crash of a Pan Am 747. Having just come over on a Pan Am 747, the news story caught my interest. I turned the volume up and sat and listened to the news story. I was shocked to find out it was Pan Am flight 103, the flight I had booked as my back up flight out of London. It had crashed in a field in Lockerbie, Scotland, after a terrorist bomb had exploded on board after take-off from London Heathrow airport. There were no survivors.

I was shaken by the thought of how close I had come to being on that airplane. I immediately called Mary Ann to let her know I was safely in Salt Lake City but did not tell her until later that I was booked on that flight. I promised her I would get my meetings done early that morning and be home for dinner that night. After talking to Mary Ann, I hung the phone up and sat back, and just started crying. My only thought was how close I had come to losing my family and leaving Mary Ann and the kids without a husband and father. I started to question if what I was doing was worth it, given all the travel time away from the family I loved. My mind was full of horrific thoughts while I finished my meetings and took the next flight home. I couldn't get the picture out of my mind of the nose of that Pan Am 747 lying in the field.

When I got home, Mary Ann and the girls were there to greet me at the door. Mary Ann had them all dressed up in some beautiful Christmas outfits. The house was amazingly decorated, with presents under the tree we had cut down shortly after Thanksgiving. I hugged them all a little tighter this time, knowing how close I had come to not being there for Christmas that year.

There would be no extra family with us this Christmas. Ray Lesin was not doing well, and my parents were spending Christmas with my brother and his family. We had celebrated Ryan's third birthday before I left for

Germany. Kristie and Karie were getting ready to celebrate their tenth and eighth birthdays, respectively, in January. Kyle was now just twenty months old, old enough to know what Christmas was all about. Mary Ann had a beautiful Christmas picture of the kids taken a week professionally before Christmas. It was framed and proudly set on the coffee table in the living room. After I gave everyone my hugs and kisses, she took me over to see it. As I held the framed picture, I just broke into tears. Mary Ann knew something was wrong. She knew those were more than tears of joy.

She said, "Stephen, is there something you want to tell me? You seem very emotional; what is wrong?"

I told her *I was just so happy to be home; it was a very long trip, and I hate to be away from the family during the Christmas season. I am not sure if I can keep on doing this.*

She said, "Go unpack and get a drink; I will start dinner. Honey, please tell me if something is wrong. By the way, I have some news about my dad, and it's not good. We can talk about it all after we put the boys to bed tonight. I have already brought the girls up-to-date on their Grandpa Lesin."

I went upstairs to unpack and get ready for dinner. As I was unpacking, I wondered if I should tell Mary Ann how close I was to be on Pan Am flight 103. It had clearly affected me emotionally, and I did not want to keep things hidden from Mary Ann. That night after we got the boys to bed, we sat down to talk. First, I wanted to hear about her dad. I knew he was having a tough time, and I was worried things were getting worse for him. He was such a great guy and a fighter, but I knew his condition was getting the best of him. Mary Ann started the conversation. As she began to talk, she began to cry. She said, "Steve, things are getting worse for both my dad and my mom. My dad seems confused all the time and is getting very frustrated. It seems they have trouble sequencing all his medicine, and his personality has changed. He is always angry and aggressive, and you know that is not who he is. It has something to do with the medicine he is taking. Now my mom is saying she can't care for him when he is like this. I don't know what we can do, but we must help my mom with all of this. I feel so helpless being out here in California. Maybe I should go back to Chicago to help. I can take the boys with me, but we will need someone to help watch the girls. They will be back in school shortly after the first of the year."

"We will do whatever it takes," I said. "But let's first get his doctors to sort out his medicine. I have read a little bit about this situation. When stroke patients start having major personality changes, they sometimes relate to all the medicine they are taking. With multiple doctors prescribing multiple types of medication, it can have a debilitating effect on patients. Your dad has had more than one doctor addressing his heart attack, his stroke, and now his high blood pressure. He needs to have one doctor in charge of everything so he can oversee all this medication. Let's call your mom in the morning and see if she can make this happen. And of course, if things don't get better after Christmas, you and the boys need to get to Chicago. I know your dad is important to you, and you want to be there for him. Whether you are there or not, this situation needs to be corrected."

With Mary Ann already so emotional over her dad's condition, I decided not to tell her about my close encounter with Pan Am 103. The next day we called Midge and told her to pick the most trusted doctor who saw Ray and put him in charge of all his meds. Midge did not quite understand why she had to do that but promised Mary Ann that she would take care of it right away.

It was now Christmas Eve, and with no family in town, we decided to share it with friends. We had started a tradition of having shrimp and lobster on Christmas Eve and a prime rib on Christmas Day. Since Mike Reidy did not like the sight or smell of fish, we would have to have our time with the Reidy family on Christmas Day. That was fine since it would give us more time to be with them. They had already become an extension of our family, and the more time with them, the better. Christmas morning had now become quite an ordeal with four young kids in the house. Our ritual was that once all kids were up, they would gather at the top of the stairs. There they would wait for their mother to get ready and for me to set up the lights and movie camera so I could capture their plunge down the stairs.

That proved to be pure agony for the kids. The staircase looked directly down onto the living room, where we had the tree and all the presents Santa had delivered the night before. As I got the camera ready and put on the coffee, the girls would always remind me that I should have set everything up the night before. I never let them know that I was simply a diversion for Mary Ann as she prepared for all the pictures that were sure to come. Once Mary Ann appeared at the top of the stairs with Kyle in her arms, the mayhem started. Mary Ann had Santa put all the kids' presents in their pile. That way, as they came flying down the stairs, they knew they had to find their name on at least one of the presents, to know they were in front of the right pile. Once the dust settled, and Mary Ann was on the couch, she would direct who got to open their presents first. Somehow, she would always remember whose turn it was to go first. This scene played out every year, and I have them all on tape. We will still watch some of those movies as we still celebrate Christmas as a family every year.

Mary Ann stayed in constant contact with her mother through the holidays, checking how her dad was doing. Midge was able to get a lead doctor assigned to manage Ray's drug regimen, and things were getting better. The doctor cut some of the drugs he was taking and then better sequenced the remaining. Ray was slowly getting back to his loving and caring personality, and Midge was starting to feel she could again handle his care. Mary Ann was so relieved that things for her dad and mom had settled down. She still wanted to get back to see him. She started to plan for a trip by looking for someone to help me care for the girls. Mary Ann and I both knew that a much sadder trip back to Chicago would come someday, and sooner rather than later. The thought of this touched both of our hearts. Mary Ann would sometimes sit on the couch in the family room playing "Ave Maria" and many Frank Sinatra songs, her dad's favorites. She loved her father so much and had always gained strength from him.

It was early January, and I had pretty much stayed around the home, not wanting to travel. I was still counting my blessings from the last trip back from Europe and wanted to be there for Mary Ann if anything happened to her dad. One afternoon I had a presentation I was scheduled to make at an investors' conference in San Francisco. We had somewhat of a standard set of slides to describe the company and the markets we addressed. I had given the pitch many times, so I was extremely comfortable presenting it. I had given my introduction, and I was well into the presentation when a lady came up to the podium and handed me a note. That was unusual, and I was curious, so I stopped, opened the message, read it, and then went on to the next slide. Half-way into the next slide, I stopped in disbelief. What was I doing? The note read, "Your father-in-law has passed; please call home immediately." I thought, *Steve, how could you have even thought about continuing your presentation? Your life is about your family, not your business.* With that, I told the audience that I had just been informed about a death in the family, and I excused myself.

I quickly made my way to my car, pulled out of the parking garage and onto a side street to call Mary Ann. Cell phones, in their earliest stages, had finally made their way into our life. Mary Ann was expecting my call and answered quickly. She was, of course, in tears and said her dad had shot himself earlier that day. I could not believe what she was saying. Ray Lesin was a deeply religious person and would never take his own life. She said, "The working theory from the family and police was that he probably knew he was a heavy burden to my mom and the family. He also knew he would not get any better and probably decided he did not want to be a burden to my mom and the family any longer. He would be out of his misery, and so would my mom."

The explanation made some sense to me. While it was tragic, it gave Mary Ann some comfort knowing that her dad had always been a caretaker, and he died knowing that Midge would no longer have to be burdened by his poor health.

The family flew to Chicago the next morning, and Mary Ann worked with Midge on all the funeral arrangements. Ray had many friends, relatives, and co-workers. The services were beautifully performed and well attended. After the services, Mary Ann came to me, still saddened by her father's loss, and asked me, "Stephen, do you think there is any chance my father is in heaven?"

I said to her, "Mary Ann, of course, your father is in heaven. I am sure he is looking down on you right now. He was a special, caring person, and he was deeply religious. Why are you asking?"

She then said, "I know all that you said is true, but he killed himself. I was taught that anybody who commits suicide could never enter the gates of heaven. I cannot live with the thought of my dad not being in heaven. What do I tell the children when they ask if Grandpa is in heaven?"

I said, "Sweetheart, the Lord is a caring and loving person as well. He knows that your dad was not himself when he committed suicide. The Lord will weigh the entirety of your dad's life, not just that one sad event. I promise you your dad is in heaven, looking down on his grandchildren and us."

It was an exceedingly tough time for Mary Ann. I think everything in her life was going well, and this was her first real family tragedy. Her father was such an integral part of her life for so many years, and now he was gone. I felt such sadness for her as I held her tightly in my arms.

We decided to stay for a few more days with Mary Ann's mom. There was a lot of cleaning up to do in the room where Ray had shot himself. Mary Ann did not want her mother to have to deal with all of that. Also, Mary Ann wanted to pack all of Ray's clothes and donate them to a local charity. She thought it best to remove all of Ray's belongings from the house so Midge could start her healing process. The loss of a lifetime partner is exceedingly difficult. Fortunately, Midge still had many friends and family in the area to help her through her loss. Mary Ann's brother, Michael, and sister, Peggy, was also there to help with her grieving mother. Our girls were old enough to understand what had happened, and Mary Ann spent a lot of time to help them properly process it all. The boys were too young to understand. So, while Mary Ann counseled the girls on their grandfather's death, I would take the boys out to play in the snow, which they were fascinated with.

As the week went on, I could see Mary Ann was still having difficulties with the reality of her father's passing. I decided to take Mary Ann out to dinner to get her out of the house, which she had not left since the funeral. I was hoping that would help clear her mind, and I wanted to let her know about a decision that I was about to make. I found a restaurant that she enjoyed in the area that was not too crowded to have a long discussion. As she became more relaxed, I told her I had some things I wanted to discuss with her. I was as distraught as she was over her father's loss, but I had to be her strength as she rightfully mourned her father. I told her that I was likely to resign Future at the next board meeting.

She was surprised by this news and asked, "Why are you thinking about doing that?"

I told her that two life-changing events had recently unfolded, and both made me realize that I needed to make a change. I told her what had happened when the lady passed me the note about her father's death. And for a few moments, I just kept presenting at the investor conference. I told her I felt like a man without a heart at the time. You needed me immediately, and for a few minutes, I was not there for you. For the first time, I told her about how close I came to being on the Pan Am flight 103.

With that, she gasped and said, "Stephen, you are not serious, are you? Why didn't you tell me that had happened? I knew something was wrong when you got home that day. How can you keep something like that from me?"

I said, "Sweetheart, I was planning on telling you that night, but we got into the discussion about your dad. I just thought at the time you had too much on your mind. Sorting out your dad's situation was the number one priority. Somehow, I felt all of this was a sign to me that I needed to be home more, and our lifestyle was just not worth it. I didn't see Future ever going public and the personal cost to our family was just too high."

She said, "Stephen, I love that you are making this decision, but what are you going to do? How are you going to find another job?"

I told her *not to worry; I was sure things would work out.* Of course, she was concerned but happy that I had come to that conclusion.

After we got back to Pleasanton, I flew over to London to resign to the Board and worked out a transition plan with them. I was not looking forward to getting on the Pan Am flight to London, but I knew this all had to be in-person with the Board.

After hanging around the house enjoying some dedicated family time, I got a call from one of the investors in Future. He was one of the investors I had the most respect for and always offered the most insight at every board meeting. One of the companies he had invested in had just bought a company in Santa Cruz, California. The company was developing and manufacturing fault-tolerant UNIX mainframe computers. He said they needed someone to run it. Santa Cruz was a long drive from Pleasanton, but at least it was in Northern California. At the time, I knew little about the UNIX operating system. However, he was a good friend, and I wanted to see if I could help him consolidate this company into one, he had invested in back in the UK. I accepted the offer and started working there a few weeks later.

To soften the commute, they rented me a townhouse in Santa Cruz so I would not have to make the commute every day. Depending on what the family schedule was, I would stay there a day or two a week.

On one of my commutes back to Santa Cruz, a few months later, the phone rang in my car. I was a bit startled because very few people had that number. Back then, whether you made a call or received a call, it was billed at one dollar a minute, so I was meticulous who had that number. Of course, one person who did have my number was Mary Ann, so I answered it right away.

I was a little annoyed when I answered the call, as it was not from Mary Ann. The person on the other line introduced himself to me and said, "I am Bob from AT&T."

I did not catch his title, but I asked, "How did you get this number?"

He said, "Steve, as I said, I am from AT&T. It was not difficult for me to find your number." That response annoyed me even more, but I decided to listen to find out why he was calling. As he started talking, he said, "We have a senior position here at AT&T that I would like you to consider. Would you be interested?"

I said, "Bob, I am not a big company guy anymore. I much prefer to work with smaller companies. They are nimbler, and it's a lot easier to get things done outside a big bureaucracy, and no one has a bigger bureaucracy than AT&T. I used to compete with AT&T when I was at Memorex, and I hardly ever saw them in the marketplace." I was pretty frank about my view of AT&T because I thought I was talking with someone from AT&T Human Resources.

Bob said, "I appreciate your honest views of the company. By the way, let me reintroduce myself to you. This is Bob; I am the President of AT&T."

I said with some embarrassment, "Bob, I am sorry to be so blunt; I thought you were probably someone from Human Resources!"

He said, "No worries, I figured as much. Listen, Steve, your critique of AT&T is exactly why we want you to join us. I know we have a cultural issue. We are bringing in senior talent from outside of AT&T to help us change that. Your work with small technology startups is exactly what we like about you. I would like you to help lead the same group that you competed with here at AT&T. I am hoping you can have the same success at AT&T that you had at Memorex. Trust me, we have superior technology, but we've done a bad job of engaging customers with it."

"Steve, you had a chance to tell me no on this opportunity. Give me a chance to get you to yes. I know you are driving right now, so let me send you an offer package to your home. Please study it and talk it over with your wife, Mary Ann. I assure you that you will find it an extremely competitive offer. Thank you for your time this morning."

My immediate impression of the call was, first, how did Bob know my cell phone number and my wife's name? It looks like he had done his home-work on this. (I later found out that Bob was a brilliant guy and always did his homework well. Bob worked on the AT&T breakup with the then chairman of AT&T. It was a complex transaction, and after that breakup, he joined AT&T as their CFO to help manage it.) My second thought was that, while flattered with the interest AT&T had in me, I was not inclined to join them unless I was somehow blown away by the offer. I still had some time before I got to the office, so I called Mary Ann. I also told her about the phone call and my early impression of it. Then told her to be on the lookout for a package from AT&T in the mail.

When I got home that Thursday night, Mary Ann handed me the package that had just arrived that day. Not expecting much, I set it aside and spent time with Mary Ann and the kids before dinner. Mary Ann could not resist asking more about the AT&T opportunity. She asked, "Where would you be based with AT&T, and what would you be doing there?"

I told her, "As far as I knew, the group he was talking about was based in the Chicago area, so I would likely be there. However, he said he wanted me to spend some time in New Jersey, where they had a big corporate campus in Basking Ridge. There is probably something in that package that will spell all of this out. We can look at it after dinner."

She said, "Stephen, you know I don't want to move, but if it were Chicago, at least we would be close to my mom. I know she is still trying to get used to life without my dad there. I could at least keep an eye on her."

The girls' ears perked up upon hearing the discussion about moving, and they weren't happy at all about the idea. After dinner and before I gave the boys their bath, I went into the living room and opened the package. After reading the offer, I was taken aback. It was a much stronger offer than I was expecting. I even thought there may have been some typos, especially in the signing bonus area. They were offering a full year's salary as a signing bonus. I thought, man, this is crazy.

Along with that was the typical stock option award. Another thing I did not expect was sixteen years of vesting into the AT&T retirement program at my then-current salary. After reading all of this, I told Mary Ann that we needed to talk and handed the package to her to read. I told her I would give the boys their bath, and after we got them to bed, we would discuss all of this.

As we sat down to discuss the offer, Mary Ann said, "Stephen, do you realize that we could pay off this house with that signing bonus? And the loan you took out to landscape the backyard. It seems crazy, but you must take a closer look at this. If it meant moving anywhere but Chicago, I would just say no, but you know I worry about my mother. It looks like your offices would be out in the Naperville area, which is less than an hour's drive to my mom's house. Why don't you call Bob back tomorrow and get more details on everything? I am not saying yes, but I am also not saying no if you think this is the right thing for you."

I called Bob back the next day to go over the details of the offer. I told him I was a bit surprised by the signing bonus and the inclusion into the AT&T retirement plan with the sixteen-year vesting. He said, "Steve, I told you I was going to get you to yes on this offer. I threw those two things to make sure that happened. Please go over the offer's details with Mary Ann, and then let's try and close this on Monday. He said, "By the way, I want to move fast on this. Do not bother selling your house. We will lease it out for you for the next year so you can get started with us right away. There will be no out-of-pocket cost for you on this."

That last part of the offer made Mary Ann more comfortable with our decision. I accepted the offer, and we moved to Naperville shortly after that.

Mary Ann was happy to be closer to her mother with our move to Naperville. We found a new five-bedroom home in a golf community called White Eagle. Naperville was a fast-expanding suburb of the Chicago area with excellent schools. It was about twenty-eight miles west of Chicago with good train service into the city. Midge would visit us often, and the girls quickly made friends with schoolmates and neighbors in the area. There was still some winter left by the time we moved in, so the boys got to play in the snow quite often. Mary Ann was also able to connect with her many friends in the Chicago area. We also enjoyed spending time with all of Mary Ann's relatives and letting the kids meet them all. Sunday dinners would often be down in Tinley Park, either at Midge's house or the relatives' house. They were all taking the time to keep an eye on Midge to help her through her loss. It was a great family, and we enjoyed the opportunity to reconnect with them all.

One Sunday night on the trip back up to Naperville, Mary Ann said, "Stephen, I know you are missing California; but I certainly appreciate the opportunity to be around mom and my family. They are all getting older, and it's good that we have the time to be with them. I am sure we will someday find our way back to Pleasanton. After all, we still have our home there, so after the AT&T lease runs out, let's keep it. We can continue to lease it out for a few years and see how things go with AT&T."

I said, "I like seeing you happy like this. If we decide to move back to Pleasanton someday, we probably ought to consider moving your mother back with us. It's only going to get harder for her to take care of herself, and she is so good around the kids."

I quickly found out why Bob was in such a hurry to get me on board. Unbeknownst to me, AT&T and Memorex had been in negotiations to combine the two entities somehow. At first, it was going to be an outright acquisition of Memorex by AT&T, but those discussions broke down. Bob really could not tell me at the time about this because they were under non-disclosure. Memorex was not public at the time, but their debt was trading publicly. He wanted my help in figuring out what the best outcome would be to combine the two companies. He also knew I was quite familiar with the management team at Memorex, so he wanted some insight on that team as well. It was the first time that AT&T would possibly spin off a significant division, so they wanted to get it right. It would be the first of the many restructurings moves that AT&T would make following the original breakup of AT&T. The discussions had lingered for quite some time, and the Memorex team and their investors were getting impatient for a deal. Memorex had massive debt at the time, and they thought the AT&T deal they would allow them to refinance that debt. To end the stalemate, they made an offer to buy the AT&T division outright. I flew to New Jersey and met with Bob and the AT&T deal team to review the proposal from Memorex.

AT&T was now anxious to get a deal done, as well. This division was not a core asset to AT&T's future strategy, so spinning it out would not be an issue for them. They were, however, deeply concerned over how all the AT&T employees would be treated in the deal, so they wanted to make sure it was a financially sound decision. There were clear synergies to be had in the deal. However, AT&T management did not want to see massive layoffs of their employees after the transaction. AT&T was an extremely employee caring corporation at the time. AT&T's investment banker had already issued a fairness report on the Memorex offer, so AT&T was preparing for final negotiations on the deal.

At Bob's request, I looked at the deal. I was able to review the offer. I looked at Memorex's balance sheet and profit-and-loss statement. I then calculated what I thought would be the synergy savings that would result from the combination. After my review, I told him that the Memorex offer was weak, and I warned him about the massive debt load that Memorex was carrying. To make this deal work, they would need additional cash to operate the business until the synergies' full value would play out.

Bob said, "Don't fight this deal if you are afraid of your role after the transaction. The Memorex team would love to have you back, and if you want to stay at AT&T, we have some great plans for you. We are even thinking about putting you on the Chairman's list."

The Chairman's list is quite an honor. At any one time, there would only be six people on that list. Someone on that list would likely be the next Chairman of AT&T. It also gave you a full salary and admission to the Sloan Institute at MIT. It was an eighteen-month high-intensity graduate studies program. Bob said, "You are the only non-legacy AT&T executive on the list, so your chances should be pretty good given we are trying to change the culture here."

I didn't feel that my analysis had anything to do with my view of my next position. With the signing bonus already in hand, I felt rather good about any outcome. As I respected Bob, I decided to go back over all the financials, including those of my division at AT&T, to make sure I was right about my valuation opinion. What I discovered was that there were $200 million of three-year equipment leases on the books that AT&T's investment bankers had missed. Those leases were to all the former AT&T operating companies, the Baby Bells, as they were referred to as. These were all AAA-rated companies. I knew that these leases could be easily sold off at a small discount given the lessee's AAA rating.

I then went down to Bob's office and waited until his schedule opened. I said, "Bob, only because I respect you, I will tell you what I saw as value. By the way, you should fire those investment bankers. They blew their analysis of the deal and the fairness report that they issued." I opened my briefcase and showed him all my analysis. I then pointed out the $200 million of Baby Bell leases we had on the books on the balance sheet. Bob was a financial genius, so he knew right away what that meant. He said, "Steve, thank you for your honesty. You didn't have to show me this. We hired the investment bankers, so we must take responsibility for their ineptitude. Had you just stayed quiet, you could have sold off these leases and bought the company in cash and still had $50 to $60 million left over? I do not know if the Memorex team was sharp enough to see this, but we are going to keep these leases here at AT&T now. I want to thank you for your integrity on this. If you still want to make the deal without the leases, I will make it happen for you, but you're going to have to raise the cash quickly. I want this deal done fast." I said, "No, sir, it would take too long to raise the money, and I know you are on a tight timetable.

I headed back to Chicago the next day. I could not wait to tell Mary Ann what all had happened on my trip to New Jersey. The story was going to be complicated, so I wanted to take her through it in person. When I got home, and after all of the kisses and hugs from Mary Ann and the kids, I looked at Mary Ann and said, "Sweetheart, I have a lot to tell you about my trip to New Jersey. Please put your seat belt on!"

With that, she looked at me and said, "Stephen, don't tell me we are going to move again. We have barely been in this house a year. Why can't you keep a job anyway?"

I said, "It's not that really, just a whole lot of things happened this week. It is complicated, and I need to take you through it from the beginning. We have a lot of options in front of us, and we are not in a hurry. But I now know why AT&T was pushing so hard to get me on board. As it turns out, they are selling my division to Memorex. Yes, the same group that I ran. In the process of me reviewing the deal, I also made an offer for the division."

She said, "Wait a minute, you made an offer to buy your division from AT&T? My God, your signing bonus wasn't that big. Where did you think, you were going to get the money from?"

I said, "It's a bit complicated, but I was thinking of buying it from them with their own money. If it all worked out, and I am sure it would have, I would have had some $50 million left over after the deal was done."

Mary Ann's head was now spinning. She said, "Stephen, why can't you just go to work, come home, relax, and have dinner with the family-like normal people do? Do you do this stuff just to drive me nuts? You know all those Memorex guys; did you have any idea that they were in discussions with AT&T when Bob called you?"

I said, "Honestly, sweetheart, I didn't. I have been out of that side of the business for a while. I can see why they wanted this deal. If done correctly, it will make a lot of sense. But quite honestly, they don't have the cash to make it work, so I am not sure what will happen post-sale. I warned AT&T about their debt issues."

She said, "OK, mister smarty-pants, where does that leave you? More importantly, where does that leave all of us?"

I said, "There were a couple of options we need to look at. One, I could go with the business, which I am not inclined to do. Two, there is this thing called a chairman's list, which, if I stay, they will likely put me on. If we choose that option, it would mean that we would live in the Boston area for eighteen months. I would get a full salary while I attend the Sloan Institute at MIT. AT&T would lease out the house here like they are doing with our home in Pleasanton, and they would rent us a comparable home to this one in Boston for us. Once I complete my studies there, we would likely move to the Basking Ridge area of New Jersey. I would love to study at the Sloan Institute and get a shot at the Chairman's job at AT&T, but that would be more moving for the family."

She said, "Oh my God, Steve, you are giving me a headache. If we keep moving around the country like this, we will end up owning more houses than we have kids. I hope you are going to give me some options here. Why don't you call your buddies in California and find a job back there? We can move back to our home in Pleasanton. We loved it there. The girls are getting too old to be pulling them in and out of schools."

I said, "Sweetheart, that's why I said put your seat belt on. A lot of things happened this week. We have options, and we do not have to do anything right now. I owe it to AT&T to help them through the transition. That will give us enough time to weigh all our options. It will also give me some time to put some feelers out in California. The opportunity at AT&T is a big one, but it's not bigger than our family. Let's see what comes up over the next month or so."

About a month later, I got a call from my good friend Mike Haltom. Burroughs had merged with Sperry, and it formed a joint company called Unisys. Mike was still running the disk and tape drive group there and was proposing a buyout of that group. Unisys had decided to exit the design and manufacture of those products. They decided they were going to private label those devices from Fujitsu going forward. That meant that Unisys would still need Mike's organization to help support the installed base until that transition was complete. Mike's idea was to buy that unit out and sign a fifteen-year support agreement with Unisys. He would use that support agreement to raise capital to fund the buyout. I had all the respect in the world for Mike. He was smart both strategically and financially, so I knew he had thought this all out. I was not a huge fan of disk drive technology, but I was a significant fan of Mike. Mike wanted me to join the team as a founding member of what became Sequel, Inc.

After the conversation with Mike, I got with Mary Ann. I told her of the opportunity and the potential of moving back to Pleasanton. She was more than excited about the idea. She said, "Steve, I know you are intrigued by the opportunity that AT&T has put in front of you, and I must admit it's a big deal. However, you must put it all in context. Another couple of moves and then life on the East Coast does not feel right for the family. We know what we have in Pleasanton, and the family would be amazingly comfortable getting back to that. You need to take one for the team. You need to tell AT&T that your family comes first, and they want to move back to California. They may not be happy with that answer, but I am sure they will understand."

I said, "Sweetheart, that is why I love you. You know how to put everything in perspective and what is vital to the family. I will let AT&T know my decision and call Mike to let him know we are coming back to California.

When I informed AT&T of my decision, they could not have been more gracious. They agreed to move us back to California at their cost and gave me an exit package that included a nice bonus for my help with the Memorex transaction. It was a hard decision to make at the time, but it was the right one for the family. We moved back into our home in Pleasanton. I would never move Mary Ann or the family out of the area again.

Moving Back to California

As we pulled into the driveway of our home in Pleasanton, I could see the excitement in Mary Ann's eyes. She could not have been happier. She reached over to squeeze my hand and said, "Stephen, thank you for bringing the family back home. We still have a family to raise, and this is where I want to do it."

There to greet us in the driveway was the Reidy family. As I got out of the car, Mike Reidy grabbed my hand and said, "Manning, you are a nut case; you should have never left for Chicago. Glad to see you and the family back!"

Mary Ann and the girls hugged Kathie and the girls, all with tears of joy in their eyes. Mike then grabbed Ryan, and with a big hug, said, "Welcome home 'garbage man,' we can take a trip to the dumps tomorrow! Let's take Kyle with us."

When we got back into the house for the first time since moving, we could see the renters did not do a particularly excellent job of caring for our home. We had a lot of cleanups and repainting to do. That was alright, though, we were home, and everyone was happy. The girls quickly ran up to their rooms to lay claim to their previous bedrooms. Ryan and Kyle would be in bunk beds in the room next to ours. Everything got back to normal very quickly.

After a few weeks of being back in our home, Mary Ann came to me and said, "Stephen, I love being back here, but I miss the kitchen and dining area we had in Naperville. Why don't we look at expanding the back of the house? We just do not have enough room anymore. I never understood why the five-bedroom floor plan had the smallest kitchen and eating area."

I said, "I agree with you. That is the one thing I loved about our home in Naperville. Let's call an architect and have him give us some ideas to expand the house's back. It will give us more room in the kitchen and possibly a larger family room."

Mary Ann took on the project, and what started as a $70-thousand, six- to eight-week project turned into a seven-month $240-thousand full remodel. It was not Mary Ann's fault. The contractor had underbid the project, and as we got into it, we decided to add an additional family room to the kitchen side of the house. We also had to re-landscape the backyard after all the construction. Overall, it turned out wonderfully, but those seven-months were painful for Mary Ann. We were basically without a functioning kitchen most of the time. Mary Ann had to make most meals on two hot plates on the family room bar. Dishes were washed in the sink in the laundry room. Needless to say, none of us missed a meal, and Mary Ann made delicious meals throughout the remodeling.

With the kids reunited with their friends and back in school, family life was back to the dream Mary Ann, and I had always had. Our life of "Camelot" was progressing nicely. After all the remodeling was finished, Mary Ann flew her mom out to stay with us for a few months. Mary Ann wanted to test the idea of having her mother in California full time, but her mom wasn't ready to leave Chicago. The house would be crowded with her in California permanently.

After being back for a few years, a developer announced that they would build a new golf course community just east of town. They were going to call it Ruby Hill and would hire Jack Nicklaus to build the golf course. It would be a Signature Jack Nicklaus course, meaning he would put his full time into its design and construction. I was intrigued by the plan and one day stopped by the sales office in Pleasanton. In the office, they had a development model, the routing of the planned golf course, and brochures on the lots. The course was scheduled to open sometime in 1996. The plan was bold as there would be four hundred custom home sites. The home values were projected to be at or above the highest-priced home currently on Pleasanton's market. A few lots had sold, but there was still a number available in phase one and phase two.

I took all the brochures home and wanted to discuss the possibilities of building a new home on one of the one-acre lots that they were offering.

There were a limited number of one-acre lots, so I knew we would have to move quickly if we wanted one. I also knew that the boys would need their bedroom at some point, and if Midge moved out to California, we would also need a bedroom for her. It was clear that the five-bedroom home we bought almost ten years earlier was going to be too small for our family and Midge.

I caught Mary Ann by surprise when I got home and started talking to her about Ruby Hill. She had read a little bit about it in the local paper but paid little attention to it. She said, "Stephen, why are you looking at this? We just got through remodeling our home not that long ago. I like what we have done with it, and I do not think we need to move. This neighborhood is perfect for us and close to the schools, the sports park, Castlewood, and the shopping center. This Ruby Hill place is way on the east end of town. I will spend all my time driving the kids around and driving to the grocery store. I don't think this is that good of an idea, quite frankly."

I said, "Honey, I knew you were going to say that, but let us think about this. You know we need eventually to give the boys their own bedroom, and if we, as we have talked about, move your mother out here, we will not have enough bedrooms. There are no six-bedroom homes around here, so eventually, we will need to build something somewhere. At least Ruby Hill is still in Pleasanton and the kid's school district. If nothing else, we can buy the lot as an investment. We will be in early, and I am sure the prices will likely go higher before we have to make a decision."

She said, "Oh, Stephen, you make things so difficult sometimes. Please put it on the coffee table. I will look it over tomorrow while you are at work."

I knew Mary Ann did not like change, but I thought my logic was sound. If we did not move Midge here, we would still have enough bedrooms for all the kids to own. It would be tight if we had a family visit, but it would be manageable.

As always, Mary Ann needed time to process new information, especially if it affected the family. I decided not to push her and gave her time to think about all the options. After a couple of days, she said, "Let's take a drive out to Ruby Hill. I want to see the location and get a feel for how long a drive it is and what is around there."

Mary Ann was, of course, right; the property was a bit of a drive. It took us about twenty minutes to get to the location.

It was in an unincorporated part of Pleasanton at the time, so the roads were narrow. Once the development started to take off, they were going to widen the streets. The property was on a sloping hillside, and there was a lot of heavy equipment cutting into the hillside, making room for the golf course and lot sales. After seeing the property and experiencing the commute, she said, "Steve, if you want to buy the lot as an investment, then go ahead. Maybe after the girls start driving in a few years, we can think about building something out there, but there is just no way we can move out there until then. I would be spending my entire day driving the kids around, and I am not up for that."

With that, we picked out one of the one-acre lots, and we bought it. As it turned out, Sequel was doing quite well, so we had sufficient capital to make the purchase. As I had suspected, Mike had negotiated an excellent fifteen-year contract with Unisys, and we were winning a lot of new business.

The kids were growing up quickly. When we bought the lot in 1994, Kristie was fifteen, Karie thirteen, Ryan nine, and Kyle was seven. Ryan and Kyle were still able to share their room and even sleeping in bunk beds. Mary Ann still found time each day to always give them all her special one-on-one Mary Ann time. Sometimes it had to be in the car as she drove them to one of their sports practices, of which there were many. We wanted all our kids to be involved in sports and felt that would give them the best opportunity to socialize with the right group of kids. Kristie, Karie, and Ryan were excellent soccer players. Soccer in Pleasanton was extremely popular and extremely competitive. The traveling teams would play other premier teams all over Northern California, Southern California, and Phoenix. I thought all the travel was a bit much since there was plenty of competitive soccer right here in the Bay Area. On some tournament weekends, Kristie would be playing in one part of the state, and Karie and Ryan would be in another part. These were weekend tournaments with two games on Saturday, another on Sunday morning. Then if you won your games, there was a final game on Sunday afternoon.

Mary Ann would take one of the kids and Kyle with her, and I would take another one. Many were far enough away that one or both would require an overnight stay Saturday night. Soccer tournament weekends were, to put it mildly, hectic. All the other games were played either at the Pleasanton sports park or another local city, so no overnight travel was needed.

Any sport the kids got involved in, Mary Ann was right there with them. Even though neither of us ever played soccer, Mary Ann became a student of the game and was at every practice and game. To the kids' chagrin, she was always yelling instructions to them from the sidelines at every practice and game. I think by the end of practice or a game, Mary Ann was more worn out than her kids were from running up and down the sidelines. Over the years, this would repeat itself whether it was a swim meet or a soccer, football, tennis, or lacrosse game. Whether it was sports or scholastics, Mary Ann kept a remarkably close tab on how our kids were doing. Her life revolved around our children; she was indeed a *very loving mother*.

It was now 1996. Kristie was seventeen and had already started to drive. We bought Kristie a car but told her that she would have to share it with her sister as soon as our youngest daughter Karie turned sixteen. Kristie and her mom knew this would never happen, but they let me declare it if it made me feel better. They shared a car for a while, but I bought both new cars a few years later for Christmas as predicted. Karie was fifteen and had her learner's permit. Ryan and Kyle were now eleven and nine, respectively. Mary Ann had taken it upon herself to teach Karie how to drive. Mary Ann would take her to a parking lot and give her the wheel. The whole experience was a disaster. Mary Ann was still the backseat/front-seat driver I knew from our drive around Ireland. Karie herself could be a little emotional at times as well. On a predictable basis, they would both return from the experience, still yelling at each other. Kristie would shake her head after having gone through the same experience with Mary Ann when she was fifteen. Finally, Karie came to me and said, "Dad, I can't take this anymore. Can you please help me learn how to drive? I am going to have to take my driver's test pretty soon, and my sessions with mom are not getting me anywhere."

Kristie quickly chimed in. "Dad, that's not fair. You didn't bail me out when mom was teaching me how to drive!"

Mary Ann was not happy with the discussion but was more than happy to hand off the duties to me. Peace was soon restored to the Manning household, and I took over teaching Karie how to drive. To be fair to Mary Ann, she did restore herself to stardom when she taught Ryan and Kyle how to drive several years later. Over time, we learned that girls are easy when they are little, and boys are harder to raise when they are young. On or around the age of thirteen or fourteen, the roles tend to be reversed.

Around this time, we had to re-address the lot at Ruby Hill. They had a rule that we somehow overlooked when we bought the lot. The rule was that you had to start building on the lot sometime in the first two years of ownership. I got a call from the developer, who was now a good friend, and he said, "Steve, you know you have to start building on your lot soon. We haven't seen any plans from you yet. There is a lengthy process of plan approval, so why haven't you submitted any plans to us?"

I said, "Jim, I don't have the go-ahead from Mary Ann yet to build a house on the property. I am not sure if she ever intends to give me the go-ahead."

Jim said, "Steve, with all due respect, you have one of my premium lots, and I can't sit back and let that lot stay empty much longer. You and Mary Ann either need to start something or you'll have to turn the lot back in. And by the way, I have no intention of buying that lot back from you at what you paid for it, so keep that in mind." The good news was that Jim had done an excellent job at developing the property. Everything he put in was first class. Jack Nicklaus also did an outstanding job designing a world-class golf course on the property that our lot backed up to. We were members there, and I often played the course, and it was always in tip-top shape. The homes that were already built were quite stunning and different from one another since they were all custom homes. Also, to get approval for the development, Jim had to turn the four hundred acres surrounding the development into vineyards. So, the setting was entirely peaceful.

I was not looking forward to this conversation, but I had to sit down with Mary Ann and discuss. I did not want to take a loss on the lot we had bought, so I suggested to Mary Ann that we should at least build a house on the lot. I told her we could hire an architect and she could work with him to design the home of her dreams. If, after completion, she did not like it, we would sell it.

She agreed, so we started to interview various architects who had been building custom homes in the area. Many had already built or at least started homes in Ruby Hill. I told her since this was going to be mostly her design, she could pick out the architect she felt most comfortable with. There were a few things that I wanted her to incorporate in the design, like a wine cellar, room for a pool table, and room for a large-screen TV, but the rest would be up to her. She selected the architect, and we started having meetings with him. I could see from the beginning that he favored all of Mary Ann's ideas. I did get my wine cellar, and the only reason we had a pool table and an area for a big-screen TV was that Mary Ann knew that would attract kids to our home. As always, she wanted to make sure that our kids entertained their friends at our house, so everything in her design was geared towards that. Mary Ann also designed a considerable pool area and spa. She wanted the space big enough so that more than one of our children could entertain their friends at the same time. She had also designed a mother-in-law suite at one end of the house for her mom. It was private enough that Midge could feel like it was her very own apartment. She even had extra soundproofing put in around the room so the kids entertaining would not disrupt her. All the kids had their own bedroom in her design. Her design was stunning and very well thought out. Once the design was complete, I had a good friend that was a builder start the construction.

As the construction of our Ruby Hill home started to complete, we had to decide. Mary Ann was getting quite excited because she saw her design become a reality. She had already picked out everything: Flooring, wall coverings, appliances, and new furniture in case we decided to move in. She and her mom were both contemplating the idea of Midge moving in with us. It would be a good deal for Midge. She could sell her house and have enough money for retirement. It would let her supplement Ray's pension, which really took a hit when Allis-Chalmers went bankrupt. Midge always worried about running out of money after Ray passed.

About two months before construction finished, we took the family out to the house for a tour. Kristie could not join us because she was in college at UCLA, where she had entered their pre-med department. The kids loved the house and the pool and spa in the back yard. The second floor, where all but Kristie's bedroom was located, was pretty much dedicated to them. Besides the three bedrooms upstairs, there was an area for a pool table and a big-screen TV. Karie's room had her bathroom with a shower, and the boys would share the one in the hallway outside their two rooms. Ryan thought it was cool to have his own bedroom, but for a few years after we moved in, Kyle was scared to be in his room alone; many times, he slept in Ryan's room. The master bedroom and bath area were well designed. It had a sitting area off the master bedroom, plenty of closet space with his and her closets, and a steam/shower room.

As we walked through the house, Mary Ann kept going back to the mother-in-law room she had designed. I am sure she was pondering her mother's thoughts about moving in with us and how that would work. Mary Ann loved her mother and wanted her to enjoy her time after Ray's passing fully. She knew Midge would run out of money at some point, and she also knew if she moved out, she would have to take care of her. Midge did not drive, so Mary Ann knew she had another person she would have to chauffeur around town. Midges move out would be a big burden for Mary Ann. As she came out of the mother-in-law's bedroom, she walked over to me in the kitchen and said, "OK, Stephen, this house came out so well. If you let me move my mother out to live with us, I am OK with selling our current home and moving to this one. I think the kids and my mother are going to absolutely love it. By the time we move in, Karie will be driving, so maybe she can help me out with hauling the boys around." The decision was made, and we moved in about three months later.

As Mary Ann had hoped, our new house became a magnet for the kid's friends. It was big enough so the kids could all have friends over simultaneously, if necessary. One group might be outside playing around the pool and others playing pool upstairs or watching movies on the big-screen TV. Karie controlled what group hung out where when there were multiple groups in the house. She was the "house mom" for the upstairs entertainment area. As the kids were getting older, we wanted to make sure we knew who their friends were. If someone new would come to the house, the kids knew their first step would be introducing the new visitor to their mother. I am sure that all our kids warned all their friends that there would be a short interrogation when they met their mom for the first time. Mary Ann had good instincts about the kids our children hung out with. More than once, Mary Ann would strongly suggest to one of the kids that someone would not be invited back to the house. When that happened, I would often hear a response from them, "Mom, you're probably right. That kid is a little weird. I don't think I want to hang around with them anyway."

Mary Ann was also able to do some screening since it was a gated community and anybody entering who was not a resident had to be cleared by the front gate. When someone would pull up to the security, they would call the house to make sure we knew the person trying to get in. Mary Ann would always ask the security guard to gather all the people's names in the car, not just the driver.

Kristie was never able to spend much time at the house when she was going to school. While at UCLA, she took a lot of summer classes. After graduation, Kristie went to Washington, D.C., to perform some research at the National Institute of Health (NIH). After a year at NIH, she entered medical school at the University of Chicago. We enjoyed her when she was home, but those were always short visits between semesters.

Karie was still in high school when we moved in. Once she graduated, she went on to Arizona State University to study criminal justice. She came back between semesters, and for most summer months, she and her friends were able to enjoy the backyard, pool, and spa. When your children are older, you find out what went on in the house when you were not there. Although Mary Ann would make repeated instructions that there were no parties at the home when we were not there, those rules were not always adhered to. We found out later from the girls as they got older that the Manning household often became party central for Kristie, Karie, and their friends. They did an excellent job hiding the evidence of such, except for a few scratches and dents on my golf cart. Thankfully, there were no apparent damages to the walls, carpet, or hardwood flooring in the house. They knew that would be a red line for Mary Ann. She always kept the house spotlessly clean. The girls knew that there would be "hell to pay" if anything was damaged in the home she designed, decorated, and loved.

Ryan and Kyle were still young when we moved into Ruby Hill, just 11 and 9 at the time. They got the most out of the Ruby Hill house since they pretty much grew up there. We enjoyed meeting their friends and checking them out as well. They were also able to spend the most time with Midge after she moved in. Midge was fantastic with all the kids, and they all loved her. Midge developed an even deeper relationship with Kyle. They had a special bond, and Kyle was never afraid to give her a big hug every time he walked into the room. Midge loved it and would light up with a huge smile each time.

Not too long after we moved into our new home, my mother and father could come out to see us from their home in Sun City West, Arizona. My mother was still playing golf, and Mary Ann and I looked forward to playing with her at Ruby Hill, but my father was not doing well, so he no longer played. A few years earlier, he had a hip replacement surgery that did not go all that well. While still recovering from the anesthesia, Ray had forgotten where he was and got out of bed to use the restroom the night of the surgery. As he made his way to the bathroom, he tripped, and his new hip came out of the socket. It did some damage to the socket, and they could never get it properly back into the socket. While not able to play, he was able to ride in the golf cart with us. Mary Ann and my mother always got along great, and it was fun seeing them enjoying their days together on the course. It was sad, though, not being able to see my dad enjoy the game he taught me and that he loved so much. They stayed with us for a little over a week and then headed back to Sun City. After they got back home, my dad's health continued to deteriorate, and he was in and out of the hospital until he passed on Oct 27, 1999. He was a great husband, father, and grandfather to us all and is still missed by everyone that knew and loved him.

Ryan also was learning to love the game and took advantage of living on a golf course. He spent many hours practicing on the driving range and the chipping and putting practice area. He got his early training while still at Castlewood, where they had an excellent junior golf program. Ryan also enjoyed caddying for me at Ruby Hill, and that experience helped increase his understanding and appreciation for the game. Ryan soon became an excellent golfer and played on his high school golf team, which also used Ruby Hill as their home course. I tried desperately to get Kyle excited about the game of golf but to no avail. Kyle never felt comfortable competing in a sport against Ryan. Possibly if I had gotten Kyle started with the game before Ryan excelled, it might have worked out.

Although tennis was Mary Ann's game of choice, she also picked up the game after moving into Ruby Hill. Indeed, after the kids had gotten older and more self-sufficient, she started at a nine-hole course in town with some of her girlfriends where she had a hole in one! She was so excited about that and could not wait to show me her scorecard when I got home from work that day. After she became comfortable with the game, she started having her friends join her for rounds at Ruby Hill.

We also started enjoying playing golf together on weekend afternoons. The most fun we had was playing with my two sisters, Michele and Stephanie, and my brother-in-law Dave while on vacation with them in Mexico. Mary Ann and my sisters did not take the game that seriously, and they had a ball playing with each other on those vacations. Dave and I would watch with joy seeing the three of them chasing their ball down the fairway, not always in a straight line. They had a favorite caddie they would always ask for who would take care of the three of them. He was a talented player in his own right and encouraged all three of them after every shot. He had the patience of a father as he would look after them through every round. I know he enjoyed it, as he would light up every time; he joined us on the first tee. Dave and I would always make sure he got a good tip for his efforts.

Kyle was very technology savvy. He pretty much taught Mary Ann how to use the computer and take advantage of an innovative technology that was hitting the internet called "Google Search." Mary Ann was fascinated with

Google and the internet in general. Over time, this also became an effective way for her to keep an eye on our kids. Mary Ann used AOL as her email provider and signed all the kids up with their own AOL accounts. Of course, she also made sure she had everyone's passwords as well. The kids at the time were OK with that knowing that their mother could read every word sent or received by them. Mary Ann also had a link to all their bank accounts and a credit card we gave each of them. We wanted them to have a credit card, so there was no excuse for not calling a cab if either they or someone they were driving with had too much to drink. Neither one of us was naive enough to think that this was not happening, and we wanted to make sure our kids always got home safely. It did not stop us from continually lecturing them about the evils of under-age drinking, but we knew it was happening in high schools across the country. The Pleasanton police would also campaign against it every chance they got. On occasion, they would park the mangled remains of a car in a parking lot involved in a drunken-driving accident for teenagers to see. We made sure our kids visited that site at least once in their early years of driving. The image was quite impactful for them. If they ever came home in a cab, Mary Ann would take them to pick up their car sometime the next day. No questions were asked unless it became a frequent occurrence. If it did, driving privileges would be restricted.

When the kids went off to college, Mary Ann also used the internet to enroll in classes. She also kept access to their student portal account. She would help them enroll in courses, and she also researched which teachers were best and were always fully aware of what classes need to be taken in their major to ensure prompt graduation. She would study the curriculum at each college the kids attended. She was excellent at helping the kids get into the right class each semester. She was the reason our kids completed their degrees in four years or less. Many schools were even telling parents to expect their kids to spend four-and-a-half to five years to graduate. Her diligence with this saved us a lot of money for tuition and room and board for all four kids. With her access to the student portals, she could also check grades, test results, and test schedules. She knew all four of our kids had a chance to do something she could never do. She wanted to make sure their college experience was a successful one.

With the help of their *loving mother,* Kristie would graduate from UCLA in pre-med and then go on to her medical degree from the University of Chicago. Karie would graduate from Arizona State University with a degree in Criminal Justice and later get her master's in teaching. Ryan earned his Bachelor's in Business from San Diego State University. Kyle went on to get his Bachelor's in Computer Science, also from Arizona State University. Eventually, to our satisfaction, they all moved back to the Bay Area after graduation. Mary Ann and I could not have been happier.

\

EMPTY NEST

*M*ary Ann loved having the kids around, but as they got older and went off to college, she found her days a little emptier. Unfortunately, they all ended up going to college outside the Bay Area, either in Southern California or Tempe, Arizona. She stayed in constant contact with them either through e-mail or by phone. And was always anxious for holidays or semester breaks to have them all home with her. The kids never disappointed her. They would always make their way home for all holidays, semester breaks, and the summer if they weren't taking classes. Mary Ann also had her hands full taking care of her mother, who was getting older and increasingly in need of more care. Not wanting to leave Midge alone too much, she took Midge everywhere she went except for her time playing golf or tennis with her lady friends.

After my father died, my mother would still visit us for some holidays and occasional summer visits to escape Arizona's summer heat. As I had mentioned earlier, my mother and Mary Ann were close and loved each other's company. My mother enjoyed good health for most of her life, but she fell ill in the fall of 2005 and was admitted to the local hospital. The health facilities at Sun City West were excellent. That being a retirement community they were used to dealing with the health issues of the elderly. Upon hearing that she was admitted to the hospital, my brother called to let us know what had happened. My brother and younger sister Kim both lived close by in Phoenix and went at once to the hospital. My other two sisters and I all flew down to Phoenix the next day. A week after being admitted to the hospital, the medical staff thought they had resolved her medical issues and released her to in-home care. We all stayed with her for four or five days, and with her doctor's belief that she was once again in good health, we all returned home. Not long after we returned home, we all got a call from my brother letting us know that she had been re-admitted to the hospital. Her condition was getting worse, and she likely had some form of pneumonia. We again made our way back to Sun City West to see her. Now more worried that whatever she was experiencing was more severe than what the doctors had suggested. Her blood levels were low and not responding to the medicine she was getting, and her breathing became exceedingly difficult. We could not believe what was happening to our *Loving Mother* and why the hospital could not help her recover. After about a week, the doctors gathered us to let us know that they had done everything they could for our mother. They then suggested that she needed to go into hospice care. They indicated that she only had forty-eight to seventy-two hours left to be with us on this earth. They strongly advised that we spend as much time as possible with her during that time. As it turned out, she lasted almost the entire week and quietly left us on October 8, 2005. Devastated and heartbroken, we all returned home and made plans for her services ten days later. I returned with Mary Ann and the kids for her services to celebrate our Loving Mother/grandmother's remarkable life.

Mary Ann became more concerned about her own mother's health after the passing of my mother. She made sure Midge was doing everything possible to maintain her health and stay on schedule with her doctor appointments. Not too long after returning from my mother's funeral Mary Ann and Midge was in church one Sunday. At the end of mass, the priest asked the parishioners for some aid in transporting some of the sick and aging to church on Sundays. They both saw this as a worthy cause and signed up immediately after mass. They were put on a call list, and generally, the church offices would contact them on Fridays to let them know if anyone needed aid getting to mass on the following Sunday. It did not happen every week, but they often got to know several parishioners that they had not previously known. One of those parishioners was an elderly lady named Ida. Ida didn't live too far from the church but far enough away that walking to and from Church was not going to work for her, and she was no longer able to drive. After several weeks of taking Ida to and from church, Mary Ann and Midge became quite attached to Ida. Ida lived alone, and her only family was a son that lived far away. Mary Ann could sense her loneliness and worried about how Ida was getting to and from the grocery store or her medical appointments. Midge also became close to Ida and felt sorry for her since she was without immediate family nearby. Midge did not drive either and often thought about how lucky she was to have family close by and a home full of people that loved her. Ida was a warm and loving person, and Mary Ann and Midge pretty much adopted her. After one of their Sunday trips to church, Mary Ann had helped Ida walk up to her house. After getting her settled, she noticed that she had extraordinarily little food in the house. Mary Ann was already concerned about Ida not being able to get to the grocery store regularly. After seeing that, Mary Ann and Midge decided to take her to brunch after mass. They would then go to the grocery store to have fresh food in the house every week. Mary Ann also kept a schedule of any appointments. If Ida needed a ride to the appointments, she would always be there to take her back and forth. Ida's son was incredibly grateful to Mary Ann and Midge for looking after his mother and staying in contact with Mary Ann to check how his mother was doing. It was just an instinct for Mary Ann to want to look after someone like Ida, and now with the kids away in school, she had the time to do just that. Ida eventually moved in with her son, but Mary Ann and Midge continued helping the sick and aged to church most Sunday mornings.

With the kids out of the house, I decided it would be appropriate to take Mary Ann on a cruise. My brother and his wife and two other couples had booked a genuinely lovely cruise to the Mediterranean that I thought Mary Ann would enjoy. We had vacationed with those same couples a few years earlier in Hawaii and enjoyed it thoroughly, so I knew Mary Ann would be comfortable with the idea. The cruise started in Athens. It had many ports of calls throughout the Mediterranean and eventually completing the cruise in Monte Carlo. After Mary Ann reviewed the itinerary, she embraced the idea right away. I was happy for her; she missed so many travel opportunities when the kids were younger. I knew this would be a special time for both of us. We decided to arrive in Athens a few days ahead of the departure date for the cruise and take advantage of Athens' sites. After disembarking from the ship in Monte Carlo, we spent a few days with my brother and Doreen and took a train with them to Venice for three days. The trip turned out to be our best trip ever together. The scenery was fantastic, the history around Athens, Turkey, and Italy were amazing, and the food and wine were over the top. During the cruise, we visited Rome for a special day and Mary Ann's first visit to the Vatican.

Shortly after returning home from the cruise, I learned that the company I was working for was going to be acquired to one of our competitors. As part of the transaction, all senior-level executives would have all their options vested, and if they stayed on to help through the transition, they would receive an additional bonus. It was a good deal for me, and it offered a chance to take some time off, maybe even retire. After the deal closed, I stayed on for an additional six months and then started spending more time with Mary Ann playing golf and cooking. Loving all the food we had enjoyed while on the Mediterranean cruise, we started trying to replicate some of the recipes. She was already a huge fan of Italian food, and I liked trying to make some of the various sauces we had with our meals. We even bought some seeds for Italian tomatoes while there, which we planted and harvested in our garden. It was a special time together, which was made even better when one or all the kids were home.

As mentioned earlier, Midge's health was failing, and it was becoming more difficult for Mary Ann to take care of her. We arranged for her to enter an excellent nursing home close to our home in Pleasanton. It was close enough for Mary Ann to make almost daily visits. The home was full of women Midge's age that she spent time playing cards or watching movies together. Mary Ann would often pick Midge up for breakfast or lunch with a group of lady friends which all referred to themselves as 'The Coffee Ladies.' They were all nice enough to let me join them occasionally. These ladies also became an important support structure in helping me care for Mary Ann after she started her chemotherapy sessions. They were all close friends of Mary Ann's, and she loved them all.

Mary Ann and her sister Peggy would also spend time together, ensuring they spent time with Midge. Midge would always be with us for our Sunday night family dinners and still helped Mary Ann prepare the dinners. Many of the recipes were original recipes from Midge, so she was always a tremendous help. We kept Midge's room before she went into the nursing home, so she would often spend the night with us after the Sunday dinners. While Midge's health and mental state continued to deteriorate, she was dealt another blow when she learned of her younger brother Tom's dying on Dec 20, 2009. Tom was a loving father, brother, uncle to the family and helped keep an eye on Midge after Ray's passing, and his sudden death was a shock to us all. Mary Ann was a huge fan of Uncle Tom and knew how much he helped her mother after Ray had passed. We all had an exceedingly difficult Christmas that year.

Losing Kyle

*W*ith all the kids back either in the Bay Area or Sacramento, gradu-ated and with jobs in their chosen profession, Mary Ann could not have been happier. Our traditional Sunday dinners were getting more prominent as the children would often bring their significant others along most Sundays. Kristie was living and practicing medicine in San Francisco. Karie had started teaching at a brand-new high school in San Ramon and was dating another teacher there named Tom Chamberlain. Ryan worked in finance in the Bay Area and dated Katelyn Schlick, who he had met while at San Diego State. Kyle worked in Sacramento in software design and imple-mentation but spent most weekends at our home in Ruby Hill. He was dating a beautiful young lady named Allison, who he had met while interning in the summer in Orange County. They had both interned in the IT department for a company down there.

While I loved being home with Mary Ann and the kids, I quickly found that I was not mentally ready for retirement. I started working on projects with some private equity firms. These projects were all with privately held technology companies, either dealing with the emergence of cloud computing or struggling to achieve their business plans. In 2009 I started traveling to Michigan. I helped a mobile electronic recycling and repair company that their private equity investors were concerned about. As I would soon find out, the company was quickly running out of cash, and their bank soon put them in default on their line of credit. The company was not professionally managed and was headed into what would be its second bankruptcy. After reviewing the operation, I told the investors that the company had some potential if

managed correctly. However, to make it work, the company would need a cash infusion to support its liquidity and restructuring. The current investors, along with a new investor and me, raised another round of financing for the company and got a new bank loan. I stayed on to help them sort out and drive the restructuring that needed to happen. Unfortunately, it began with a substantial reduction in headcount until new financing was secured.

As I started traveling back and forth from the Bay Area to Michigan, I started to miss my time at home with Mary Ann and the kids. I would go back there for a week and then return for a week to be with the family. The company had arranged for a townhouse for me to stay in while I was back there. We had no plans to move there permanently since I believed this to be a twelve- to the eighteen-month assignment. Mary Ann did not love it while I was gone, but she loved the benefit of having the kids around, and she and her mom kept busy with them always. Her sister Peggy would also stop by often to check in on Mary Ann and her mom.

On Sunday, June 6, 2010, I got a call from Mary Ann. I had just finished a golf game with our new CFO and was pulling out of the parking lot heading to my townhouse. Mary Ann was clearly upset about something, and with a shaken voice, said, "Stephen, Kyle is dead!"

I said, "Calm down, sweetheart, I am sure it's not that bad. What did Kyle do?" I thought she was just upset about something he did and used that expression.

She said, "No, Stephen, your son Kyle is dead. We found him this morning, and he was not breathing!"

My heart just dropped, and I started having a difficult time breathing. I could not comprehend what I was hearing. I said, "Sweetheart, please tell me what exactly happened. I cannot believe Kyle is dead. Who is there with you right now?"

She said, "The police are here, and the coroner is on the way. Midge, Allison, Ryan, and Karie are here, and Kristie is on her way home. Steve, I can't believe this is happening; you need to get home right away."

With that, the policeman who was first on the scene got on the phone. He said, "Mr. Manning, what is your location?"

A little surprised by the question, I said, "I am in Michigan. Why are you asking?"

He said, "Mr. Manning, I am sorry for your loss, but we need to know the whereabouts of anyone close to your son Kyle over the last twenty-four hours. We are starting an investigation into his death."

Those words were so hard to hear, *an investigation into your son's death.* The fact that Kyle was dead was starting to sink in, and I hated it. It was a phone call no parent ever wants to get.

I quickly had to pull to the side of the road and try to process what I had just heard. I sat numbly in my seat before I just started crying out of control. With that, a picture of my last time with Kyle entered my head. It was clear as day. Just a week earlier, he had hugged me and told me he loved me as I left for the airport. It was surreal, almost like he was reaching down from heaven telling me goodbye for the last time. As it turned out, after I had left that day, he was outside playing football with his buddies. As he was running to catch a pass, he had tripped and fractured his ankle. When he told me he thought it was broken, I told him to have his mother take him in to get an x-ray. I told him if it is broken, they will likely put a cast on it, but I told him, "Don't let them give you any pain pills. You won't need them, and they are just too dangerous. You can handle the pain with Advil and by keeping your weight off it."

In his incredible, sweet voice, he said, "OK, Daddy-O, no pain medicine, love you."

That would be the last time I would ever talk to my son.

All I could think about now was how was I going to get back to Pleasanton. I knew Mary Ann needed me home to help her with the family and get through this awful tragedy. I also knew all the direct flights back to the Bay Area had either taken off or were about to. In my grief, I was having a challenging time driving back to my townhouse. Worse, I was in an area of Detroit that I was not familiar. I turned on my GPS and started driving home. It was awful because I was unable to process the instructions my GPS was giving me. If it said turn left, I would turn right. I was missing turns and ended up in a not-too-desirable part of Detroit. More worried that I would not get to the airport in time to catch even a connecting flight to the Bay Area, I pulled into a bank parking lot for safety. It was Sunday, and I knew the bank was not open, but it looked safe.

I needed time to gather my thoughts and call to see what flights were available for my return. Not knowing all the fight schedules for all the airlines, I decided to call American Express. I had a platinum card that I always used for travel, so I knew the concierge service would help me sort this all out. As the lady got on the line, I started crying again and told her my dilemma and needed to get home as soon as possible. She said, "Mr. Manning, I am sure I can help you. The airlines are used to this emergency type and even offer special rates for these types of last-minute bookings. I assume you can land at any airport in the Bay Area, so let me see what the quickest route back for you is. Unfortunately, the last direct flight is about to take off, so I will need to put you a connecting flight."

It was brilliant how she handled this situation. She booked me on the most practical connection she could find using two different airlines. The flight took me to Denver and then into Oakland. With the three-hour time change between Detroit and the Bay Area, I would be able to get in by 5:30 that night. But I needed to get to the Detroit airport in time to make the first connection. I then called my limo service and asked them to send a driver to my townhouse to get to the airport.

I had little time to get home, pack and get to the airport. I could not afford to get lost anymore, and I need to stay focused and follow my GPS instructions. When I finally got to an area that I was familiar with, I called my brother Mike to let him know what happened. It was hard to speak the words, but I had to let him know what had happened to Kyle. I then asked him to inform the rest of the family. We had already lost my father and mother, so I knew Kyle was already in heaven with them, but my sisters needed to know. When I finally got to the townhouse, I quickly packed my bag and got into the limo and called Mary Ann. I wanted to let her know what time I was arriving and at what airport. She said that the police were still at the house and the coroner had arrived. All the kids were now at home, along with Midge, Mary Ann's sister Peggy, Allison, Mike, and Kathie Reidy.

I knew with that much support around her, and Mary Ann would be better able to process the horrible news of Kyle's passing.

I also knew she would be blaming herself for the tragedy, which I assured her was not the case. I knew it was vital that she did not think I was going to blame her in any way for what happened to Kyle. If she even thought that for a moment, her life would have been destroyed. She was still very emotional and was having a tough time talking between her tears of sorrow.

I asked her if she had gotten any more information on how Kyle passed. She said, "Stephen, we still don't know exactly. The police have interviewed everyone who was around Kyle over the last twenty-four hours. They seem to have developed a working theory. Kyle, Allison, and their friends spent most of the day yesterday in the backyard and around the pool. They were drinking some beers, throwing the football around, and barbequing dinner on the grill. Sometime around noon, a friend of his who I did not like having around the house gave him one of his pain pills. I guess Kyle was complaining about his ankle hurting and that the Advil was not helping. It turns out this kid had become addicted to pain pills, and his doctor was prescribing increasingly stronger doses to him. Later that evening, the kid gave Kyle another pain pill. The police have questioned the kid and have taken away the pain pills he had given Kyle for evidence. Kristie asked the officer what the pain medicine was and how strong the dosage he gave Kyle was. It turns out that the dosage he gave Kyle was *eight times* more potent than the standard prescription he would have gotten from his doctor. She is sure the autopsy will show that Kyle died from that drug. His body just couldn't take such a high first dosage, and it caused him to die in his sleep. Thankfully, it was likely a painless death, but a death all the same." She then burst into tears and handed the phone to Kristie.

Kristie reconfirmed what she knew of the events and said, "Dad, you need to get home right away. Mom and Midge are having a challenging time dealing with all of this. Karie and I are trying to stay calm and care for mom. Ryan has not left Kyle's side since he got home. The police and coroner made us all come downstairs because it was a crime scene, but Ryan won't leave the bottom of the stairs. Dad, we all need you here."

I let her know my flight details and that I would be landing in Oakland. I said, "Kristie, you and Karie need to keep an eye on your mom until I get home. Please don't let her alone for a minute or think that any of this was her fault. She needs you guys now more than ever. And please tell her that I love her."

She said, "Ok, daddy, I just can't believe this has all happened. Safe travels home, and oh, by the way, Mike Reidy will pick you up at the airport when you land."

I got to the airport in time to make my flight to Denver. When I checked in, they told me that they had changed my seating, gave me a seat in the back of the first class, and blocked the seat next to me. I am sure American Express had told them what had happened and thought it best that I had my time alone. Everyone was terrific to me, and I certainly needed my time alone. As we took off and started the journey to Denver, all I could do was look out the window. With my eyes towards heaven, I began to think about how a life without Kyle would be. He had such a warm smile and a great personality, always there to help others, and a growing and loving relationship with Allison. Allison was great for Kyle, and I was looking forward to seeing them someday married and starting a family. I then started feeling guilty about telling him not to accept pain medicine for his ankle. I knew doctors were over-prescribing pain medicine to their patients. At least had they done so, it would have been at a much lower dosage than what that kid gave him. The thought about what "could have been" for Kyle was driving me crazy, and I was becoming quite restless. I knew the flight crew was keeping a close eye on me. They knew I was distraught and wanted to make sure I did not do something stupid.

I decided I needed to start making some notes about Kyle and our life with him. I knew that I would have an opportunity to speak about Kyle at the wake and funeral, and I wanted to make sure I had all the correct words for him. When I got out of my seat to get my laptop from the overhead compartment, the flight attendant at once came over to me. She said, "Mr. Manning, what is wrong? What do you need? Please, sit back down. I will get you whatever you need."

I said, "Thank you, you all have been accommodating. I just need my laptop so that I can write down some words about my son, Kyle. You were all kind enough to give me a seat alone, and I want to take advantage of this time." With that, I started my "letter to Kyle." I could not complete it for a few days, but when I finished it, I emailed it to him at the AOL email account his mother had set up for him years earlier.

Dear Kyle Raymond,

I write this letter with great sadness. It is Thursday, your mother's birthday, the day before your wake on Friday, and your funeral mass on Saturday. I have been spending the week trying to digest how something so terrible and so meaningless could have happened to you. You were so much coming into your own with your life. Your job was becoming just what you wanted. Your relationship with Allison was so much going in the right direction, and our relationship was continuing to get stronger. In a lot of ways, we were very much alike, and by the way, I think that is a good thing.

I know you wanted a big family because you were so comfortable with life in this family. I so much wanted that for you. In recent years as I got to know you better and we had time to talk about the future, I started to see you becoming the family rock. One that, over the years, would always make sure the family stayed connected. You, like I, were becoming the Uncle Tom for your generation of the family.

I remember after I retired, you helped me digitally copy all the family videos. It was such a precious time as you and I could re-live the times together as you were growing up. Family gatherings, your birthday, and others, and of course, Christmas mornings. I think that you could see that we had a closer relationship when you were younger than you remembered. And it really wasn't all about Ryan when you were little. I should have done more with you, and I always regretted that. That is why I so much looked forward to being with you as you got older and promised that I would be your kid's greatest grandfather. That will not happen for us now.

You had so much in front of you, and I think even you started to believe that. I know that someday I would have had the great pleasure of walking into a movie theater and viewing one if not more of your screenplays you would have written. You were so creative. You started a project of writing that I told your mother years ago that I wanted to do. You really could have had it all.

You are in heaven now with some very special people. Two grandfathers, a loving grandmother, and some special uncles and aunts, some of whom you are meeting for the first time. You had a great sense of family, and now you can research it all firsthand. You are going to be able to build the family tree in person and understand our family roots. Please keep the family safe from above, and allow me to talk to you through the stars above and in my thoughts and my words. I love you!
Dad

I changed planes in Denver, and my connecting airline afforded me the same courtesy as the one out of Detroit and gave me an isolated seat in first class. After drafting my letter to Kyle, I started to put some words together for his wake and funeral mass. There would be no alone time when I got home, so I wanted to get a jump on getting my thoughts together. As I was writing, I started thinking about what I would say to Mary Ann and the family when I got home. I knew they were all grieving deeply, and I knew I would have to be strong for them. When we landed, I went outside to look for Mike. He was already at the curbside, and I walked quickly over to his car.

He gave me a big hug and said, "Steve, I am not going to pretend that I know what you are going through. Kyle's death was horrible news, and I just can't believe something like this has happened. How are you holding up? We have been at the house for most of the day. The police and coroner left a couple of hours ago."

I got in the car and told him, "Mike, this is all like a nightmare. I would just like to wake up and find out it has all been a bad dream, but I know that is not true. Please tell me how Mary Ann is holding up." He said, "Steve, I have to tell you she is taking it hard. She had been in her room for a good part of the day. Kristie, Karie, and Kathie have tried to console her, but they are having a tough time of it as well. Ryan stayed inside the entire time until they took Kyle's body away. Steve, it's just a big mess. It would help if you let Kathie and I know what we can do for you and the family. Anything, anything at all, just ask." Mike and Kathie were great friends, and it was good to get the update on everything before I entered the house.

We pulled in the driveway and up to the front door. Mike said, "Get in there with your family. I will park the car and bring in your luggage. They really need you."

As I opened the door, I could see everyone gathered in the family room. I walked through the kitchen and saw Mary Ann together with the kids. The look on her face just broke my heart. I put out my arms and gave her a big loving hug, told her that I loved her, and held her tight to me. As we were both crying in each other's arms, I said to her, "This is nobody's fault. Kyle didn't know what that kid was giving him, and no one here is to blame. Kyle would turn over in his grave if anyone thought they were to blame. This is a great loss for us all; let's not add to it by trying to assign blame to anyone."

With those words, the kids all came up, and we all started hugging each other. Our lives changed forever that day, just four days before Mary Ann's fifty-seventh birthday, a day she always wanted to be special, and a day we would never celebrate in any meaningful way again. She grieved heavily for Kyle until she passed. June would become an extremely uncomfortable month for her and all the family.

We quickly had to get ready for his celebration of life. I had told Kristie when I talked to her from Detroit to immediately contact the parish office to let them know we have had a death in the family. They would know exactly what to do. They notified the funeral home in town and arranged for us to meet with the people who ran the Catholic cemetery. Our pastor, Father Green, was an excellent grief counselor, and he arranged for a meeting at the parish office with him the next day. They said he wanted the entire family at the meeting if possible. The thought about going to meet with Father Green did not sit well with the family. Mary Ann and the kids were not feeling too strongly towards God at that moment after Kyle's passing. All felt strongly that God had betrayed them by taking Kyle early that morning. That night, after all the friends who had stopped by to console us and to keep an eye on Mary Ann had left, I gathered the family. Along with Midge's help, I told them that it was unfair for them to blame God for what happened to Kyle. Clearly, the loss of Kyle was a tragedy, but it was not a reason to turn away from God and the Church. We also had little time to waste planning for Kyle's funeral, and they needed to join their mother and I to meet with Father Green the next day. They all agreed to attend the meeting with Father Green. The night was getting late, and I suggested that we all go to bed and get some sleep. We would have many long and sad days ahead of us, and we would need whatever sleep we could get.

Mary Ann was still very emotional and trying to hold back her tears. As I walked Mary Ann down the hall to our room with my arm around her, she turned to me and said, "Steve, I am not sure I want to live anymore."

Her words shocked and scared me. I said to her, "Mary Ann, please don't say that. I know it's been a shock to your system, and the loss of Kyle could not be more tragic, but we still have three fine children who need you. We must be there for them; they need us both to be strong for them. I know you are exhausted and depressed. Please try and get some sleep tonight. We have a lot to do over the next couple of days to honor Kyle's life."

Mary Ann was restless all night, likely reliving her time with Kyle. I laid there in bed thinking; how can this beautiful, *loving mother* get past the loss of her youngest son. I felt helpless, and I was also grieving over the loss of Kyle.

The next morning the family slowly got up from what was indeed a restless night of sleep. As I made coffee and started to get some things for breakfast together, Mary Ann began making notes. She was thinking of all the things we would have to do in preparation for Kyle's funeral. She knew we had to pick the day for the funeral and no funerals on Sunday. And Thursday was her birthday, so that was out. We decided to have the wake on Friday and the funeral mass on Saturday. That would also give the family members living out of town time to get to Pleasanton for at least the funeral mass.

After breakfast, we headed to the parish offices to meet with Father Green as a family. As we all gathered around the conference table, Father Green turned to Mary Ann and me and said, "So please tell me how the family is holding up?"

Mary Ann sat silent, so I spoke up. "Father Green, this is day two of the worst day of our lives. We are all grieving very deeply, and quite frankly, many here today think that God has abandoned us. No one can understand why He took Kyle from us yesterday morning."

Father Green said, "Please understand that those types of feelings are not rare when such a tragedy occurs. Please let me assure you, God did not take Kyle from you. Hopefully, the Lord received Kyle into his arms after his passing. And he is there in heaven right now looking down on all of us. Please, if you don't mind, let me speak to each one of you about Kyle's passing."

With that one-by-one, he tried grief counseling each one of us. He, of course, started with Mary Ann. He then went around the table asking everyone what their relationship with Kyle was. From his grief counseling experience, he knew every individual would have a different impression of what had happened. Often in that session, he had to defend God and handled it in a very spiritual way. Father Green probably had this type of session multiple times a week, and he was particularly good at it. We left that session in a much better frame of mind than we had entered. Not all were yet ready to forgive God for what happened to Kyle, but their heads were not hanging as low as they were when we entered the parish offices.

As we got back home, I could see that Mary Ann was still not herself. She excused herself and said she needed to be alone, and went back to the sitting room in our bedroom. I gave her about an hour to be alone and then went back to see her. Mary Ann was just sitting on the couch staring at the ceiling when I walked into the room, clearly still trying to process the loss of our youngest son.

I said to her, "Sweetheart, I am so deeply sorry for how you are feeling. I know the loss of Kyle has been exceptionally hard for you. You are a wonderful *loving mother,* and you did everything right in raising Kyle. He is gone now, and we really must spend some time quickly completing the plans for the celebration of his life. I want your input on all of this. Can you please join us in the family room so we can discuss all the planning? It's not healthy for you to sit here alone; please come be with the family."

She said, "Stephen, I am so sorry I am having such a tough time with this. I just still can't believe that Kyle is gone. I sit here and still hear his voice playing in the backyard with his friends, still hoping he will walk in from outside. Steve, please tell me that Kyle is in heaven."

I said, "Trust me, Mary Ann, our son is in heaven right now. Kyle was a very caring and loving person. I am sure he is sitting there with your dad, my dad, and my mom looking down on us right now. He knows he broke your heart, and he is so sorry for it. Kyle cherished you and Midge and would never have knowingly done anything to hurt you or Midge. Kyle will always be missed by us all, but let's, please focus on his life. We need the next few days to be about who Kyle was and what a wonderful person he grew up to be." With that, she got up from the couch, hugged me, and we went back into the family room together.

Karie had a lovely friend, Amy Harbottle, who was particularly good at putting videos together. She had come over to comfort Karie and the family and was already busy gathering all the pictures and videos we had of Kyle. She also asked the kids what Kyle's favorite songs were so she could put his montage together with those songs. The spirit of celebrating Kyle's life was already starting to come together, and thankfully Mary Ann was already beginning to engage in that. As Amy was playing the videos on the TV, many of which Kyle and I had copied earlier, Mary Ann was pointing out the ones that she wanted to be included. Of course, Mary Ann had Kyle's iTunes password, so the kids started selecting his favorite songs to be included. Amy did a perfect job on that video, which we played at his wake, and we handed out copies to all the family and his friends. I still play it today when I want to see and hear our Kyle. A friend of Kyle's, Kyle Freitas, also put together a disk of many other songs Kyle liked and distributed those to family and friends. It took a little getting used to listening to the songs since the first track recorded Kyle's voice mail message. "You have reached the phone of Kyle Manning, please leave a message."

Tuesday night, Kyle's friends organized a candlelight vigil in the Grotto behind St. Augustine. It was meant for the friends of Kyle, so we were not invited, but our kids were. All were amazed by how many showed up, with almost a hundred people in attendance. Some of them spoke at the vigil with great praise for Kyle's friendship and loving nature. Prayers were made, and some of his favorite songs were played. Not knowing it was only for young adults, some of our friends were in attendance with their kids. Many of the adults in attendance spoke with admiration and surprise at how many people were in attendance. They said with a heart of love, "Your son was so well thought of. The attendance at the vigil was amazing, and the words spoken about Kyle would have made your hearts warm." While our hearts were broken, those actions and words helped our healing process immensely.

The next day as the kids talked about the vigil, we started to focus more on who Kyle was and the life we had with him. I asked everyone to tell their favorite story about Kyle. Pretty soon, funny stories started to be spoken about Kyle. They were all loving stories, but funny, nonetheless. That put a lighter note in the house for the first time since Kyle's passing. I could quickly see it was putting Mary Ann in a better mood. While her heart was still bleeding from his loss, she started to focus more on who he was and how much we all loved being around him. It wasn't long before she began to add some of her own stories. Kyle was our youngest, and Mary Ann was naturally protective of him. They had such a close relationship that she knew every-thing about his insecurities and ambitions. As Mary Ann told her stories about Kyle she would be laughing and crying at the same time. It was so good to see Mary Ann coming out of her deep depression, but I knew it was a fragile recovery.

Mary Ann never recovered from Kyle's loss, but she was able to start focusing on his life. Much of that played out in the speeches that were made at his viewing and the following day at his funeral and burial. Family and friends from all over came to the celebrations, and the attendance at both was overwhelming. The funeral home where we held the viewing had to open an added section for the overflow crowd on Friday night. We also had to move the funeral mass to the main chapel to accommodate the overflow atten-dance on Saturday. I am sure Kyle would have been shocked to see so many of his friends attending the two events. Kyle was still a little shy and did not always appreciate how much he was loved by so many of his schoolmates.

His remarkably close friend, Pete Georgatos, had some great words to say about Kyle both at the vigil and the night of his viewing. Kyle and Pete were like brothers, and both traveled to Europe together after graduation.

Mary Ann did not enjoy public speaking, so she asked me to say our last words to him at the funeral mass, but she edited them very closely. This was our youngest son, and she wanted to make sure we said goodbye to him with all our love. I had written the words and reviewed them with her many times. They were heartfelt and intense for our love for Kyle. Not knowing if I could get through it all, I asked my brother Mike to stand behind me as I spoke them. These were words that both Mary Ann and I thought needed to be said. I knew Mike would be able to pick up from where I left off if my tears were too heavy. RIP our son, Kyle Raymond Manning, 6-06-2010. Thank you for sharing your 23 years with us. The words we spoke to Kyle from Mary Ann and I are as follows:

Mary Ann and I want to thank all of you on behalf of Kyle for coming today. We also want to thank all his friends that attended the candlelight vigil Tuesday night at St. Augustine's grotto and the viewing last night. Father Green, the family wants to especially thank you for your kind words and thoughts Monday to help us deal with Kyle's passing. As you stated, dealing with his life and not his death is the only way one can get through what we need to get through. Now is a time to celebrate Kyle's life.

Mary Ann and I have often thanked the Lord for giving us such a remarkable family. We have been fortunate beyond all measure. Kyle was an essential part of our family, and he will be deeply missed. It's hard to make sense of some things in life. But I think the Lord last Sunday morning decided that the stars in the sky were not bright enough and didn't sparkle the way he liked. He decided to enlist the help of Kyle. One so selfless and caring with that wonderfully bright smile and those sparkling eyes to help brighten the night sky for all of us. Kyle, I know your star is out there already; you are smiling down on us and wanting to help us all. Just as I know you would be doing if you were still with us.

Kyle was maturing into quite a young adult, and his future was bright. He met and fell deeply in love with a lovely young lady, Allison. He was pursuing his career goals at a great software company in Sacramento. There he was already starting to make a difference. He had a family, including a grandmother, parents, two sisters, and a brother that sincerely enjoyed being around him. We were all very close.

His invigorating presence, unwavering companionship, and his contagious smile will be truly missed.

Kyle wanted and expected a lot out of life. He loved to write, critique movies, and cheer on his favorite teams. The 49'rs, Arizona Sun Devils, and the Phoenix Suns win or lose. He often talked of entering politics because he was passionate about making a positive difference. He was well-read on most significant issues beyond the interest of most kids his age. Kyle was very shy as a young person, but as a flower does in the spring, he blossomed into a dynamic young man. Being the last of four was both a blessing for our Ky-Ky (Kyle) and a burden. He had the love and leadership of his older brother Ryan and sisters, Kristie and Karie. But the spaces in life were crowded by them. It took Ky-Ky some time to find some of his own spaces. Once he did, he flourished in them. He could fix anything electronic. He was both a writer and a dreamer, and he knew the meaning of both family and friend.

While there were many beautiful postings on his Facebook page from his friends and family, the one I would like to share with you is this, "When a love becomes a memory, the memory becomes a treasure."

We will never know what could have been for Kyle. What we do know is that the critical job he now has is to look down on us. Guide us to do the right thing and keep God's sky at night brighter than it was before you arrived, with that sparkle we so very much now miss.

We All Love you, Kyle.

Life after Kyle's passing never got back to normal in the Manning household, but the event's enormity brought the family closer together. Hugs and kisses from everyone were more robust and more frequent. Sunday dinners always started with prayers to Kyle, usually followed by a remarkable memory or two of our life with him. His friends would often check in with us to see how we were doing, and they would often share one of their favorite Kyle stories with us. Everyone was affected by his passing.

The problems with opioids at the time were not well understood and seldom reported. Kristie decided to use her medical training to better research the opioid situation to help the family better understand how it caused our loving Kyle to fall asleep one night and never wake up, but then later to help inform others. Karie and Tom, as high school teachers, became very interested in Kristie's research. They knew if their students better understood their bodies' effects from opioids, others might avoid the tragedy our family suffered. Both asked Kristie to present her research at their science and health classes next fall. Kristie first presented to their high school students, and it was very well received. As word got out within the school district, the other high schools in the district asked Kristie to do the same, including Amador High School, which Kristie, Karie, Ryan, and Kyle all attended.

This soon became a regular routine for Kristie for several years to follow. It was so successful Kristie perfected it and copied it to DVDs that she could forward to other high schools in and around Northern California. I am confident that awareness of this issue with Kyle's death through his immediate friends, and those who saw Kristie's presentation, had some positive impact on others' lives. That is a legacy that can never be taken away from our Ky-Ky, and just maybe why the Lord took our son that early morning of June 6th.

Karie and Tom's Wedding and Their First Child

A few months after Kyle's passing, I had a surprise visit from Tom. Tom and Karie had been dating for a while, and both Mary Ann and I knew their relationship was strengthening. Tom was a rock for Karie and the family after we lost Kyle. As I heard the doorbell ring, I went to let Tom into the house and led him to the family room.

As he sat down, he said, "Mr. Manning, I have something to ask of you."

I said, "Tom, this sounds serious; I hope nothing is wrong with you or Karie." He said, "No sir, nothing is wrong. I would like to ask your permission to take Karie's hand in marriage."

This was not a total surprise to me. Mary Ann and I were hoping for this day. We just didn't think it would come so soon. I said, "Tom, Mary Ann, and I both think the world of you. However, the family has just experienced a huge tragedy, and I am not so sure a life-changing decision like this should be made so soon after such a tragedy."

I think Tom was a little surprised by my response, but in his usual mature manner, he said, "Mr. Manning, this is not a reaction at all to the loss of Kyle. We were already planning on announcing this before Kyle died. Unfortunately, you were out of town when we decided it was time for me to ask you for Karie's hand in marriage. Trust me; this decision was made before the loss of Kyle."

I thought for a minute, absorbed his response, and then I said, "This is great news. Please let me go get Mary Ann so we can properly accept you into the family." I quickly went to get Mary Ann.

From a family and indeed a Mary Ann point of view, this was precisely the change in scenery we needed, something incredibly positive to focus on and steer our energies. Mary Ann was excited for them both. She thanked Tom for coming over and quickly asked if I had behaved when he asked me for Karie's hand in marriage.

Tom, used to being put on the spot by Mary Ann on anything to do with her children, laughed and said, "Mrs. Manning, yes, he was very well-behaved."

She said, "Good, then I have trained him well. Please, in the future, Tom, please address us as Mary Ann and Steve, and welcome to the family!"

Tom was happy with our response, but both knew it would be difficult for Mary Ann to keep this pending engagement a secret. Everyone in the family knew that it was almost impossible for Mary Ann to ever keep a secret. I thought, *if I cut the line to the internet and telephone and hide Mary Ann's cell phone and car keys in the freezer, maybe I can buy some time for Tom to pop the question to Karie.* I was sure Tom was worried as well, knowing Mary Ann.

As it turns out, Mary Ann did keep the proposal a secret long enough for Tom to make his proposal of marriage to our Karie. A few weeks later, the proposal became official, and Karie and Tom came over to show off the beautiful engagement ring Tom had given Karie.

With that, Mary Ann's sweet smile finally came back to her face. I had missed so much not seeing that happiness on her face the previous months, and I started to cry. The joy was for the great news on Tom and Karie, but along with that, it was seeing my lovely bride coming back to life.

Quickly Mary Ann started getting into the details with Karie. *When do you guys want to get married? Have you thought about a venue? How about a wedding in the backyard like your Aunt Peggy and Ron did in 2000?* Of course, Karie and Tom had already put some ideas together and thought a summer wedding would work best since they were both teaching at the time. Having the summer off would give them plenty of options on dates and their honeymoon. As far as venues go, there were many options to choose. Our backyard was large enough to host the event, and it had a beautiful setting, being just off the golf course. The pictures from Peggy's wedding were stunning. After eleven years, the trees around the property had grown, offering increased privacy. The Ruby Hill clubhouse was also a possibility. There were also two unique wedding venues just outside Ruby Hill's gates, both nestled in the wine vineyards. Mary Ann and Karie would soon have their hands full choosing a venue and a date for the wedding. The fact that they were planning a summer wedding gave them time to find the venue that Karie and Tom wanted. It was precisely the project Mary Ann needed to focus on, and she went all-in on it.

With Mary Ann in full wedding-planning mode, life was quickly improving in the Manning household. Mary Ann was busy every day with thoughts of making our first family wedding a roaring success. While the doors to our "Camelot" home had a severe crack in them, we were now starting to focus on the positives happening in our family. Sunday family dinners were in full swing. The kids were so happy to have their mother fully back in their lives, as was I.

After many visits to the various venues in and around our home, Karie and Tom chose a delightful place, just south of the Ruby Hill front gate. It had recently opened and was specifically designed for weddings. Beautiful wine vineyards surrounded it. There were a couple of dates still available in July. Oddly enough, it was either Saturday, July 23rd, which would have been our thirty-fourth wedding anniversary or Friday, July 29th. Karie wanted their wedding date to be unique, as would anybody, so they chose July 29, 2011. Friday weddings were cheaper than Saturday ones, so I was more than OK with that decision. I also knew that Mary Ann would be going overboard on the wedding, so saving a few bucks would be helpful. I remember saying to Mary Ann as all the planning got started, "Sweetheart, I know I will never know what we are spending on Karie's wedding, but please don't go crazy with it." Years ago, Mary Ann took over the family finances, so she pretty much had total control of everything financial. I remember once when the kids were younger, she said, "Steve, can you please watch the kids? I have to go to the bank." One of the kids then asked, "Mommy, what is a bank?" I quickly answered, "Well, that is a building that daddy goes to put money in so mommy can go and take it out." I was too far away from Mary Ann when

I said that, so no punch in the stomach was received, just an *Oh, Stephen, you're not being funny!* The kids always knew who to go to when they needed money.

Karie and Mary Ann did a fantastic job planning the wedding and getting everything done. As with Mary Ann's wedding, they hired a wedding planner, and they scripted the entire event perfectly. The wedding list grew, as I knew it would, but that was OK. It was our first family wedding, and the first time we would be able to re-engage with family and friends from out-of-town since Kyle's funeral. Most of the family came into town early so that we could host several family lunches and dinners the days before the wedding. We set up extra seating by the pool and spent many hours chatting with friends and family there. No one wanted to mention or think about the family gathering we had at the house just thirteen months ago, especially not Mary Ann. Nobody really needs an excuse to come to the Bay Area in the summer, and all took advantage of some tours beforehand.

The weather in the Bay Area in July is predictable and very accommodating to outdoor activities. The venue that Tom and Karie had selected had a beautiful patio area surrounded by vineyards. It afforded us a great patio area we could use for pre-dinner cocktails and other events after the ceremony. The wedding ceremony itself was very well done. One of Tom's favorite uncles was a Minister, and he performed the ceremony. Karie looked stunning in her wedding dress, as did her mother. With a smile on my face and a tear in my eye, I proudly walked her down the aisle. Kristie was her maid of honor and looked equally stunning. The look on Mary Ann's face as we walked down the aisle was to die for, so proud of her little angel that she did such an excellent job of raising her into a thoughtful and loving adult. We all knew that Mary Ann had developed in Karie, by example, another rendition of a *Loving Mother*.

After the ceremony, we went to the dining area and patio for cocktails and socializing before the wedding dinner started. As the dinner was getting ready to start, I got the pleasure as the father of the bride to make a toast to Karie and Tom. I would only have two opportunities to make such a toast, and I took full advantage of my first one. At the end of my toast with the permission of both, I also made a toast to Kyle. To my surprise, Karie had also arranged for something to honor Kyle. After all speeches and toast were made, she asked everyone to gather in the patio area outside. There, Karie had arranged for some helium-filled baby blue balloons, one for each family member, including Allison. We gathered, and after she said some great words about her brother Kyle, we all let them go. As I write this, I still have a tear in my eye, thinking just how special Mary Ann and I thought this gesture was. Of course, Mary Ann was the last to let her balloon go, not wanting to let anything go associated with her loving son.

It was now time for the party to start. Karie first had to toss her wedding bouquet, and of course, Kristie caught it! Tom then threw out Karie's garter. Karie and Tom then had their first dance as husband and wife, and then I had my first dance with Karie. Karie had chosen for our dance the same song Mary Ann had selected at our wedding for our first dance, "Evergreen" by Barbara Streisand. Tom has also picked his mom's wedding song for his dance with her. Mary Ann and I thought that was a genuinely lovely touch. The wedding was an enormous success, and dancing went on well into the night.

Karie and Tom moved into a house in the town next to us, Livermore, only about ten minutes away. They continue to this day teaching high school at the school they met at and helped to open. They have gone on to give us our first two amazing grandchildren, Jeremy and Parker Chamberlain. Like her mother, Karie is a *Loving Mother* to those wonderful two young children who are the light of my life.

Unfortunately, only a few days after Jeremy was born, Midge died unable to see her new great-grandson.

Finding Out Mary Ann Has Breast Cancer

$\mathcal{W}$ith Karie and Tom's wedding behind us, we started to get ready for the holidays. Mary Ann was still living the high from seeing her Karebear (Karie) happily married and was in a good mood for the holiday season. She would spend hours decorating the house, first for Halloween, then Thanksgiving, and finally Christmas. Midge could not help Mary Ann as much now as in years past, since her health was failing, and we had to move her into a senior care center close by our home. Midge was restricted to a wheelchair but always in good spirits while at home with the family. Mary Ann would spend time with her there and would bring her home for Sunday and holiday dinners. Peggy was also spending time with her mother and helped Mary Ann keep a close eye on her. We all knew it would be a tough holiday season that we would be celebrating without Kyle, but all were trying to stay positive and happy that we would be doing it all as a family. As usual, Mary Ann went beyond to make the holiday season memorable but did not have her usual energy. She was also having severe back pains that had been bothering her on and off for a few months. It had gotten to the point that she went into the doctor for an exam and some x-rays of her back. The doctor also decided to do a CAT scan of her back. She was still waiting for results when I had to fly back to Michigan for one more trip before the end of the year.

Five months after Tom and Karie's wedding, and just before Christmas, we found out that Mary Ann had stage-four breast cancer. It was devastating news. Mary Ann had gotten breast cancer in 2000, but her doctor had diagnosed it incredibly early. He noticed a small spot on her breast after one of her breast mammograms. It was a little spot, but her doctor was good enough not to let it go unchecked. Thanks to his diligence, they were able to catch it early. Her initial treatment allowed her to recover and go cancer-free without chemo or invasive surgery. She did have to undergo some limited radiation, and her doctor removed the spot with a small outpatient surgery procedure. Unfortunately for Mary Ann and the family, that doctor moved out of the area, and Mary Ann had to find another doctor. She was not so fortunate with this one.

I remember getting the call from Kristie while I was back in Michigan. Mary Ann had gotten all her test results back from her appointment on her back. After several tests, they detected that cancer had spread into the vertebrae around her spine. Tracking the source of the cancer, they found that the source was her left breast. What started as breast cancer had spread through her body and into her bone marrow. Kristie was calling me to share this horrible news with me. I knew something terrible had happened by the way Kristie was crying. She said, "Dad, something terrible has happened. Mom has been diagnosed with breast cancer, and it is bad. They caught it late, and it's already started to spread through her body. Dad, she has stage-four breast cancer." With that, Kristie started crying uncontrollably.

I was devastated by the news but not understanding what stage-four breast cancer was. *I asked Kristie to catch her breath so I could ask some questions relative to the diagnosis.* I said, "Kristie, what is the significance of stage-four breast cancer? From what you are saying, there seems to be some significance to her cancer being stage four; what is that?"

Before she could answer, she had to regather herself again. She then said, "Dad, stage-four breast cancer is in most cases terminal. Mom is going to have to likely go through a long cycle of treatment including chemo, probably some radiation, and possibly some surgery."

I then asked one of the most challenging questions I have ever asked anyone. "Kristie, how long does your mother have to live? You said it was likely terminal. What is the doctor telling you?"

Still, in tears, she said, "Dad, they don't know yet. They still have a lot of testing to do on her. Daddy, I can't believe this is happening. We just lost Kyle not that long ago. Why is God doing this to us?"

I said, "OK, sweetheart, please calm down. We have a lot to get through here. Let's not take the Lord on right now; we need him to help your mother and us through this. Please get as much information as you can and please stay with your mother until I get home. I will catch the next available flight as soon as possible. I think I still have time to get to the airport and catch the last direct flight to San Francisco. Please tell your mother that I love her. Please let the rest of the family know what is going on. I love you too, sweetheart. I will be home soon."

I could not believe our family was now facing another tragedy. As I gathered my things together and started towards the airport, I started thinking of how devastating this news was for Mary Ann. I decided to wait to call her from the airport once I knew what flight I would be able to get on. She, of all people, did not deserve this horrible outcome. She was finally getting through her depression caused by Kyle's passing, and now she had been issued her own death sentence. It was hard to put any logic behind this or why our family was being hit with back-to-back tragedies. The Lord had been so good to us for so many years, first even to let us meet and then to help us build the family we had always hoped. I was just not able to process all of this, but I knew I had to get on the phone with Mary Ann before I got on the flight. After securing my flight back to San Francisco, I went to the Delta lounge to find a quiet place where I could call Mary Ann. I knew this would be a difficult call, but I had to talk to my bride to see how she was handling her diagnosis.

Once settled in the lounge, I gave Mary Ann a call. She answered right away, already aware that Kristie had called me with the news. She said, "Stephen, I know you have already talked to Kristie; she is here with me right now. I am shocked by the news. I have been getting breast screenings every six months. I have no idea how my doctor missed this. For it to be stage four means I have had it for a while, and now it has spread throughout my body. I don't understand how this has all happened. When are you getting home? I need you to hold me."

I said, "Sweetheart, I am getting on the plane in about a half of an hour. Please trust me; I will be there for you as I know you would be there for me.

We will get through this together, and I assure you I will work with Kristie to find you the best cancer specialist available. Wherever that doctor is, I will take you there, no matter where, no matter what the cost. We will fight this together." I could tell by her voice she was dealing with the news in a rational sense. Kristie used her medical learnings to help Mary Ann better understand what was about to be in front of her.

What Kristie and Mary Ann could not understand was how her doctor missed this. The medical protocol for any breast cancer survivor was that you got two screenings a year. One would be a mammogram, and the next one would be an MRI. That process would repeat itself for the rest of your life. Mary Ann was disciplined and always followed the rules. If she were scheduled for an exam every six months, she would be there in five months. She never missed one of her exams. Unfortunately, her doctor, in my opinion, failed her. He did not give her the MRI's, just merely the mammograms. Later, when I challenged him on this, he just said the insurance company complained to him that he did too many MRIs! He took absolutely no responsibility for what I believe to be his medical malpractice. When he said that, it took all my strength not to come across the table at him.

With Kristie's help and research, we quickly changed doctors for Mary Ann. Kristie was working in a hospital in San Francisco that had a relationship with UCSF. UCSF had an excellent reputation for its research and management of women with breast cancer. Along with MD Anderson in Houston, they were the two that came up most often in my research. With Kristie's persistence and diligence, we were able to get Mary Ann assigned to the medical team led by Dr. Rugo, the head of the breast cancer team at UCSF. Dr. Rugo was an excellent doctor and was very patient and friendly. Her mother died of breast cancer, and afterward, she became dedicated to its prevention, treatment, and cure.

Unfortunately, there would be no cure for my lovely wife and my children's *Loving Mother*. In fact, with our first meeting with Dr. Rugo, after she personally reviewed all of Mary Ann's medical records, she turned to Mary Ann and said, "Mary Ann, the medical profession has done you a great disservice. This is not a wrong that we can right, and not something that can be undone. I want to be honest with you; your condition is terminal. There is a lot we can do, and we will do, to prolong your life for as long as possible, but this is something that you will die from."

As I looked at Mary Ann, she sat quietly staring at Dr. Rugo as tears started flowing down her face. Kristie had already explained to Mary Ann what the likely outcome was to be. Hearing it from someone so well regarded in the field of breast cancer just made the news that much worse. She finally spoke up and said, "Dr. Rugo, I appreciate your honesty. I still have three children I need to live for. With your help, I will fight this for as long as I can. I am a strong woman, and our family has been through a lot recently. When it gets too hard to continue, I will let you know. Until then, please give me as much time with my family as possible." At the end of our session with Dr. Rugo, there was no dry eye in the room. That would be the first of many meetings with Dr. Rugo and her team over the next thirty-two months.

Mary Ann's schedule would have her come in every week for three weeks for blood work, chemo treatment, and a meeting with Rugo's team. The fourth week she would have off to recover from the three earlier chemo treatments. Every six months, we would go into the city for her to get a PET scan.

In the early days, she handled the chemo well. That was expected since they started her out with lighter doses. As time went on, they started to increase the chemo's strength, and as was forecast, she started losing her hair. She handled all of this very well. Before she started losing her hair, she had gone out and bought several scarves and a couple of wigs. Mary Ann was going to fight this with every tool in her tool bag.

Chemo days were long days. We would get to the city early in the morning. Spend time together between appointments, blood draws, and her chemo treatment, and always had lunch together. We faced rush hour going both to and from the appointment, which gave us time to talk about her cancer, the family, and our life together. I knew the conversations would always be better on the way in since as the treatments went on, she would often nap on the way home. When this all started, I felt terrible for not knowing more about breast cancer or its treatment.

After her diagnosis, and with Kristie's help, I started researching her particular form of cancer. It was different from the type of breast cancer that she had in 2000. I found in my research that many positive things were going on in breast cancer research. Many developments pointed to an eventual cure for some forms of breast cancer using innovative new forms of treatment, treatments like immunotherapy, and others that try to use the immune system to attack the cancer cells proactively. Researchers know that the cancer cells continue to change their structures so they can hide from our immune system. These treatments were trying to attach markers to the cancer cells somehow. The markers could help the immune system identify the cancer cells so they could not hide from it and could be attacked. I would always share my research results with Mary Ann on our chemo days, not just to give her hope, but because it was something I was starting to believe. I would tell her to keep fighting so we could buy time for this research to get to a clinical trial level. Once it did, I would do everything in my power to get her into one of those trials. She became interested, and she started doing her own research. After reading the research, she started getting encouraged by it. We both felt that if she could hang on for a couple of years, she might have a realistic chance of beating this awful disease, a disease that strikes way too many women in our world today. As we talked about it, we decided to set specific future goals where she could focus.

One goal was quickly set for us by Karie and Tom, the month after Mary Ann was diagnosed, Tom and Karie proudly announced that they were expecting their first child, our first grandchild. Being the *Loving Mother* that Mary Ann was, the child's birth would be an easy first goal to set. The baby was to be born sometime in December of that year. We knew that Mary Ann would likely live long enough to hold what turned out to be our first grandson, Jeremy. And she did. The look on Mary Ann's face when Karie first handed Jeremy to her was amazing. It brought a tear to my eye because I knew what Mary Ann thought as she held Jeremy for the first time. *How happy, yet sad, I will not be able to watch this beautiful baby grow up, graduate college, and get married.*

On the way home that day, she confirmed what I had thought at the time. She said, "Stephen, I am so happy for Karie and Tom. Jeremy is just beautiful and so full of life. I know I will not be around for him, and that makes me incredibly sad. Please, Stephen, be there for Jeremy, Karie, and Tom. I know that Karie will be a *Loving Mother,* but please make sure you give them everything they need. They reminded me of us when we had Kristie. We were young, and we were not sure what our parenting skills were. I will not be there to help Karie figure it all out, and they both will be working. If they need something, make sure you are there for them."

I said, "Sweetheart, I love your love for your children and your love for Jeremy, our new grandson. Unless you know something that I don't know, you are not going anywhere. Karie and Jeremy need you right now, so please stay in the game. I will always be there when you are not, but I assume that we are still a long way away from that point. Let's get home and get some sleep so we can get back up there and see Karie and Jeremy."

She grabbed my hand and said, "I know, it just breaks my heart that I won't be there for Karie, Tom, and Jeremy as he grows up. He was just so special today; you could already see his personality coming out in him."

I said, "Yes, you are right, especially how he smiled at you when you were holding him. Sweetheart, you will have time with Jeremy, and I know you will take full advantage of it. Tom, Karie, and I will always make sure he knows who you were and how special his grandmother was."

I felt so sorry for Mary Ann on our way home that night; she was so special and a *Loving Mother.* It was likely that her grandkids would never have the opportunity to know who she was and how she worked so hard to raise their parents. Through this writing, I can only hope that they will have a chance to know her and love her as much as she would love them. She so wanted to hold all her grandchildren and, of course, help their parents to become better parents. I think that she, by example, achieved the latter, but she never achieved the former. God love you from us all, Mary Ann; you achieved it all. I am sure as you are sitting in heaven, with our son Kyle, you are likely holding him tightly and enjoying every minute of our children's family development.

Mary Ann kept up her fight against her cancer for quite a while. During her treatments, they would change the chemo she was taking when they saw her blood levels or platelet count decrease. It was hard for her to stay optimistic when those levels decreased, but all those levels would rise when the new chemo kicked in. For her, like I am sure all cancer patients do, when you see those levels going up, you start to believe there still might be a cure for you. It's an unbelievable roller-coaster ride, and all the time, the chemo is eating away at your body.

A new goal was soon set for her when Ryan and Katelyn proudly announced they were getting married. We loved having Katelyn around, so we were both overly excited about the new development. Katelyn was also a rock for us when Kyle passed. Kyle adored Katelyn, and the feeling was mutual. On the day of Kyle's viewing, Mary Ann wanted Kyle's hair combed out how he always liked to wear it. The mortician did a surprisingly excellent job getting Kyle ready for the viewing, other than his hair. When Mary Ann asked for one of the kids to fix Kyle's hair, they looked at her with a blank stare. I don't think they felt comfortable touching Kyle's body. With that, Katelyn just said, "Someone, please find me a brush or comb. I will do it; I know exactly how he likes it." Mary Ann was happy with her response and the job she did getting her little boy ready for his final viewing.

Ryan and Katelyn had set a date for Labor Day weekend 2014. They knew they needed to keep the date as close as possible due to Mary Ann's health and her fight with cancer. Ryan wanted his mother there and to be able to dance with him at his wedding. As a backup, Ryan and Katelyn planned to hold a private ceremony in front of a justice of the peace if Mary Ann could not hold on until then. At her next chemo appointment, Mary Ann proudly announced to Dr. Rugo and her staff that Ryan and Katelyn were getting married. The first thing out of their mouths was, "When is the wedding date?"

When Mary Ann quickly responded, Labor Day weekend 2014, I could see the look of concern on their faces. I don't think Mary Ann noticed it, but I did, and it scared me. My heart sunk, thinking maybe we had all been too optimistic with that date. Mary Ann had already suffered a stroke earlier and had to start taking blood thinners. The blood specialist at UCSF had discovered that cancer had already entered her bloodstream. It was causing a series of small strokes in her brain. When he did a brain scan and saw those small strokes' results, he was surprised at how well Mary Ann was functioning mentally. We were at the start of a new chemotype, so her blood and platelet levels were acceptable. But it was just the start of another roller coaster ride, and the medical staff knew it.

It was becoming increasingly clear that Mary Ann was getting to the point that she would soon need 24/7 care. Because of her condition, the medical staff also told us she could no longer drive. That was going to take away Mary Ann's feeling of independence. It would make her homebound, which I knew she was not going to appreciate. I knew it was time for me to do for Mary Ann what she would have done for me. I ended my work in Michigan and returned to the Bay Area full time to care for my lovely bride. We also decided to sell our house in Ruby Hill and downsized to a home in Dublin, California, the neighboring town just north of Pleasanton. With the help of the kids, Peggy, Kathy Reidy, and many of Mary Ann's friends, we made sure she was never left alone at any time. It was a tough time for us. We both knew her time on earth and with us was ending. She was still having some good days and still fighting to hang on, but her body became more fragile. We talked a lot about the kids and her sister and what I would likely do after she passed. I think our love for each other became even stronger during those final twelve months of being together. We relived many times all the great experiences of our life together, and she took pleasure in the thought of sometime soon being with our beloved Kyle.

In June of 2014, Kristie had taken Mary Ann to the store to pick up some of her medicine. Mary Ann felt strong that day, but Kristie was home and offered to drive Mary Ann to the store. While at the store, Mary Ann suffered a seizure, and they had to call an ambulance. Kristie was in shock and was extremely concerned about her mom. Thankfully, she knew what to do with her medical training and stayed by her mom's side until the ambulance arrived. Once they got Mary Ann into the ambulance and Kristie found out what hospital they were going to take her to, Kristie called me. In panic and tears, she said, "Dad, mom just had what seems to be either a seizure or a stroke. She is unconscious and on her way to the hospital in San Ramon. I am going to follow the ambulance there. Please come quickly. I am not sure if she is going to be OK. Please also let Ryan, Karie, and Peggy know what has happened."

Shaken by the news, I quickly got in the car and headed to the hospital. On the way there, I called the kids. The staff at the hospital took Mary Ann immediately to the emergency room to start their examination. As I pulled up to the hospital, I saw Kristie pacing back and forth in front of the emergency room entrance. Still, in tears, Kristie told me that Mary Ann was still in the exam room. She said, "Dad, I don't have any new information on mom. They took her at once in, so I haven't even talked to the ambulance team. Dad, this could be serious."

I asked, "How did this all happen?"

Between tears of sorrow, she said, "Dad, it was crazy. She was acting fine all morning. We went to the store to pick up her meds, and as we were waiting for them to fill her prescriptions, she felt faint and dropped to the floor and then started shaking. Thank God we were sitting in that little waiting room they have off to the pharmacy side. It was carpeted; otherwise, she would have fallen on the hard-tiled floor. I immediately screamed for them to call 911, and the ambulance showed up a few minutes later. Dad, I am so worried for mom. I think this is what Dr. Rugo's team was concerned. Her body has been through so much from all the chemo they have been giving her. Please tell me it's not going to end like this."

The kids and Peggy showed up quickly, and before we had any report back from the medical team at the hospital. We were all worried but together. Finally, the attending doctor came out to the waiting area to update us on Mary Ann. He said, "Mary Ann is awake and is breathing fine. They will be taking her to intensive care, and there you can see her, but only in small groups. It appears that she suffered a seizure, but there does not appear to be any added brain damage. We will need to perform more tests. I understand from what Kristie told the ambulance team that she is undergoing chemo treatment for breast cancer. The two may be related, and we will be getting in contact with her team at UCSF to coordinate care. I see that she is under the care of Dr. Rugo, who has an excellent reputation. Mary Ann should feel good about being under her care. Mary Ann will be here for a while until we understand what has happened and what follow-up care she is going to need."

Mary Ann recovered from the seizure within a few weeks, but unfortunately, her mental status waxed and waned from there on out.

RYAN AND KATELYN'S WEDDING

For those final twelve months, Mary Ann's final goal was to get to Ryan and Katelyn's wedding and dance with him there. She also wanted to help them both in any way she could to help make that day as unique for them as she could. Mary Ann was never afraid to share her opinion on anything that had to do with her children, and she was all in on helping with their wedding planning. Ryan and Katelyn had chosen a delightful venue for the wedding in Southern California. The venue was not too far from the beach we earlier took our girls to when we lived down there. They chose the St. Regis in Dana Point, California. It is a beautiful hotel and resort that overlooked the Pacific Ocean and the Monarch Bay Golf Club. The setting for the ceremony could not have been more stunning. Ryan and Katelyn had hired a great wedding planner who had done several weddings at the St. Regis. They also hired a video company that would help document the entire event.

As it got closer to the wedding, Mary Ann was busy getting ready for it. She had already bought a new dress, and her hair was already starting to grow back. She had lost quite a bit of weight through all her treatments, so she pretty much had to replace her entire wardrobe. The kids would come by the house often to visit with Mary Ann. It was cute to listen to Ryan and Katelyn discussing the wedding and going over everything with Mary Ann on one visit. I was especially taken back by discussing what song Mary Ann wanted to dance to with Ryan for the Mother/Son dance. They eventually chose "Somewhere over the Rainbow" by Israel "IZ" Kanakawiwo'ole. Besides being a great song, it was one of Kyle's favorites. It was featured in the album Kyle Freitas had put together for Kyle after he passed. Mary Ann was more than happy with that choice. Mary Ann was getting excited about the wedding and, at the time, looked like she would have no trouble getting to that special day. To make the trip easier for her, Ryan's boss offered to have his private plane fly Mary Ann down to Orange County and back after the wedding.

We rented a big house in Dana Point for the week of the wedding. We knew there would be a lot of family at the wedding, and Mary Ann wanted to spend as much time with them as possible that week. We also wanted the kids to stay with us, so we needed a lot of bedrooms and an area to entertain everyone. Labor Day weekend was going to be busy for the area, so Kristie and Karie started searching for a house as soon as Ryan and Katelyn picked the date and venue. It worked out great because we had a lot of the extended family come into town for the wedding. They certainly wanted to see Ryan and Katelyn get married, but they all knew that the time for Mary Ann was passing quickly.

About four months before the wedding, Mary Ann asked Dr. Rugo if it would be OK if she took some time off from her chemo treatments. They were wearing her down, and her blood and platelet levels were again decreasing. She was getting weekly blood transfusions to help keep her blood levels up, but it was only effective for a few days. It was likely the last chemo regimen that she would get, as there was little left for them to do for her. I think even in their eyes, she had survived longer than they had initially thought she could. Dr. Rugo agreed that a respite was well deserved. Her only request was that she continues to get her blood transfusions and that she stays on her blood thinner medicine. All agreed that she would come back in a month for a checkup. The medical team would monitor her blood levels through the lab by our house, giving her the transfusions.

At the follow-up meeting, the staff suggested that they had done everything medically possible for Mary Ann. They said that she should consider going into hospice care. While not unexpected, it was horrible news. We all felt so helpless and sad for Mary Ann. She had fought such a brave and hard battle for so many months. Now the only care she would be receiving would be focused on her comfort. This awful disease continued to destroy her body, the body of my sweetheart, and the *Loving Mother* of my children. Kristie arranged for the local hospice group in Dublin to enter Mary Ann into their treatment program. About a week later, one of their nurses came by to interview Mary Ann and describe how they work with patients in their program. It was one of the most painful times of my life. I sat next to Mary Ann, holding her on the couch as the nurse took Mary Ann, Kristie, and me through their process. Mary Ann fought to hold back her tears as the nurse described what was ahead for her. As she finished, Mary Ann's only words were, "I will be going to my son's wedding on Labor Day weekend, and I will be dancing with him to 'Somewhere Over the Rainbow' that evening."

Kristie quickly grabbed her mother's hand and said, "Yes, mom, of course, you will!"

Karie was terrific through all of this. She kept in touch with her sister Kristie to better understand what was going on with her mom medically. She would always join us when she could at the weekly chemo treatments, and if not able to, she would stop by the house to see how Mary Ann was doing. It also gave her an excuse to bring Jeremy by, so he and Mary Ann could have as much time together as possible. She wanted to make sure Jeremy knew who his grandmother was and what a special person she was. Even when Jeremy was young, he seemed to know grandma was sick. When he was still little, he would often just lie quietly on her chest and softly hug her as she patted him on his back and sang to him. By the time of the wedding, Jeremy would be eighteen months old, full of energy, and able to walk and talk. He was so much fun for us to be around but getting too big for Mary Ann to hold. She was getting weaker, and she always worried that she might drop him. She was now also pretty much in a wheelchair most of the time. Ryan and Katelyn also found every excuse to stop by to see how Mary Ann was doing, and all would be there for Sunday dinners. She was no longer doing much cooking but was always the most loved at the table. The kids all knew how much their *Loving Mother* loved to be around them.

Even before Mary Ann entered hospice, she was struggling with daily life. She was often confused about what time of day it was and often thought it was nighttime even though the sun was high in the sky. She even complained to the kids that I was feeding her dinners in the morning and breakfast at night. As it turned out, she was suffering from what the doctors called "non-24 disorder," and she could not tell day from night. She was sleeping in a separate room where we had a hospital bed delivered with proper guardrails on each side of the bed. We did not want her rolling out of bed at night and hurting herself. We also installed a baby monitor to listen if she was having trouble during the night or trying to get up. She needed help with going to the bathroom, showering, and eating. We were becoming more concerned that she was not going to make it to the wedding. It was clear that she was still having those small strokes in her brain even though she continued to be on blood thinners. Because of this, we were told by hospice that she could not fly to the wedding. The pressure from takeoff and landing could cause a more significant stroke to occur. Although she was becoming more confused during the day, she still had periods of awareness and could hold a conversation. When she learned of her flight ban, she worried that we would cancel plans to take her to the wedding. I let her know that would not be the case, and we would drive down to Dana Point. If necessary, we would stop every hour if she needed to rest or use the bathroom. It would typically be an eight to nine-hour drive depending on traffic in and around Los Angeles, so we planned for a twelve-hour journey.

As we started getting ready for the trip, the hospice informed us that they would not authorize the journey. They did not want Mary Ann to leave the area for any reason. We all knew that hospice was trying to do the right thing by Mary Ann. It was a great organization and very caring for their patients. The problem with this was Mary Ann's dream to be there for Ryan and Katelyn, and we were not going to let that dream vanish from her. We let hospice know that the family would be taking their *Loving Mother* to the wedding at all cost. We asked them to support that decision, which they did, and put us in contact with a local hospice service down by Dana Point. We then arranged through Katelyn's mom, Penny, a registered nurse, to arrange a nurse to be with Mary Ann during the ceremony. After arrangements were made, we packed up Mary Ann's SUV and headed south to the wedding.

Mary Ann handled the drive well and mostly slept in the front seat, which we tilted back, and with blankets and pillows in place to make it comfortable for her.

The home the girls had found was perfect. It was large enough for everyone to have a room, a large kitchen area, and a patio with a pleasant but slightly obstructed view of the Pacific Ocean. The look on Mary Ann's face once we got settled was heartwarming. She knew her lengthy battle with cancer was not going to stop her from dancing with her son at his wedding. While the wedding was still a few days away, she was well settled, only a few miles away from the venue, surrounded by the family she so much loved and was devoted to. Soon the extended family started to arrive. It was beautiful to see everyone and heart-lifting to see them spending time with Mary Ann.

Mary Ann was in good spirits and genuinely enjoyed her time around the extended family. The patio above the garage had plenty of seating so that Mary Ann could hold court out there for most of the week. My sisters, who Mary Ann loved, got there early, so they spent many hours together with some of the cousins who came in for the wedding. Mary Ann was also close to my brother's second wife, Doreen. We had a wonderful cruise with them in 2007 around the Mediterranean that my brother, Mike, had arranged. Two couples they were very close to and that we both liked and had vacationed before also joined us on the cruise. It was a great cruise, and Mary Ann and Doreen reminisced about how much fun it was for us all to be together as they sat together on the patio.

As I sat and listened to all the memories Mary Ann and Doreen were reliving, I could not help but think of how happy our family life was back in 2007, not that many years before. The children we had raised were all healthy, wonderful, and loving individuals. They were either well into college or had already graduated. They were all notable examples of Mary Ann's dedication to their lives and the strength and willpower of a "*Loving Mother.*" All the excitement and emotions of the week did wear Mary Ann down. As the week went on, we had to start limiting Mary Ann's time on the patio so she could rest and take some naps, but it was good to see her so engaged.

It was time for the prenuptial dinner that Mary Ann and I were hosting. Katelyn's family helped us find a nice restaurant in the dining area where we hosted the wedding party and some of the extended family. It was the first time for Mary Ann and me to meet much of Katelyn's family, including her father. Katelyn's mother, Penny, had remarried a fine gentleman named Rod when Katelyn was young. We had already been able to spend time with Penny and Rod over the last couple of years, which was always fun. We enjoyed meeting her dad for the first time, and we thanked him for what we knew was going to be a magnificent event the next day at a simply fantastic venue. He was sparing no expense to make that day memorable for both Katelyn and Ryan.

Mary Ann had rested well during the day, and she was in good spirits for the evening event. Of course, Katelyn looked beautiful, and both she and Ryan were excited about their upcoming wedding. They were both undoubtedly happy and relieved that Mary Ann would make it that next day to the wedding and the dance floor with Ryan. The restaurant was one that Rod and Penny frequented, so they knew the owner well, and they served a wonderful dinner to us all. As the evening started to get late, I could see that my bride was getting tired. With apologies, we left the party early and headed back to the house we had rented. Everyone understood our early departure. All were excited for Ryan that his mother would be there to see him marry Katelyn the next day and dance with her.

It had been a big week for Mary Ann, and as we all awoke that next day the girls could see that Mary Ann was exhausted and a bit confused. After breakfast that morning, the girls convinced Mary Ann to lay back down for a nap before they would help get her ready for the big event. The girls laid out Mary Ann's dress for the wedding and made sure they got ready ahead of time themselves to help their mother when she got up from her nap. I had warned Ryan the night before that he should have a backup plan if Mary Ann were too weak to get out of her wheelchair for the dance. I suggested that putting two chairs together side by side might be a suitable alternative. That would allow Ryan to put his arm around his *Loving Mother* through the song. They both agreed that this would be a good backup plan. Our plan all along was to have Mary Ann attend the wedding in her wheelchair to help her keep her strength through what would be a long day. Once the girls had Mary Ann ready, we made our way to the St. Regis for the event.

As I mentioned earlier, the St. Regis sat on a hill overlooking the Pacific Ocean. It had lovely grounds surrounding it and a well-maintained golf course between the hotel and the ocean. The setting could not have been more beautiful. The wedding altar was at the end of the lawn area, with the pool area and ocean directly below it. The seating was arranged to see the altar and then the ocean's blue seas beyond it. It was a bright, sunny day with blue skies and not a cloud in the air. Being so close to the ocean provided a gentle breeze to keep everyone extremely comfortable for the ceremony. Mary Ann was alert and excited for what was about to unfold. Once everyone was seated, the music started. The wedding party started to stream down a large white stone winding stairway just off the hotel's back. It was a large wedding party including friends of both Katelyn and her little sister, Kaylee. Once the wedding party reached their positions in front of the altar, Ryan appeared at the top of the stairs. His mother would not be able to walk with him down the stairs and onto the altar, but she was seated right in front of the altar, beaming at her son. She was so thankful to be there, and Ryan was overwhelmed with emotion to see her there.

It was now time for the bride to appear at the top of the stairs. All stood and looked back towards the hotel to see Katelyn appear. Katelyn looked stunning. She had a beautiful wedding dress that flowed behind her as she made her way to the altar. As the ceremony started, I turned to Mary Ann and said, "Sweetheart, you made it, and I am so enormously proud of you. We all knew you were going to do whatever it took to be here today. Ryan and the girls love you for what you stand for, and you have made them all a better person with your strength and devotion to them."

Tears were in both of our eyes when I kissed her. I held her hand through the ceremony and their vows of marriage. We stayed seated after the ceremony, hoping to get through the family pictures quickly. I wanted to take Mary Ann somewhere quiet for her to rest before the celebration started.

LAST DANCE

The post-wedding pictures took some time because of the size of the wedding party. And the fact that so many family members were in attendance. A cocktail area on the hotel's back patio, where many went to meet with family and friends before the evening celebration started. We found a quiet place in the lobby area where Mary Ann and I sat to relax and talked about how perfect the ceremony was.

She said, "Stephen, it was such a delightful wedding. The setting and the views could not have been more stunning. I do wish that I could have walked Ryan down the aisle. I am just so happy I was able to make it here. I know you and the girls were worried for me, and I thank you all so much for your help. I want to dance with him tonight; I just don't know if I can."

I told her, "Don't worry, one way or another, you will be on that dance floor with him tonight. Worst case, I will have Anthony arrange some chairs that you can sit with him. I love the song you both picked for this. Kyle will be proud of you both tonight!"

As the pictures finished and everyone made their way to the dining room, we went to our assigned table. The tables were large enough that the girls and Tom, Jeremy, and the nurse we had with us for Mary Ann were all able to sit with us. Next to us were Peggy, Mike, Doreen, my sisters, brother-in-law Dave, and close by, Mike and Kathie Reidy. Before dinner, there were many speeches made by the wedding party and a great toast made by Katelyn's dad, mom, and Rod. The bar was opened, and a perfect dinner was served along with some delightful wines. Katelyn's dad had spared no expense. I turned to say something to Mary Ann when I noticed she was asleep in her wheelchair. I quickly turned to the girls and said, "Damn, I don't think your mom is going to make it to the dance with Ryan.

Please tell Anthony we need to move to plan B. I will wheel her out to the dance floor, and Ryan can grab a chair and sit next to her for the song."

They got the message to Anthony while Katelyn and Ryan had their first dance. Then Katelyn had her dance with her father and another one with Rod, her stepfather.

It was now time for Mary Ann to join Ryan on the dance floor. The girls had already gently woken their mother up to let her know it was time for her dance with Ryan. As the dance floor cleared and as Ryan stood there waiting for his mom to arrive, I got up and started wheeling Mary Ann out to the middle of the dance floor. All of a sudden, she jumped out of the chair and started slowly walking toward Ryan. Standing there in shock, Ryan walked quickly towards Mary Ann and gently put her arms around his neck. He put his arms around Mary Ann's waist to give her support, and the music started.

As "Somewhere Over the Rainbow" began to play, everybody just stood in shock. Everyone knew about Mary Ann's condition and their desire to have that dance together. No one could believe what they were seeing. As the dance continued, people started openly crying in admiration for what they saw happening. They all knew that they were seeing first-hand the incredible power of a *mother's love for her child*. The sheer strength and will power of that wonderful mother to fight through everything to get to that dance.

Ryan dancing with his mother, Mary Ann, at his wedding. Ryan knew how unbelievably this time with his mother was and what it took her to get to that dance floor for her Last Dance. He fights back his tears as he holds his *Loving Mother* in his arms.

Kristie, Karie, myself, and Ryan's best man Anthony watching Mary Ann's last dance with Ryan at his wedding. We knew what we were witnessing, an extraordinarily strong and *Loving Mother* struggling to have one last dance with her son at his wedding. What we didn't realize at the time was that we would lose her a few days after this dance.

When the dance ended, there was tremendous applause from all in attendance. Along with the girls, I went onto the dance floor to help carefully walk Mary Ann back to her wheelchair. Mary Ann was shaking from exhaustion and crying uncontrollably. She was proud of what she had accomplished, but it had taken everything in her body to do it. Many family and friends came by the table to congratulate her on her remarkable accomplishment. As things calmed down and as she sat in that chair, I could see she had little strength left in her body. Since we were not staying in the hotel, I asked my brother if we could use their room to lay Mary Ann down. Of course, he agreed, and he and Doreen escorted Mary Ann, me, Kristie, Karie, and her nurse to their room. Once there, the girls helped get Mary Ann out of her dress and into bed. The nurse stayed with Mary Ann, and out of respect for Ryan and Katelyn, we returned to the wedding party. About an hour later, Kristie and Karie went back to check on their mommy.

When the girls came back from checking on their mother, they told us that she was sleeping well. The nurse suggested we let her rest for a little longer before taking her back to the house we were renting. As the evening was getting late, I could see Mike and Doreen were getting anxious to go to their room for the night. I asked the girls to go get their mother up and dressed. Mary Ann was barely awake when we rolled her in her wheelchair to the car. We gently got her into the car, and I headed back to the house with Mary Ann and her nurse.

Once back at the house, the nurse and I got Mary Ann ready and into bed for the night. Still amazed at the incredible vision of Mary Ann and Ryan dancing to "Somewhere Over the Rainbow," I went to bed.

The next day started with a late morning breakfast for all. The girls had stayed at the wedding, catching up with all the friends and relatives who were there. Mary Ann slept in, still exhausted from all the activities the day before. When she finally got up, you could tell she was not fully aware of what was going on. She would have moments of awareness but would then drift off. We decided that there was no way we could drive her back to Pleasanton in her current condition, so the girls contacted the landlord and asked if we could stay at least one more night. The landlord could not have been nicer and told us he would arrange for the party coming into the rental to occupy one of his other properties. Many of the friends and relatives at the wedding stopped by the house to check on Mary Ann. We kept the activities light for Mary Ann and allowed her to take some naps during the day. I went to the store and got some food for dinner, and we all made it a short evening, hoping for a restful and peaceful night of much-needed sleep.

At around 2 a.m. Screams from Kristie awakened me. "Dad, please come into mom's room. I need your help!"

As I entered the room, I could see Kristie struggling to calm Mary Ann down. Mary Ann was in a rage, and even though Kristie was much stronger than Mary Ann, she was having a challenging time controlling Mary Ann. Her arms and legs were swinging in all directions. I quickly got on one side of Mary Ann, and with Kristie, on the other, we struggled to control Mary Ann's arms and legs. The strength of her rage was unimaginable and quite scary. We didn't want to hurt her, and because of the blood thinners she was taking, we certainly didn't want her bruising herself. Soon Karie and Peggy came into the room to help after hearing all the commotion. We all worked diligently to calm Mary Ann down and placed cold towels on her head because she was sweating from her struggles.

Once we got Mary Ann calm, I asked Kristie what had happened.

She said, "Dad, it was surreal. I was awakened by hearing mom screaming 'Michael' in the middle of the night. I couldn't figure out what was going on, so I rushed into her room. She was pacing around the room just yelling, 'Michael.' I assume she was calling out to her brother, Michael, who had passed in 2002. She then started calling out for her dad. That is when I called out to you for some help. Dad, this is really weird. That is what people do before they die. Dad, please don't tell me mom is dying."

I said, "Sweetheart, I just don't know what is going on. I have never witnessed someone dying before. Let's see if we can get her back to sleep, and we can call hospice or a doctor in the morning. I know Penny can help us find someone to help your mother."

After Mary Ann calmed down, Kristie agreed to stay with her, and we all went back to bed. By now, it was past 4 a.m., and everyone needed their sleep. We knew the next day was going to be a tough one.

Mary Ann did get back to sleep that night, and the next day we called Penny, who immediately came over to help. Kristie called hospice, and they told her that Mary Ann was experiencing what they called "terminal agitation" and that she was starting the process of dying and we shouldn't try to drive her home. Hospice had given us sedatives and pain medication and said if those don't work, we should call 911. Penny and Kristie both examined Mary Ann, who was not very responsive, and we decided to call 911. Quickly the fire department responded along with an ambulance. Penny negotiated with them and asked them to take Mary Ann to a hospital that she used to work. She felt they had the best staff in the area, and it was a short drive away. They allowed Kristie to ride in the ambulance with her mother since she was a doctor and could help get Mary Ann admitted. We let Ryan know and Katelyn that we were admitting Mary Ann to the local hospital, and then we drove there.

When we got to the hospital, they had already started to examine Mary Ann. Fortunately, with Kristie's medical training and her knowledge of Mary Ann's current health status, the attending doctor was able to ascertain Mary Ann's condition quickly. As we got to the room where they were examining Mary Ann, Kristie finished her briefing to the medical staff there. As she finished, the attending doctor said, "Excuse me, are you a doctor or something? Your briefing has been very precise. What kind of medicine are you in?"

Kristie said, "Thank you, doctor; I am a hospitalist in San Francisco at a children's hospital. I am not that familiar with adult medicine, but I have been closely following my mother's health."

The doctor then said, "Well, Dr. Manning, you have done an excellent job of briefing me on your mother's condition. By the way, I am a hospitalist, as well, and hospitalists need to stick together. The hospital will not want to admit your mother, and they will try and push you to a hospice group here in the area. Let me assure you I will not let that happen. They will resist me for sure, but I will refuse to sign any release forms for your mother for at least the next forty-eight hours. We have a hospice group here that is particularly good. I want them to evaluate her and update the status of her condition fully. I will make sure she gets a private room. There is a Denny's just around the corner from the hospital. It is a leisurely walk. Please go get some break-fast, and by the time you get back, we will have your mother admitted and in her room." The doctor could not have been kinder or more professional.

When we got back to the hospital, the kind doctor had already brought Mary Ann into her room. It was a large private room with plenty of seating and a fold-out couch. They had Mary Ann all hooked up on monitors, and the nurse was checking her vitals as we entered the room. The nurse was exceedingly kind as well and said, "The doctor said to call him as soon as you all got back. He should be up to see you in an hour or so. In the mean-time, please spend time with your mother; she will likely be in and out of consciousness. We are giving her fluids right now and are prepared to give her any pain medication that she might require during her stay with us."

Mary Ann looked so peaceful as she lay there. Her eyes would occasion-ally open, and we assumed that she could hear what we were saying. All of us were crying when the doctor came into the room. When the doctor entered the room, he first turned to Kristie and said, "As you can imagine, right now I am not a favorite of the hospital administrator, but I can confirm that your mother will be with us for at least the next 48 hours. Now let me tell the Manning family what you probably already suspect. Mary Ann is in the process of dying. It is clear she has fought a hard battle, but she is quickly losing the battle to cancer. The staff in this ward are outstanding, and the second-shift nurse is one of our best. She will be checking Mary Ann's vitals, and she will be able to tell you with surprisingly good accuracy how long she has left. Mary Ann can hear you when you talk to her. Even though she may not react or answer you, you should assume she can hear you. I think this would be an appropriate time for each one of you to speak softly into her ear your final words. Take your turn with Mary Ann one at a time. We will give her fluids and some pain medicine just to make sure she is comfortable. The nurse will continue to monitor her vitals and, again, with some degree of accuracy, be able to tell you how long Mary Ann will be here on earth with you all. From what I can tell, it is not likely that she will be leaving the hospital alive. Any or all of you are welcome to spend whatever time Mary Ann has left in this room with her."

As the doctor was talking, my heart and I am sure everyone's heart in the room just sank. Our time with Mary Ann was quickly ending, and everyone knew it. Although her battle with cancer was long, the end seemed to come too soon. Just two nights before, she was dancing with Ryan at his wedding, and now we were getting ready to say goodbye to my sweetheart for the last time.

Everyone took their turns saying goodbye to Mary Ann. I asked the kids to go first since I knew that Mary Ann would miss the most. As they all took their turn softly talking into her ear, my heart broke, seeing their faces anguish. The *loving mother* that they all so much loved was about to leave them, and there was nothing any of us could do about it.

When it came time for me to say my goodbyes, I got up close to her, held her hand, and told her how much I loved her and would miss not being with her. I also told her how proud I was of her and how well she did raising our children. I promised her I would do anything in my power to try to continue to help and guide them as she did for so many years. I apologized for not caring for her as well as I knew she would have cared for me during her fight with cancer. As I was talking to her, I could see tears coming out of her eyes. I will swear to this day; I felt her squeeze my hand, as she so often did when we talked of love and family. In my final words, I said, "Sweetheart, I love you. Please say hi to Kyle when you are with him and make sure he knows how much I loved him and miss him." It was an incredibly moving moment that I remember to this day.

Once everyone had their time with Mary Ann, the nurse came into the room.

The nurse could feel the emotion in the room. Everyone was in tears praying for Mary Ann's safe passage into heaven. As she again checked Mary Ann's vital signs, she said to us, "Mary Ann is peaceful and without pain. All her vital signs suggest that she won't pass for at least another 18 to 24 hours.

My strong suggestion is that you all go home, get some food and a good night's sleep. You all have had a long day, and you need your rest. Tomorrow will be a long day. If anything changes with Mary Ann's condition, I will call Kristie's cell phone. For now, it looks like she will be with us until late afternoon or evening tomorrow."

After the nurse left the room, we talked and decided to take her advice. I suggested that I pick up some food on the way back to the house, and we all gather there and talk about all the good times we had with our angel. The kids were a wreck, and I wanted them to focus on the positive things that their mother's life meant to them. I knew that, at least for a few hours, they had to pick themselves up from the deep depression that they were all feeling. Their mother knew how much they all loved her, but she did not need to hear the sobbing that was happening all around her if she could hear us. When we got back to the house, everyone gathered around the kitchen and the bar. As we were preparing the food, I asked everyone to grab a drink and tell two stories about Mary Ann: One being the most treasured memory they had of her and, two, the funniest moment they remembered about her. The mood in the room started to change from deep sadness to something much more positive. Many took more than one turn at their storytelling of Mary Ann, and tears slowly turned into smiles and laughter. I told them all as the evening progressed that this was how we would get through this great tragedy, together and with positive thoughts and memories for this great lady. Everyone needed their sleep for the next day, and I did not want everyone going to bed depressed and unable to sleep.

The next day we all gathered once again in Mary Ann's room. The nurses told us that not much had changed with her condition, and we should expect her to pass later that day. As it got closer to the end for Mary Ann, I gathered the kids together. I asked them, "Are you sure you want to be in the room when your mother passes? It will be a vision in your mind that you will never be able to erase. If you are not comfortable with that thought in your mind, I am sure she would understand. You can still say your goodbyes one more time right now, and if you are not comfortable, we can leave the room."

Unanimously the kids all said that they wanted to be with her until her last breath.

That last breath came at 5:30 p.m. that day. Precisely 72 hours after Ryan and Katelyn said their I-do's.

Mary Ann was pretty specific on how she wanted to be remembered. She was cremated and had a small funeral mass in the same chapel where we celebrated her mother's life. It would also be in the same church where we celebrated the life of Kyle. Afterward, she would be placed in the same crypt that housed Kyle and her mother. She did not want a viewing as we had for Kyle. We were committed to honoring her wishes. As we got closer to the funeral, it became clear that the chapel would not be big enough to house the funeral mass. When the Last Dance was about to begin, Kristie had given her cell phone to Meagan Reidy and asked her to record the dance with Mary Ann and Ryan. A few days afterward, Kristie posted that video on YouTube with a special note to her mother.

You can view that video "Mother's Last Dance" by going to this URL, https://www.youtube.com/watch?v=4HJ3b44WAL4.

The video quickly went viral and has been viewed by close to two million viewers worldwide. A local TV station in San Francisco picked up this story and the announcement of Mary Ann's passing. The news director decided to do a story on Mary Ann for the ten-o'clock evening news. They did an excellent job with it, and you can view that video by going to this URL, https:// www.youtube.com/watch?v=0UZ2Q6eBAQM.

In this story, they interviewed all three kids after doing some quick research on Mary Ann. This piece was viewed live by many in the Bay Area and over 1.6 million on YouTube. I was soon getting messages from friends all over the world who had viewed one or both videos.

Even without these two videos, we knew that the chapel would not hold all our family and all the many friends who would be coming out for Mary Ann's celebration of life. Mary Ann had also asked that Father Green perform her ceremony just like he did for Kyle and Midge.

As expected, the church was packed. Many of the same family and friends who traveled down to Dana Point were there and many others. Mary Ann was loved and admired by many, and their presence and kind words to the family were heartfelt by everyone.

Following the mass, we placed Mary Ann in the crypt with Kyle on her left and Midge on her right. Sadly, for Mary Ann, shortly after her death, Karie and Tom found out that they were pregnant with their second child, Parker. Karie was never able to tell her mother about the wonderful news, which has always saddened me. I do not know...... if Mary Ann had known that there was a new goal for her to achieve, to see and meet her second grandchild, she might have lasted another nine months. After witnessing her struggles to get to Ryan and Katelyn's wedding and that dance floor, I certainly would not put anything past her.

Life after Mary Ann and Her Legacy

Shortly after Mary Ann's passing, I wrote the outline for this story about her. I intended to spend my time as I mourned her to celebrate her life and who she was. Unfortunately, at the time, I could not bring myself to author the story. I was too depressed. It took me over two years to get over Mary Ann's loss, and I went back to work to help fill my days. Fortunately, I was able to work for a great gentleman named George Huang. He and his able partner Clarice Liao, Executive Director of Operations, ran a mobile software company George had founded several years earlier called FutureDial. The company was growing nicely, and I was able to stay busy as I tried to move beyond Mary Ann's loss. Time was getting away from me, and I knew I had to get back to my original plan of writing Mary Ann's story while I still had the energy to do so. After about three and a half years there, I retired to author this story finally. The good news about being delayed with my story of Mary Ann is that I can now write about her remarkable legacy that has developed since her passing.

Kristie, our eldest, has now married an extraordinary gentleman by the name of Garrett Morgan. After their wedding, they moved into the Pleasanton area and have delivered our fourth grandchild, Weston Kyle, our third grandson and our second granddaughter, Macy Ann. That would have completed the circle for Mary Ann, seeing her oldest daughter married and raising her own family with Garrett. She will miss not being here to guide her through the challenges and wonders of motherhood, but I know her legacy of a *Loving Mother* lives inside Kristie and all our children.

As mentioned earlier, Karie and Tom gave birth to our second grandson just eight months after Mary Ann's passing. Parker is a beautiful child and admires his parents and his brother Jeremy immensely. As Karie has often said, the two of them remind us all how Ryan and Kyle were when they were their age. Mary Ann would so much have loved watching the boys grow up together. Karie and Tom still live a short distance from my house and bring the boys to see their Papa every Sunday night for dinner. Jeremy remembers his grandmother, both from the pictures we show of him and the frequent visits Karie makes with them to Mary Ann's final resting place. Tom is a great father to the boys, and Karie is a *Loving Mother* to them both.

Ryan and Katelyn are now happily married with a gorgeous little girl named Decklyn Marie, and a healthy young man named Kallen Lee. Mary Ann would have certainly enjoyed this one, our first granddaughter. After Decklyn was born, they moved out of San Francisco and close by. They join us often for Sunday dinners. Ryan has quickly become a proud and loving father. Katelyn's love for children allowed her to become a Loving Mother to Decklyn quickly. So, while all the grandchildren will not have benefited from knowing Mary Ann or being held in her arms, I hope that by writing this story of her, they will always know her legacy. Mary Ann and Kyle's smiles are the stars I look at in the evenings knowing how proud they are for being key parts of our family......

Peggy still lives in the area and joins us often for our Sunday family dinners. Jeremy, Parker, and Decklyn love her, and she always spends special time with all three. She makes it to most sporting events that the boys are involved in and still joins me when we help walk the boys around the neighborhood for trick-or-treating on Halloween. Like I, she knows how much her sister Mary Ann would love to be with us for all these events.

God Bless you, Mary Ann; your incredible legacy is living on through the children you so well cared for and raised so successfully.

Mary Ann pictured with her children's baby pictures shortly after finishing her second round of chemo letting her babies know she was fighting for them.

Made in the USA
Monee, IL
04 January 2023

24198701R00163